D0635968

Microcomputers and Clinical Psychology

THE WILEY SERIES IN CLINICAL PSYCHOLOGY

Series Editors

Fraser N. Watts
MRC Applied Psychology Unit,
Cambridge, UK

J. Mark G. Williams
Department of Psychology,
University College of North Wales,
Bangor, UK

Further titles in preparation

Microcomputers and Clinical Psychology

Issues, Applications and Future Developments

Edited by
ALASTAIR AGER
Chancellor College, University of Malawi

Editorial Assistant
Sue Bendall
Chelmsley Hospital, Birmingham, UK

JOHN WILEY & SONS
Chichester · New York · Brisbane · Toronto · Singapore

Copyright © 1991 by John Wiley & Sons Ltd,
Baffins Lane, Chichester,
West Sussex PO19 1UD, England

All rights reserved.

No part of this book may be reproduced by any means,
or transmitted, or translated into a machine language
without the written permission of the publisher.

Other Wiley Editorial Offices

John Wiley & Sons, Inc., 605 Third Avenue,
New York, NY 10158-0012, USA

Jacaranda Wiley Ltd, G.P.O. Box 859, Brisbane,
Queensland 4001, Australia

John Wiley & Sons (Canada) Ltd, 5353 Dundas Road West,
Fourth Floor, Etobicoke, Ontario M9B 6H8, Canada

John Wiley & Sons (SEA) Pte Ltd, 37 Jalan Pemimpin 05-04,
Block B, Union Industrial Building, Singapore 2057

Library of Congress Cataloging-in-Publication Data:

Microcomputers and clinical psychology : issues, applications, and
    future developments / edited by Alastair Ager.
        p.   cm. — (The Wiley series in clinical psychology)
    Includes bibliographical references and index.
    ISBN 0-471-92770-8 (ppc.)
    1. Clinical psychology—Data processing.   2. Microcomputers.
    I. Ager, Alastair.   II. Series.
    RC455.2.D38M52   1992
    616.89′00285′416 – dc20   91–12241
                                                                          CIP

British Library Cataloguing in Publication Data:

A catalogue record for this book is
available from the British Library.

ISBN 0-471-92770-8

Typeset in 10/12 pt Palatino by Dobbie Typesetting Limited, Tavistock, Devon
Printed and bound in Great Britain by
Biddles Ltd, Guildford and King's Lynn

Contents

List of Contributors

ALASTAIR AGER   Department of Psychology, Chancellor College, University of Malawi, Box 280, Zomba, Malawi

SARAH BALDREY   Department of Psychology, Polytechnic South West, Plymouth, Devon PL4 8AA, UK

J. GRAHAM BEAUMONT   Department of Psychology, University College of Swansea, Swansea SA2 8PP, UK

TONY C. CARR   Department of Psychiatry, Hamilton Civic Hospitals, Hamilton, Ontario L8L 2X2, Canada

CHRISTOPHER J. COLBOURN   Department of Psychology, The University, Highfield, Southampton SO9 5NH, UK

JO DOUGLAS   Department of Psychological Medicine, The Hospitals for Sick Children, Great Ormond Street, London WC1N 3JH, UK

NEIL FRUDE   School of Psychology, University of Wales in Cardiff, PO Box 901, Cardiff CF1 3YG, UK

KELLEY HARRISON   Department of Psychology, State University of New York at Binghamton, PO Box 6000, Binghamton, New York 13902-6000, USA

STEPHANIE B. LOCKSHIN   Department of Psychology, State University
                             of New York at Binghamton, PO Box 6000,
                             Binghamton, New York 13902-6000, USA

TOM McMILLAN   Department of Clinical Psychology, Wolfson
                             Medical Rehabilitation Centre, Atkinson
                             Morleys Hospital, Wimbledon, London
                             SW20 0NE, UK

RAYMOND G. ROMANCZYK   Department of Psychology, State University
                             of New York at Binghamton, PO Box 6000,
                             Binghamton, New York 13902-6000, USA

CLIVE SKILBECK   Department of Clinical Psychology, The Royal
                             Victoria Infirmary, Queen Victoria Road,
                             Newcastle Upon Tyne NE1 4LP, UK

SARAH WILSON   Department of Psychology, University of
                             Surrey, Guildford, Surrey GU2 5XH, UK.

Series Preface

The Wiley Series in Clinical Psychology aims to include books on current advances. Recent developments in microcomputers promise to make a substantial impact on clinical practice. There has probably been no technological revolution with comparable implications. This book aims to review what has already been achieved in introducing microcomputers into the practice of clinical psychology, and to survey future possibilities.

The chapters of this book present a comprehensive guide to the various domains of application of microcomputers in clinical psychology. Assessment software, of course, is one of the best developed, though, there is also growing use of microcomputer software in treatment and rehabilitation. However, this book is not solely concerned with uses of microcomputers with individual patients. Consideration is also given to higher-level issues such as the development of expert systems and the use of microcomputers in service delivery and management.

One of the most intriguing issues in this field at the present time is why microcomputers are not already used more widely, despite the range of applications that have already been developed. Is this due simply to a lack of the necessary familiarity and expertise, or is there some other kind of resistance to their use in clinical work? If so, is there a rational basis to this resistance, or does it amount to a kind of 'phobia' of information technology? These issues are also explored in the present volume.

Clinical psychology is a field that has close links with many other professions. I hope that the series will have a broad appeal to all those concerned with psychological approaches to clinical problems. Many of the applications of microcomputers discussed here will also be of interest to other professions such as psychiatry, and to other branches of professional applied psychology.

FRASER WATTS
Series Editor

Preface

I have greatly enjoyed editing this book from the perspective of a sceptic. Although I had been involved in the clinical application of microcomputers from the early 1980s, my enthusiasm for the new technology had—in all truth—considerably abated by the time I was invited to assemble the current volume. That invitation gave me the ideal opportunity to examine the field in some detail, and decide on a rational basis where I stood concerning the future role of microcomputers within clinical psychology.

Although I am tempted to cite some sophisticated technical objection or therapeutic principle as the cause of my declining commitment through the 1980s, in retrospect its origins were considerably more plain. One focus of discontentment was the matter of plugs and cables. Their repeated and continual incompatibility was a cancer, a growing malignancy that sapped my allegiance to the technology. For want of appropriate connection, system after system, application after application, limped along, hinting occasionally at what could be achieved, then just as surely reverting to an unresponsive, unforgiving complexity unrecognized from the manual.

The other major factor which influenced my loss of enthusiasm for what microtechnology had to offer the clinician was the loss of a human environment supportive of such an interest. From being in a team of individuals who readily shared problems and insights regarding microcomputers, through changes of appointment I came to be isolated in my interest. I had no one close to share problems with, and soon tired of my internal conversations regarding alternative strategies to overcome a difficulty.

I share these experiences here for a number of reasons. First, I suspect that they are, in fact, far from atypical. I believe that the vast majority of those who have worked with microcomputers will at one time or another have experienced the viscera-twisting anguish of incompetence that new technology can face us with. I hope that acknowledging this may encourage perseverance in those facing such problems.

Second, my difficulties illustrate the key importance for success in this field of basic issues such as the presence of a supportive network of other users. I am delighted that contributors have not neglected such factors in their discussions—and particularly commend the chapter by Colbourn as a wise guide to such concerns.

Third, from a state of some equivocation, I must report that the contributors to this volume have managed to rekindle a commitment in me to the application of microcomputers within clinical psychology. My commitment now, I would like to think, is of a more mature variety than a decade ago, discerning both value and danger and, I hope, distinguishing the principal sources of each. It is of course the reader's ultimate judgements that are important, not the editor's. I do hope, therefore, that you find the contributions before you stimulating, and that they help you determine the appropriate role of microcomputers in your work.

The approach readers take to this volume will obviously depend heavily upon their prior experience of clinical applications of microcomputing. I have tried to keep this variation in mind when planning the structure of the book. Those with little experience may find it useful to begin with Chapters 1 and 2, before selecting a subsequent chapter discussing specific applications in their major field of specialism. More experienced users may prefer to focus directly on chapters discussing particular fields of application, backing up this information with the reviews of more general applications found in Chapters 9 and 10. A group of which I have been particularly mindful, clinical psychologists in training, may wish—along with others no doubt—to gain a comprehensive assessment of the potential role of the microcomputer within clinical practice by working through the complete text. Such individuals should find the presented sequence of chapters the most satisfactory for such a programme. Irrespective of a reader's prior experience, I strongly commend Frude's final chapter of thought-provoking futurology concerning the potential impact of microtechnology on the culture in which our profession operates.

Finally, there are the expected—but no less unwarranted for that—acknowledgements of thanks to friends and colleagues who have assisted in this work. Above all, there is a major debt of gratitude to Sue Bendall who contributed immensely to the coordination of this project.

ALASTAIR AGER
Zomba, Malawi
January 1991

Chapter 1

The Role of Microcomputers in Clinical Psychology

ALASTAIR AGER

In the guise of the wordprocessor or patient record system the microcomputer has won access to many clinical psychology services. However, compared with many professions—such as banking, journalism and architecture—the general impact of the microcomputer on clinical psychology practice has been negligible. It is the purpose of this chapter to consider this state of affairs, and to examine both the technical feasibility and clinical desirability of a significantly broader role for the microcomputer within clinical psychology.

The legitimate role for the microcomputer in clinical psychology is an important question to address at the outset of this volume. There is considerable danger that the adoption of microcomputers within clinical practice will become marginalized as a concern only of that minority of practitioners with an existing interest in things technological. Such "technophiles" will be tolerated by their profession, and may be considered to be making a valuable contribution in certain areas. But their concerns will be seen as essentially peripheral to "mainstream" clinical psychology.

The thrust of this volume is that the application of microcomputer technology within clinical psychology is not such a marginal concern. All clinical psychologists need to consider the manner in which microcomputers could facilitate their work. This is an ethical imperative. Clinical psychology is a profession where service quality has a direct influence on human well-being, and practitioners must therefore be continually mindful of developments and innovations that may serve to improve the quality of their work. Also, in a profession where shortage of resources is frequently cited as a major constraint on clinical impact, clinical psychologists cannot afford to ignore any resource savings that may be attainable through the use of new technology.

Microcomputers and Clinical Psychology: Issues, Applications and Future Developments. Edited by A. Ager
©1991 John Wiley & Sons Ltd

This is not to say that all clinical psychologists should consider the microcomputer a panacea to all the major ills of the profession. The crucial issue is one of role. To which roles is the microcomputer best suited? What new possibilities for clinical practice are made available through microtechnology? In which roles should particular caution be exhibited regarding computer use?

Subsequent contributions in this volume go some way towards answering these questions. In this opening chapter, however, I want to suggest a framework that may assist such evaluations. Such a framework begins by appreciating the range of tasks tackled by clinical psychologists and, in consequence, the diversity of roles that the microcomputer may potentially fulfil.

THE TASKS OF CLINICAL PSYCHOLOGICAL PRACTICE

Clinical psychology represents a broad and diverse discipline, encompassing many differences in therapeutic approach. Nonetheless, at a functional level, it is possible to identify key tasks which are common to much—if not all—clinical practice. Figure 1.1 is a schematic representation of the tasks which may be undertaken at various stages of a therapeutic intervention. This scheme may readily be identified as in line with the "scientist–practitioner"

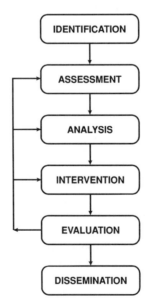

Figure 1.1 The key tasks of clinical psychological practice.

model of clinical psychology, though other approaches—for instance, models based upon Kolb's experiential learning cycle (Kolb, 1984)—serve to generate a similar picture.

The scheme is inevitably a broad characterization of clinical practice, attempting to be applicable to both individually and organizationally focused interventions. However, it is at a suitable level of abstraction for its purpose here: by highlighting the discrete tasks that a clinical psychologist may undertake, I simply wish to enumerate the numerous distinct roles that a microcomputer may potentially fulfil for the clinician.

The scheme suggests that the initial task for the clinical psychologist is that of *identification*. This may involve problem identification within some service setting or perhaps receipt of a referral from some other agency.

Such further action will usually involve some form of *assessment*, either formal or informal. Assessment is here defined in the narrow sense of the gathering of relevant information regarding a presenting problem.

Such assessment is then inevitably followed by some form of *analysis*, using the information obtained to build some understanding of the origin and/or maintenance of the presenting difficulties.

Such analysis may lead to referral on to another agency, when that agency is perceived to offer relevant services. In many other circumstances, however, it will be followed by the formulation of an *intervention* by the clinician and its subsequent delivery.

The ongoing *evaluation* of intervention is then a central element of most clinical psychological practice, feeding-back to previous stages and prompting further assessment, re-analysis etc.

Most therapeutic work also involves some process of *dissemination*. This might involve communicating information regarding therapeutic outcome to other agencies, or perhaps sharing information regarding intervention techniques with professional colleagues.

APPLICATIONS OF MICROCOMPUTERS IN CLINICAL PSYCHOLOGY: AN OVERVIEW

The above scheme can be used as a structure with respect to which we can overview current applications of microcomputers in clinical practice. Applications listed are merely a sample of those discussed in considerably more detail later in the volume, the principal intention here being merely to illustrate the diversity of roles that the microcomputer may potentially assume within clinical practice.

Identification

The client record systems described in the chapter by Romanczyk are representative of a number of systems that have been used to assist psychologists and other therapists in the identification of targets for intervention. These may be local systems as in the case study here of the Children's Unit for Treatment and Evaluation. The microcomputer-based Special Needs Registers which have been developed for many disabled populations across Britain in the last few years are an example of more extensive systems, which may serve a broadly similar function for a much larger and widely spread client population.

Such systems have a relatively long historical pedigree, but there are a number of more contemporary developments. Colbourn, for instance, describes the communication possibilities arising from the connection together (or "networking") of microcomputer systems. Cross-referral between agencies and monitoring of service goals across multiple sites are two examples of the resulting facilities now readily accessible to clinical psychology services. Carr describes how a computerized information system enables self-referral of clients for professional assistance.

Assessment

Assessment, defined narrowly here merely in terms of the gathering of relevant information, is perhaps the clinical task with respect to which the largest number of microcomputer applications have been developed. Between them, the chapters of Lockshin and Harrison, Wilson and McMillan, Baldrey and Beaumont document numerous systems which serve to provide the clinical psychologist with data for clinical analysis.

Lockshin and Harrison focus on applications involving the computer conducting a behavioural interview of clients. Programs may present a general screening interview, or focus on specific areas, such as sexual dysfunction (Binik et al., 1988). In either case, they essentially emulate the manner in which a clinician is likely to conduct such an interview.

Wilson and McMillan focus more on formal psychometric assessment. They consider both the automation of existing psychometric tests and the development of novel procedures (utilizing the special features available with the microcomputer). For many of these tests the computer controls the complete assessment session, and the presence of the clinician is not required.

Baldrey, in reviewing applications relevant to people with profound and multiple handicaps, describes how the computer may serve as a "perceptual tool", detecting patterns and progress in the learning performance of such individuals that would otherwise be imperceptible.

Beaumont describes how assessment procedures may now be readily automated through the use of expert systems "shells"; that is, open-ended programs which allow information to be structured in a formal manner. Whilst most of the expert systems described by Beaumont attempt some form of analysis of information (the concern of the next section), inevitably they also frequently involve the actual gathering of such information. Beaumont, in fact, identifies psychometric assessment and the assessment of vocational adjustment as two of the areas within clinical psychology where expert systems may have their most significant impact.

Analysis

Analysis of psychological information is a task for which a number of computer systems have now been developed. Each of the contributors mentioned in the section on assessment above also describes applications where microcomputers, having facilitated in some form the gathering of information, may then be used to provide some form of analysis of this data.

Lockshin and Harrison, for example, describe how real-time behavioural observation using a portable microcomputer allows subsequent analysis of the temporal—and therefore potentially functional—relationships between observed events and behaviour (Felce et al., 1987). A number of interpretive report writing programs are now available for analysis of data obtained through either manual or computerized administration of psychometric tests (Roid and Gorsuch, 1984). Wilson and McMillan note the availability of computer-based test interpretation systems for a number of established psychometric tests including the MMPI, 16PF, and Rorschach, as well as for the Halstead–Reitan and Luria–Nebraska neuropsychological test batteries.

Baldrey, and also Douglas, consider the ways in which the progress of computer-based instructional programs can be controlled by instantaneous analysis of a student's pattern of responding. Such programs are structured according to some form of instructional theory, usually either behavioural (e.g. Ager, 1986) or cognitive (e.g. Rotheray, Sewell and Morton, 1986) in nature. Beaumont discusses the ultimate extension of this principle: the capture of psychological expertise within a microcomputer-based "expert system". Analysis of assessment data for the framing of neuropsychological diagnoses is at an embryonic stage, but clearly suggestive of future capability. Beaumont also identifies the potential application of expert systems in advising clinical psychologists in the analysis of complex information with which they may have limited expertise—for example, regarding the interaction of drugs and nutrition with behaviour.

Intervention

The microcomputer serving in the delivery of psychological intervention is the central focus of the chapters of both Carr and Skilbeck. The former specifically addresses intervention with respect to anxiety and addiction, as well as more general psychotherapy and counselling applications. The style and scope of these applications vary widely. In some instances the computer serves as an adjunct to the work of the therapist, perhaps providing a client feedback on the attainment of treatment goals. In other circumstances, however, the microcomputer displaces the therapist from the key therapeutic role, directly supervising and controlling the course of intervention (e.g. Binik et al., 1988).

Skilbeck considers the role of the microcomputer in the specific field of cognitive rehabilitation. This is a field where the arrival of microtechnology has led to genuine therapeutic innovation, microcomputers presenting training exercises effectively unimplementable without such technology. Alongside a microcomputer version of the familiar game "hangman", therefore, a battery of programs to encourage recovery from aphasia (Katz and Nagly, 1984) includes a number of innovative procedures with no manual or "pencil-and-paper" equivalent.

In her chapter, Douglas examines the "non-specific" effects that having access to a computer may have on a child. She also considers, however, how particular programs may serve as specific interventions for children. She reviews applications for physically disabled children, communication impaired children, children with severe learning difficulties, children with mild, moderate and specific learning difficulties and socially, emotionally and behaviorally disturbed children. Such programs take a variety of forms, from those offering an individualized "tutorial" function to those facilitating group discussion and decision-making.

Baldrey's focus is the provision of computer-aided instruction for adults with severe learning difficulties, describing interventions framed with respect to behavioural and cognitive models of learning and skill. Again, the format of applications varies. Some are individually focused, others involve groupwork; some function independently, others operate as an adjunct to the work of a teacher or therapist.

Evaluation

In describing computerized treatment applications, both Skilbeck and Carr note the accessibility of such automated interventions to formalized evaluation. By recording all responses to presented items, microcomputers can readily compute and present (in a suitable form) information regarding a client's progress. This is obviously of value to the clinician, but may also be capitalized upon for direct feedback to clients.

Douglas and Baldrey both identify the potential value of the microcomputer in evaluating the progress of individuals with severe learning difficulties, where otherwise changes in behaviour may be sufficiently small to go undetected.

Romanczyk, however, broadens the issue of the microcomputer's role in evaluation much further, by discussing applications at the level of the clinical service. Romanczyk shows how the development of a service-wide database regarding clinical inputs and client progress can, with accurate and comprehensive information recording and management, facilitate the monitoring and evaluation of service delivery.

Dissemination

The increasingly ubiquitous wordprocessor is obviously a major aid to clinical psychologists in the dissemination of their findings and analysis to others. There are now numerous other ways in which the microcomputer can assist in this task, however. Colbourn, for example, notes the potential utility of "networking" with other computer systems. Using an electronic mail facility, for example, a clinician can instantaneously notify all other clinicians known to have a shared clinical interest of a particular intervention and its outcome. Preparation of clinical research reports can be facilitated by shared access to computer-based conferencing systems, where ideas from a number of clinicians can be canvassed and integrated into a developing document.

Lockshin and Harrison's discussion of interpretive report writing systems is also clearly pertinent here. Not only do such systems conduct analysis on data obtained, they produce a prose report of a form suitable for presentation to a client, referring agency etc. In a less formal fashion, Douglas notes how the hard information commonly arising from computer-based activities with children can be very useful for demonstrating to parents the progress that their child is making and encouraging them to pursue related activities at home.

The above overview is intended to give readers a flavour of the applications of microcomputers discussed in some detail subsequently in this volume. It should be apparent that, in relation to the scheme presented earlier, applications have been developed which are relevant to all the major functional tasks faced by the clinical psychologist. For some of these tasks, notably that of assessment, there are very many applications available indeed. For others, there are somewhat fewer. The number of applications available, however, tells us little about the appropriateness of the microcomputer taking a particular role. In going through the preceding sections readers will inevitably have reacted to the listed applications with varying sentiments. Some will perhaps have been viewed with enthusiasm, as well-conceived and of real utility. Others may have been considered inappropriate, perhaps even unethical. Such variation in response is inevitable. But it is important to move the discussion of the appropriate role of the microcomputer away from individual sentiment alone. Some rational framework is required with respect to which the various merits and demerits of applications may be discussed.

The next section attempts to identify such a structure, which readers may wish to use as a basis for evaluating their own views regarding the individual applications subsequently described within the volume.

However, before leaving behind the above discussion, it is worth highlighting an issue to which we will subsequently need to return. This concerns the manner in which—for any specific application—the microcomputer relates to existing clinical practice. I want to suggest that there are three distinct ways in which the microcomputer can assume a role within clinical psychology.

The first of these is when the application essentially involves a technical *elaboration* of existing practice. The clinician uses the microcomputer to accomplish a task in much the same way that it would have been accomplished previously. The task—by virtue of the microcomputer—is, however, accomplished more efficiently, or perhaps more elegantly, than previously. Most automated client record systems are in this sense a technical elaboration of existing manual file systems.

The second way in which a computer can relate to existing clinical practice is when the computer actually *emulates* the previous work of the clinician. The computer essentially replaces the clinician in the accomplishment of a specific task. Much of the automated assessment and instructional programming applications described above would fit into this category.

Finally, the microcomputer can be used in the *innovation* of clinical practice. There is no prior equivalent to the procedure accomplished by—or done with the assistance of—the microcomputer. Many of the cognitive rehabilitation applications are examples of the computer assuming this sort of role.

It seems clear that judgements about the appropriateness of specific microcomputer applications will depend, in part, on the manner in which the application relates to clinical practice as categorized above.

FACTORS INFLUENCING THE ADOPTION OF MICROCOMPUTERS WITHIN CLINICAL PSYCHOLOGY

Lockshin and Harrison discuss a survey by Farrell (1989) of clinical and counselling psychologists regarding their use of microcomputers. Together

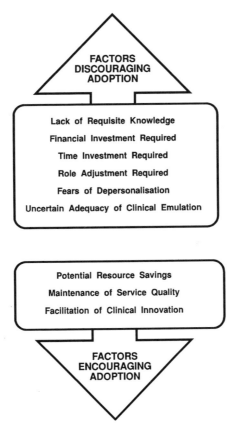

Figure 1.2   Factors discouraging and encouraging adoption of microcomputers within clinical psychological practice.

with informal surveys of the type reported by Colbourn, a number of factors influencing clinicians' decisions regarding the adoption of microcomputers in their work become apparent.

Figure 1.2 shows some of the major factors identified, presented in the form of a "force-field analysis". This depicts the opposition of factors encouraging and discouraging adoption, emphasizing that clinicians' behaviour—like that of their clients—is influenced by functional considerations. In these terms clinicians will move in the direction of adoption only when the costs of adoption are clearly outweighed by the benefits.

Lack of requisite knowledge

The chapter by Colbourn examines issues in the selection and support of a microcomputer system for clinical use. Many of the decisions that have to be made by clinicians when adopting such systems are complex, and require technical and strategic, as well as clinical, judgement. In such circumstances it is not surprising that many clinicians feel they lack the requisite knowledge to make appropriately informed decisions (Farrell, 1989).

Obviously, texts such as the present volume and those of Norris et al. (1985) and Romanczyk (1986) can assist clinicians to a certain degree, in providing access to relevant information. However, the importance of support and guidance from individuals with some degree of expertise with microcomputers cannot be over-emphasized. Knowledge is not only required during the setting-up phase of a microcomputer system, but throughout its development and integration within clinical practice.

Colbourn commends recruiting assistance from colleagues with some experience of microcomputers, but not those who may be considered "computer buffs". The issue here, well illustrated by Romanczyk in Chapter 9 regarding the implementation of a technically primitive but highly successful system within a service facility, is that technically sophisticated information can seldom be satisfactorily assimilated by the naïve user. As with all good instruction, assistance needs to be matched to the present level of an individual's understanding. Those very involved in the use of microcomputers can find it difficult to pitch their advice at an appropriate level.

Technical guidance may also be gained from computer dealers with, as Colbourn points out, local suppliers likely to prove the most useful. With their restricted profit margins, small customer base and relative reliance on income from after-sales service and support, it is no surprise (applying our psychology to the situation) that local dealers will usually be motivated to assist small-scale users.

Microcomputer user groups are another potential source of guidance. In addition to national user groups associated with specific machines, there are now a very large number of more local networks that can be of great assistance. User groups within health authorities or universities, or those focused on geographical communities, can provide the means for the exchange of ideas and difficulties and, perhaps most usefully, to gain "hands-on" experience of equipment or programs before committing oneself to purchase.

There are, then, numerous ways in which clinicians may seek to become better informed regarding microcomputer applications in clinical psychology. There is still, however, unquestionably a role for broader education on this topic within the profession. Clinicians involved in such work should disseminate their experiences on a far broader front, not simply to the readers of "computer columns". The key, perhaps, is for such experience to be clearly related to substantive clinical issues. Too often reports focus on the use of the microcomputer *per se*—rather than on the manner in which technology has assisted in a particular clinical intervention—and are consequently seen as of marginal significance by the average clinician.

The financial investment required

Despite dramatic increases in its technical sophistication, the cost of microcomputer equipment has, in real terms, dropped significantly over the course of the last decade. With this trend likely to continue, concerns over the amount of financial investment required in setting up a microcomputer system are likely to be an increasingly insignificant influence on clinicians' attitudes towards such developments. The survey by Farrell (1989) did, however, find some clinicians citing the financial outlay required as a reason for their decision not to use computers. As Lockshin and Harrison suggest in Chapter 3, however, these clinicians were perhaps working within small private practices, where resources for such investment would be severely limited. Within larger private practices, and public services, such concerns are generally likely to be less. In the UK, where the vast majority of clinical psychologists work within the public sector, the National Health Service has developed a culture particularly receptive to applications of new technology and few Departments of Psychology would nowadays be unable to make a good case for the purchase of computer equipment and a fair amount of supporting software.

The time investment required

Whilst the adequacy of financial resources may seldom now be a substantive problem regarding the adoption of microcomputers within clinical work, the time required of clinicians and support staff for the appropriate implementation of systems remains a key issue. In Chapter 2 Colbourn notes that "you need to feel that time spent learning to use a computer is time well spent, because that time may not be especially productive in terms of your clinical work . . .". For many clinicians this describes a major dilemma. They perhaps believe that familiarity with a computer system will ultimately assist them in the quality and efficiency of their clinical work. But in the short term, sitting in front of the computer seems time-consuming, frustrating and apparently unproductive. I have known many clinicians who—despite enthusiasm for what new technology has to offer—have never invested enough time in learning about applications to inherit their promise.

Many clinicians will justifiably claim that they simply do not have the time required. Large active caseloads and pressing waiting lists force them to abandon all activities not immediately instrumental in achieving short-term goals.

We can approach this issue in two ways. One way is to assume the paucity of time clinicians have to become familiar with any application as a "given" in many service environments. In such circumstances, we need to consider ways in which the time investment required by clinicians to become familiar with a system might be significantly reduced. For instance, the "learning curve" with some computer systems is considerably faster than others. Most naïve users appear to find systems requiring recall of commands and their entry via the keyboard difficult in comparison with systems where the user selects options from a series of displayed "menus" using a simple pointing device (Norman, 1988). This observation would tend to favour use of machines such as the Apple Macintosh, which feature the latter form of user interface (though as Colbourn points out, this style of interaction may become increasingly available on other machines). Locally arranged, in-house training for a specific application may prove to be another time-efficient route to competence, certainly when compared with the more usual strategy of independent sessions on the computer guided only by a written manual.

The second way to approach the issue is to help clinicians find more time for the necessary learning. The key here is likely to be rigorous cost–benefit analysis over the longer term. If application of microcomputers is to be of only uncertain future benefit to clinical practice, there is clearly little justification for investing appreciable amounts of time in training. If, on the other hand, clear benefits are to accrue, it is ultimately in the interests of patients that time be found in the short-term for such learning. Such an approach requires considerable discipline, but is imperative if clinical practice is not to become subject to the tyranny of the immediate need.

The role adjustment required

The implementation of any microcomputer system inevitably has implications for existing work patterns and practices. When a system has a service-wide role its introduction will affect the work of many individuals, many of whom may be dubious of the ultimate benefits of the innovation. In such circumstances there are two broad strategies available: fitting the people to the system, and fitting the system to the people.

The former strategy is probably the more typical of computerization programmes within commerce and industry. Private sector organizations tend to have a greater role flexibility than those in the public sector, though retraining programmes, job counselling and some redeployment are still often necessary to bring about the required adjustments. In public sector organizations—particularly those in the field of health and social services—such a strategy is likely to be severely problematic. With the complex organizational ecology of such settings (Ager, 1991), the strategy of fitting the system around the staff and their existing roles will commonly be the more productive. Romanczyk discusses in Chapter 9 the implementation of a curriculum management database at a children's treatment unit, which explicitly sought to accommodate to existing patterns of staff activity. He argues that the efficiency and sustainability of the system is far in excess of what would have been achieved by a "state-of-the-art" system which took no regard of the manner in which teachers previously taught and recorded the progress of their pupils.

When a system is primarily for the individual use of a clinician, things are obviously likely to be rather more simple. This is not to say, however, that there will be no problem of role adjustment. Even if a clinician is very keen on making use of microcomputer technology, there may be "costs" to the clinician which create some discomfort. A clinician may see real benefits of a client record system, for instance, but still find it difficult to keep up with the regular record-keeping which the system demands. Where the adjustment required involves an individual's clinical role rather than just an administrative procedure, conflict is likely to be particularly acute. Many psychologists will feel uncomfortable at the prospect of what they consider skilled tasks being handled—in part at least—by a machine. There are aspects of this discomfort, of course, which relate to matters other than straightforward role inertia, and it is to these that we turn next.

Fears of depersonalization

The survey of Farrell (1989) indicated that for many clinicians there are certain clinical tasks for which use of a microcomputer is considered inappropriate. This view is most commonly expressed with respect to applications where the microcomputer may function independently of the clinician, emulating the clinician in some discrete clinical task such as assessment or treatment supervision. Much of this concern seems to relate to fears of depersonalization, and the feeling that certain clinical tasks should involve professional contact. When teaching regarding clinical applications of microcomputers, this is the issue which I find most commonly arises. Many argue that psychological intervention involves processes not reducable to the level of technique, and thereby not captured by essentially mechanical applications.

This is clearly a huge issue, and I will not try to tackle it comprehensively in this introductory review. What I can sensibly attempt, however, is to place certain "markers" in the debate which may help to structure readers' consideration of the issue. Let us begin by stereotyping the argument into two extreme positions: one suggesting that the computer can emulate, and perhaps even surpass, the clinical competence of the average clinician, the other that the computer cannot capture the essential qualities of clinical interaction.

A number of pieces of evidence can be marshalled towards support of the former position. Angle et al. (1979), for instance, found that computer-administered screening interviews yielded more complete information than those conducted by clinicians. Wilson and McMillan suggest that psychometric tests may be both more reliably and validly administered by computer than by clinician. Baldrey describes teaching programmes for individuals with learning difficulties that work with a subtlety and complexity beyond the competence of most clinicians. Beaumont's review of expert systems demonstrates the considerable capability of computers to capture true analytic expertise.

In support of the latter position—that computers cannot capture the essential qualities of clinical interaction—much of the above evidence can, however, be dismissed as tangential to the issue of debate. This evidence may suggest that many technical skills of the clinician can be successfully emulated by the computer, but says nothing of the non-technical, non-specific aspects of clinical interaction. Evidence reviewed by Lockshin and Harrison concerning the non-acceptability of computer interview to certain clients lends some support to this contention, though such studies must be interpreted in the context of the generally favourable ratings given by clients to computer interview and, indeed, therapy (see Chapter 4).

A belief in the importance of specifically human interaction may best be construed as just that—a belief—rather than a proposition open to scientific appraisal. Defending human worth on scientific grounds may, indeed, turn out to be an increasingly perilous business, especially if the "intimate machine" arrives, as envisaged by Frude in Chapter 11, to provide clients with necessary "social support". Frude's image of individuals whose self-worth is asserted by machine is perhaps a good test of our views on this issue. On purely scientific grounds the effectiveness of the "intimate machine" in supporting "psychological health" may be unimpeachable. For some, however—and I must include myself here—clinical practice has a moral dimension which, in the final analysis, asserts the personal and spiritual in the face of the scientific reductionism that generally underpins our methods.

While these extreme positions may clarify the essential nature of the arguments surrounding the issue of depersonalization, for most clinicians a pragmatic compromise between the two is probably the most likely outcome. For example, for many clients depersonalization is not a major fear for the clear reason that there is no person involved with them in a therapeutic role. Debate between computer-based therapy and therapy by clinician is vacuous when there is no therapy available. Few will be disturbed if applications of microtechnology extends genuine therapeutic impact beyond the restricted few who presently have access to clinical services. Beyond this, clinicians will inevitably make personal judgements regarding those clinical tasks for which they consider a "human touch" imperative. Such criteria are unlikely ever to be scientifically based, and will reflect the personal style and inclination of the indivdual clinician.

Uncertain adequacy of clinical emulation

This next issue is closely related to that discussed above, but focuses on technical concerns rather than the importance of human interaction within clinical work. A clinician may, in principle, be prepared to devolve a clinical task to a microcomputer application, but be uncertain, in practice, how satisfactorily the computer will perform. I will illustrate the issue with respect to two major classes of application: client record systems, and automated assessment and report writing.

Client record systems may serve not only to reduce the time spent on administrative tasks, but may make a positive contribution to the quality of clinical intervention. Many clinicians are, however, justifiably concerned whether such systems emulate clinicians in their determination to maintain strict standards of confidentiality. Handwritten case notes, test protocols, lists of therapeutic goals etc. are traditionally guarded by clinicians as strictly confidential material. Is such material stored within a computer system similarly guarded?

The short answer to this question is that it depends upon the system and the way it is implemented within a clinical setting. Computer disks storing confidential information can, of course, be locked away, but they are often treated with considerably less sensitivity than the case note files they replace. Data stored on a hard disk will be accessible to all users unless some form of "codeword" protection device is implemented. Suppliers of computer systems may not always appreciate the confidentiality standards of a clinical psychology service, and clinicians need to emphasize these when specifying their system requirements. In the UK the whole issue of confidentiality is further complicated by the Data Protection Act 1984 (see the discussions by Colbourn and Carr). With similar legislation arriving in many other countries, all clinicians need to be aware of their legal obligations to divulge certain information kept on computer systems.

For clinicians interested in using a test administration and report writing system to take some of the burden of routine psychometric assessment, an obvious question to be addressed is whether their own expertise in the presentation of items, their scoring, recording and subsequent analysis, and in the formulation of an analytic report, is adequately emulated. As noted above, Wilson and McMillan claim the validity and reliability of microcomputer-based test administration to be in most circumstances, if anything, superior to that attainable by clinicians themselves. Subsequent analysis of performance by computer, and construction of formal reports, is a considerably more controversial issue, however.

Many computer-based test interpretation systems are now available for a range of psychometric instruments. The manner in which these packages analyse an individual's performance is usually modelled in some form on the decision-making processes followed by clinicians. However, the adequacy of these systems in genuinely emulating clinical deduction, and the resultant validity of their analyses, has been queried by a number of studies (Moreland, 1987; Groth-Marnat and Schumaker, 1989; see also discussions by Lockshin and Harrison, and by Wilson and McMillan, in this volume). Of particular concern is the fact that many systems do not indicate the manner in which they have made deductions, and their analysis is thus not open to subsequent clinical scrutiny. Beaumont suggests that with the advent of true expert systems in clinical psychology this form of difficulty may be circumvented. There remains, however, concern over the psychological status of reports produced by test interpretation systems without adequate professional clinical supervision.

The above examples should make it clear that clinicians need to take considerable care when devolving to a microcomputer system tasks which they have previously tackled themselves. Lockshin and Harrison emphasize that clinicians must always assume ultimate responsibility for such applications, being fully familiar with the procedures undertaken by machines in their service.

Potential resource savings

When we turn to consider incentives for the adoption of microtechnology, a common factor to virtually all planned programmes of computerization is the promise of resource savings. Cash savings through improved efficiency may be an increasingly important goal for clinicians, whether operating as private practitioners or within increasingly cash-conscious bureaucracies. But it is likely to be the potential savings in human resources that motivate most clinicians towards the application of new technology. Whether assisting a clinician in the performance of a task, or directly emulating some function previously tackled by a clinician, microcomputers save time. And time, within clinical psychology, is not necessarily money. Time is increased breadth of service. Time is shorter waiting lists. Time is the opportunity to tackle frequently neglected long-term needs, such as mental health education and primary prevention.

Maintenance of service quality

Microcomputers potentially contribute to the maintenance of service quality in two distinct ways. First, as described in Chapter 9 by Romanczyk regarding the Children's Unit for Treatment and Evaluation at Binghamton, they can provide an efficient and effective means of abstracting information on clinical process and clinical outcome. In facilitating feedback on the success of a service, they prompt a crucial element of any system of quality assurance.

Second and far more broadly, in addition to their role in service evaluation, microcomputers may themselves directly contribute to service quality. This is ably illustrated in Romanczyk's second case study, where the implementation of an agency-wide computerized treatment planning system had a generalized positive effect on many aspects of service quality.

Contributions to service quality may be far more narrowly focused than this, however. Any clinical task completed efficiently and appropriately with the assistance of a microcomputer marks a contribution of micro-technology to the maintenance of high standards of clinical practice. Applications which involve the elaboration of existing practice illustrate this most clearly, as technology is self-evidently fostering the extension of clinical competence.

For many clinicians the promise of such extension is likely to prove a major motivation for the adoption of microcomputer technology within their work. Clinicians who are sceptical of the potential of the computer in emulating clinical functions and for whom the development of novel assessment and intervention procedures holds little attention, may yet enthusiastically accept a role for the computer in helping them to improve on what they presently do. The chapter by Douglas, for example, is replete with examples of how the microcomputer may be used to help clinicians tackle established difficulties in their work with children. Functioning as communication aid, teaching machine or facilitator of group interaction, the computer's role is firmly defined with respect to established therapeutic goals and principles. Such clear definition of the role of the microcomputer with respect to existing clinical goals is a principal guarantee of its facilitation of genuine service quality.

Facilitation of clinical innovation

In their review of microcomputer applications in the fields of psychometric and neuropsychological assessment, Wilson and McMillan begin by considering the translation of established tests into an automated form. This mirrors the preoccupation of workers in this area in the first major phase of such applications, running up to perhaps the mid-1980s. Since that time, however, there has been an increased realization of the potential for developing totally novel procedures, many of which allow the assessment of functions previously inaccessible to psychometric examination.

A similar realization regarding the possibility of genuine clinical innovation has increasingly emerged in a number of other fields. Baldrey, for example, discusses the possibilities that have arisen, as a direct result of advances in microtechnology, for treatment intervention with individuals with multiple and profound learning disabilities. Carr describes a number of treatment innovations—ranging from self-treatment programmes to groupwork tasks mediated through a computer—that are based upon the unique facilities offered by microcomputer systems.

Perhaps Beaumont's discussion of expert systems, however, gives the clearest indication of the potential for innovation made available to our profession through microtechnology. Facilities for the modelling of psychological dysfunction and for the generation and test of clinical hypotheses are just two examples of the sophisticated means that may soon be at the disposal of the clinician.

SUMMARY

In this chapter I have attempted to provide readers with an overview of applications of microcomputers within clinical psychology and, in particular, how these applications relate to the distinct tasks addressed within clinical practice. As a device for facilitating critical appraisal of the applications discussed in subsequent chapters, I have then suggested some of the key factors which are likely to influence clinicians' decisions regarding the adoption of microcomputer technology.

REFERENCES

Ager, A.K. (1986) Performance contoured programming: a structure for microcomputer-based teaching of individuals with severe learning difficulties. *Programmed Learning and Educational Technology*, **23** (2), 130–35.

Ager, A.K. (1991) Planning sustainable services: the importance of the behavioural analysis of service environments. In B. Remington (ed), *Applied Behaviour Analysis and Severe Mental Handicap: Facing the Challenge*, Wiley, Chichester.

Angle, H.V., Johnsen, T.J., Grebenkemper, N.S. and Ellinwood, C.H. (1979) Computer interview support for clinicians. *Professional Psychology*, **10**, 49–51.

Binik, Y.M., Servan-Schreiber, D., Freiwald, S. and Hall, K.S. (1988) Intelligent computer-based assessment and psychotherapy: an expert system for sexual dysfunction. *Journal of Nervous and Mental Disease*, **176**, 387–400.

Farrell, A.D. (1989) Impact of microcomputers on professional practice: a survey of current practices and attitudes. *Professional Psychology: Research and Practice*, **20**, 172–8.

Felce, D., Saxby, H., de Kock, U., Repp, A. and Blunden, R. (1987) To what behaviors do attending adults respond?: a replication. *American Journal of Mental Deficiency*, **91** (5), 496–504.

Groth-Marnat, G. and Schumaker, J. (1989) Computer-based psychological testing: issues and guidelines. *American Journal of Orthopsychiatry*, **59**, 257–63.

Katz, R. and Nagly, V.T. (1984) CATS: Computerized Aphasia Treatment System. *Cognitive Rehabilitation*, **2** (4), 8–14.

Kolb, D.A. (1984) *Experiential Learning: Experience as the Source of Learning and Development*, Prentice-Hall, New Jersey.

Moreland, K.L. (1987) Computer-based test interpretation: advice to the consumer. *Applied Psychology: An International Review*, **36** (3/4), 385–400.

Norman, D.A. (1988) *The Psychology of Everyday Things*, Basic Books, New York.

Norris, D.E., Skilbeck, C.E., Hayward, A.E. and Torpy, D.M. (1985) *Microcomputers in Clinical Practice*, John Wiley, Chichester.

Roid, G.H. and Gorsuch, R.L. (1984) Development and clinical use of test-interpretive programs on microcomputers. In M.D. Schwartz (ed), *Using Computers in Clinical Practice: Psychotherapy and Mental Health Applications*, pp. 141–9, Haworth Press, New York.

Rotheray, D.R., Sewell, D.F. and Morton, J.R. (1986) The design of educational software for children with learning difficulties. *Programmed Learning and Educational Technology*, **23** (2), 119–23.

Romanczyk, R.G. (1986) *Clinical Utilization of Microcomputer Technology*, Pergamon Press, New York.

Chapter 2

Issues in the Selection and Support of a Microcomputer System

CHRISTOPHER J. COLBOURN

Perhaps because I have been a user of computers in my work as an academic psychologist for a long time now, I am often asked by colleagues, students, and others for advice on the type of computer that would help them in their work. This used to be a relatively simple matter, because many of the parameters were well-defined and one did not have to seek too much information before making a recommendation, which also came from a relatively narrow range of options. However, the pace of change and development of information technology has been relentless and it has become no easy task to assess individual situations. One only has to scan a few of the plethora of computer magazines that are now available to see the truth of this, and sources such as Capron (1990), Day and Athey (1989) and Zorkoczy (1990) show the incredible range of possibilities that this technology can now offer us.

My aim here is nevertheless to attempt an outline answer, and in a relatively non-technical way to accommodate as wide an audience as possible. I shall also try to do this in terms of *principles* since any specific recommendations may be rapidly superseded. After an initial consideration of the main issues in selecting an appropriate computer system—and the focus here will be on personal or desktop computer systems—I will deal with three other main points that need to be taken into account when dealing with computers. These are: networks, since the value of interconnecting machines is now considerable; training and support, which are often forgotten in the rush to put machines to work for us; and finally data security, important in most contexts but crucial for clinicians.

Of course, to some degree all of these factors interact and there will be no one perfect solution to the selection of a suitable system. Compromise is inevitable, but I hope that this chapter will help to guide you through

Microcomputers and Clinical Psychology: Issues, Applications and Future Developments. Edited by A. Ager
©1991 John Wiley & Sons Ltd

some of the key decisions to be made in selecting and supporting a microcomputer system and assist you in arriving at the best compromise for your particular circumstances.

DECIDING UPON A COMPUTER SYSTEM

Initial considerations

The traditional recommendation for selecting a computer system, constantly reiterated in the many computer magazines that are not dedicated to one particular manufacturer's products, but all too rarely followed, is that you need first to define exactly what you want to do with a computer. You should, if possible, take some account of the future as well as immediate requirements. You should then select or take advice on the software that will allow you to do these things, and finally choose the machine that will run the selected software. Again, if possible, you should try out some likely combinations, since it is rare that one solution and one only will emerge. Of course, usually we do not have the time or the capability to judge alternative systems adequately, and what may seem wonderful at a demonstration and for a short time of using it yourself, may turn out to be far less suitable or even irritating to use when you have become familiar with it.

The best advice is probably to consult with friends and colleagues who have implemented a solution to the same or similar problems to your own and go, observe, and try their solutions. This is better than depending on vendors of the equipment who may not have encountered your particular requirements previously, or have a vested interest in selling you a particular solution. Such consultation with others will be especially important if you are working within an organization that either already uses computers or is intending to introduce them in the near future. It may be that your organization already has a purchasing policy for microcomputers and software which you will have to follow unless you can show that the "approved" machines cannot fulfil your requirements. A useful discussion of organizational factors in buying hardware and software has been presented by Barden (1988).

Setting out your requirements

The initial target is to narrow down the possible range of systems to look at. First of all, what do you want to do with a computer system? Most people will have *one main answer* to this—for example, easing "office" work, the automated testing of patients, or sophisticated statistical analysis of data collected in the course of research. However, there soon follows the realization that a computer system can have several uses and more can be made of the investment (in terms of time, money, and skills developed) by planning for several other areas of application. I have outlined the major application areas of computers for clinicians elsewhere (Colbourn, 1989) and many of the other chapters in this volume go into some detail on these matters. Suffice it to say here that all currently available computer systems can offer some sort of solution to these application areas, although many of them will be rather elementary solutions which the user may quickly find unsatisfactory in one way or another. Thus taking a family of five on a touring holiday in a small car is possible but much easier and less fraught using a large estate car. So it is with computers.

Before proceeding any further with your considerations you should write down a definition of your requirements in terms of:

- what the system is supposed to do;
- what output will be required (e.g. high-quality printing, coloured screen displays, etc.);
- how much information will need to be stored (e.g. likely quantity of patient records, research data, etc.);
- how often this data will need to be accessed or edited;
- how the data will be input to the system (e.g. keyboard entry, automatic data logging, via telecommunications, etc.);
- who is going to use the machine, and therefore what training will be needed;
- whether the system will need to be linked with other electronic systems.

This kind of list—and the above is not necessarily exhaustive for any given circumstances—will help when you consult others about your needs and compare various suppliers' products.

What will it cost?

The cost is unfortunately often looked at in unidimensional terms, i.e. the purchase cost should be minimized. However, costs need to be looked at in overall terms, not simply as the purchase price of the hardware and software. Value for money is important and it is well known that for the price of some powerful single-user scientific workstation computers you could buy a small network of less powerful but equally useful (to you) personal computers! For the price of one manufacturer's hardware, you could buy cheaper alternative, yet equivalent, hardware and all the software that you require! However, over and above this is whether the cheaper alternatives actually handle the tasks in the way you require and whether the running costs (e.g. consumables, training, repairs, depreciation, upgrades, etc.) are also lower. Costings need to be made on at least an annual all-in basis, and it is sometimes surprising that initially expensive equipment can turn out to provide a better solution at an all-in price equivalent to much more cheaply purchased equipment. It is also worth remembering that, whatever computer is chosen, the list of 'extras' required—cables, display monitor and printer stands, perhaps more suitable office furniture, floppy disks and paper—can add considerably to the overall cost.

Portable computing?

Where do you want to do your computing? That is, do you need genuine portability? Although many microcomputers and personal computers are relatively compact and reasonably light, they were designed to be used on a desktop, and not to be portable in the sense of being opened up and used immediately and easily almost anywhere.

In recent years truly portable or "laptop" computers have become available, often in a form that offers the equivalent power and facilities of desktop machines, and runs the same software. While these devices are very attractive there are still many drawbacks in terms of, for example, cost (they tend to be much more expensive than the equivalent desktop machine), battery life, storage capacity and screen readability. They are often a compromise in some areas and so you need to consider carefully what, if any, uses that you have for a computer actually demand such portability. Clearly the disadvantages will diminish as development continues; but at present it seems that if portability is essential to your work you might consider a dual purchase of a desktop machine and a simpler, cheaper type of portable computer that could be used for data capture in the field. The data so obtained can subsequently be transferred to the desktop machine upon your return to base, or via a telecommunication link while you are still in the field. Such a telecommunication link could also provide you with access to material held on your office-based system.

BASIC CONFIGURATIONS: SOFTWARE FIRST

We need to concentrate first on the tasks to be carried out on the computer, and thereby select the appropriate *software*. As Barden (1988) indicated, there are really just three distinct types of software:

- *Bespoke software* is specially written to carry out tasks to your own specification.
- *Application-specific software* is designed and written to carry out specific tasks for a wide range of people and organizations who require it. In a clinical context, automated testing programs come into this category (see Morris, 1985, and Chapter 5 in this volume), as do statistical analysis programs.
- *Package software* is designed for general use. Examples are the almost "standard" wordprocessing (e.g. Microsoft Word, WordPerfect), spreadsheet (e.g. Lotus 1-2-3, Microsoft Excel), and database (e.g. dBase, FoxBASE) programs.

Each of these types has advantages and disadvantages and it is highly likely that you will need to select more than one of them to fulfil all your requirements.

Bespoke software can be expensive and time-consuming to produce, depending on the complexity of the design. Nevertheles, if you have some skill in programming (or can employ someone who has) and/or you feel your needs cannot be adequately met by "off-the-shelf" programs, then you can purchase a suitable programming language package and produce your own applications. Most of the current programming languages such as C, Pascal, Fortran, etc. are available on microcomputers, and many come with the BASIC programming language as standard. Norris et al. (1985) provide some good examples of this "bespoke" approach in the context of clinical psychology practice and a detailed overview of all that it entails.

Both application-specific and package software are likely to be cheaper and more efficient to implement than the bespoke type, unless you have plenty of time and skill available. There is also the advantage of a larger number of users who will report problems and bugs in the software, which are likely to be corrected by the producers. Commercial software producers commonly offer telephone "hotline" support to their users to sort out difficulties. A community of users could also be available to share their expertise with novices through user-groups and bulletin board systems. Quite often package software may be the only type actually required since many packages are so flexible that they can be used either alone or in combination with other applications to fulfil all the tasks you require. Many spreadsheet and database packages come with their own programming languages—usually referred to as macro languages—which enable customized versions of the program to be produced to fit your requirements. An example of this in clinical practice was discussed by Kapur (1984). However, it must be noted that here we are bordering on the "bespoke" approach, and the user must be prepared either to devote some time to such development or to pay others to do it.

There is also a vast wealth of public domain or freeware and shareware (i.e. "try before you buy") programs available for many microcomputers.

This type of software is generally produced by professional programmers, academics and enthusiasts as a sideline to their main activities. The type of application is most commonly small utilities or simple versions of standard package applications. The quality is variable but most are very good and have the key advantage of being very cheap, or even free—except perhaps for the cost of media and/or copying fees. However, along with this goes relatively limited or no support from the software author, and no guarantee that it will work with all your other software and be regularly updated or debugged.

Clearly the strategy adopted in deciding on suitable software will evolve from discussions with colleagues, consultants and suppliers. It will often be the case that more than one solution will arise, and where a number of uses are to be made of the system there may be conflicting answers. This is most likely to be so when it is appreciated that many programs are only designed to be run under one type of computer operating system (OS), the overall executive supervisor program that runs on a computer (e.g. MS-DOS, UNIX). Thus, the program that provides the best solution to, say, your assessment problem may require an OS that is different from the best program that would solve your data analysis problems. Since most microcomputers are designed to run only one OS (although there are now some notable exceptions that will run several different OSs and at the same time) this could be difficult to resolve. Clearly, then, one needs to consider the software in conjunction with the hardware that will run it.

BASIC CONFIGURATIONS: HARDWARE NEXT

The choice of software may well dictate fairly specific hardware requirements, although increasingly application-specific and package software is produced for several different hardware platforms. Thus the likelihood of being able to satisfy all your computing needs with one type of machine has increased somewhat, at least for most of the standard types of application. There has also been a fair amount of movement by manufacturers towards implementing the so-called "open systems interconnection" (OSI) standard, which allows easier and improved ways of interconnecting different hardware. These factors mean that machines will increasingly be able to allow interworking, and the constraint of always buying what is already used within an organization will be less compelling.

There is still, however, a vast range of microcomputers to choose from, although it is easier now to summarize the basic choices. For simplicity and in the context of use by clinicians and other professionals, we can resolve the current choice of microcomputers into:

- the IBM PC (personal computer) range of machines and their many clones manufactured by other companies (or "IBM compatibles" as they are known) which run the MS-DOS operating system;
- the newer replacements for the IBM machines known as the IBM PS/2 range, and similarly their clones (which are far fewer than for the earlier machines);
- the "non-compatibles" or proprietary machines, of which the Apple Macintosh family of computers is the most significant in my opinion.

It is worth noting that some of the "non-compatible" machines can emulate the IBM PC by the addition of extra hardware or software (e.g. the Apple Macintosh, and the Acorn Archimedes computers) and can thereby run programs designed for use on IBM PC type machines. This could give you the best of both worlds and is worth considering if your chosen software comes from the different camps.

With more sophisticated machines the above simplified distinctions become blurred. The scientific workstation market offers very powerful desktop/deskside machines that are aimed primarily at high-speed complex graphical processing and multi-user applications. These machines are correspondingly expensive and often more powerful than needed in most clinical psychology contexts. Therefore I will say no more about these here.

A host of other and older proprietary machines are currently being used by clinicians, particularly Apple II computers and BBC 'B' microcomputers (the latter nearly all in the UK). While these can and still do sterling service, they use older technology that is no longer manufactured or as well supported as it once was. In fact the IBM PC itself uses "old technology"; but because it became an "industry standard" very quickly by selling large numbers worldwide, and was allowed to be cloned, there is a substantial investment of human and financial resources in this technology that users are loathe to relinquish for the latest, more expensive, developments.

Returning to what I have specified as the current choices, I feel that your decision can be further resolved into choosing between IBM PCs and compatibles (the later IBM PS/2 range can be included here for present intents and purposes), and other proprietary machines, especially the Apple Macintosh family. Barden (1988) summarizes what he sees as the advantages and disadvantages of each choice in terms of standards, software available, cost, and quality. Unfortunately, these often balance out and the choice becomes an emotive one. There are enthusiasts on both sides, and again I would urge you to choose the software and hardware combination that seems to most fully and adequately meet your current and likely future needs, that will fit easily into your organization, and that you feel happiest in using. The latter principle is often overlooked but is important if the computer is to be used as effectively as possible (Hutchins, Hollan and Norman, 1986).

It is perhaps also worth pointing to the psychological principles that have influenced the design of some computer interfaces, i.e. the way in which people are required to use them. Most early microcomputers, including the IBM PC, used a "command-line" interface whereby the user had to type in specific commands to get the machine to carry out functions. Some application software displays on the screen a list or menu of things that can be done next, and the user selects one of these by typing in a number or a letter or by moving a cursor to the item selected using the arrow keys on the keyboard. A further development of the latter idea was the "direct manipulation mode" of interaction that is evident on graphical user interfaces (GUI) first made commercially successful by the Apple Macintosh computer. In this case the user operates a "mouse" pointing device to directly select words or images on the screen that initiate the functions. Together with some access to command-line features for executing repetitive tasks, the direct manipulation mode seems easier to use, easier to learn, and less prone to error (see e.g. Norman, 1988, pp. 177–86). Macintosh computers currently present the best commercially available version of a GUI on a microcomputer, but these interfaces are becoming available on the IBM-type machines and others, although few as yet show such an integrated interface across all the software as in the case of the Macintosh. However, in the longer term it is unclear what weight should be attached to such "user friendliness" over and above other factors mentioned. I return briefly to this issue in a later section.

Caution should be exercised when purchasing the very latest machines since, as with any new product, there may be some teething problems that are sorted out over the first year of manufacture. It is also probably best to avoid less well-established manufacturers (of which there are many in the IBM-clone business) unless you feel assured of their long-term stability and quality of their products. They will often be the cheapest products to purchase but, as I pointed out earlier, one needs to account for overall costs rather than just the purchase price. Again, advice from others on any specific products should be sought. Ideally you should be able to try out your selected system before finally committing yourself to purchase, but it is likely that you will only be able to do this for a relatively brief period. By taking as much advice as possible and by using a helpful supplier, most problems should be minimized.

There is the possibility of purchasing secondhand equipment, but all the previous advice would still apply. While bargains are possible so are bad mistakes, as with secondhand cars. Barden (1988; pp. 52–4) discusses secondhand purchase, but I think it is worth noting that few if any computer dealers handle secondhand equipment.

Rental and leasing of equipment are possibilities, although the way in which funds are likely to be made available to clinical psychologists make such options less attractive than outright purchase.

More about options

Before leaving the topic of the equipment—or "kit" as the computer professionals tend to call it—I shall say a little about the various options that you may have to decide between even after choosing one manufacturer's kit.

General aspects

Any particular range or even model of microcomputer has a variety of options available with respect to the amount of RAM, storage capacity (i.e. disk drives), maths co-processors (to drastically increase the speed of numerical computations in data analysis), input devices and ports (i.e. keyboards, mouse, graphics tablet, analogue to digital convertor, etc.), output devices (monochrome or colour displays, high or low screen resolution, serial and parallel ports for printers and other peripheral devices, etc.), network connections (see subsequent discussion), internal expansion slots for adding other facilities like high-speed graphics processors, internal modems for connecting to telecommunication networks, faster central processors to speed up the basic machine, extra hard-disk drives to expand the backing store capacity, etc.

Detailed discussion of these features is beyond the scope of this chapter. The information is commonly obtained through reading equipment reviews in computer magazines, but further advice should be sought to establish the best price–performance combination for the software that you wish to utilize. The best general advice would be to select the most RAM you can afford, since software is becoming increasingly sophisticated and requiring more memory space in the machine; and always get a microcomputer with a high-capacity hard disk if it is to be used as a stand-alone machine most of the time—the slow speed and relatively low capacity of floppy disks as a storage medium will often make computer usage a chore because of the need to handle several "floppies" for all but the most mundane of tasks. The choice of a colour or monochrome display largely depends on your requirements, but unless crucial, colour can be considered a luxury.

Printers

There may be some peripheral devices that you need to complete your computer system, the most likely being a printer for hardcopy output. There are four main types: *dot-matrix* (characters are formed by preprogrammed combinations of wires held in a printing head matrix striking a typewriter-like ribbon on to paper); *daisy-wheel* (using a wheel of preformed characters); *ink-jet* (a fine jet of ink is sprayed through an electric field which shapes the jet into the character); and *laser* (essentially using photocopier technology, whereby a laser beam temporarily etches the image on to a rotating drum for transfer to paper). As with computers themselves, there are many manufacturers, and a wide range of prices.

The types differ primarily in terms of printing speed, print quality, noisiness, and costs, although the cheaper ones of all types may not be robust enough to handle lots of daily output. Daisy-wheel printers produce output like a good-quality typewriter, but they are slow and noisy, and cannot handle graphics. Laser printers are the fastest type, produce the best quality output, handle graphics, are relatively quiet, but rather expensive to buy and to run. Dot-matrix printers are perhaps the most widely used because the latest versions are fairly flexible in being able to trade speed for output quality and also handle graphics. They can be rather noisy but there is almost bound to be one that suits many of your requirements. The latest generation of ink-jet printers provide a good compromise between dot-matrix and laser types at a cost that is generally lower than the top-end of the dot-matrix range.

As with the choice of computer, it is essential to ensure that the printer works with your other software and hardware selections, and will stand up to the kind of usage you require.

Other peripherals

An increasing number of other peripherals can be connected to micro-computers. Examples are video digitizers (for taking input from video cameras and recorders), image scanners (for inputting images on paper), CD ROM systems (based on compact-disk technology for the storage of very large quantities of mixed alphanumeric, sound and image data), tape drives (for rapidly making back-up copies of the contents of hard disks) and optical/magnetic disk systems (like hard disks but offering vastly more storage capacity). One can see many applications of most of these devices in psychological research and practice, but currently the expense is beyond most budgets.

CONNECTING TO NETWORKS

The value of networking

Microcomputers of the type discussed above offer good local processing power, but when also connected to networks (via cables or the telephone) they can access a considerably larger number of facilities and software that are available on larger, remote computers. The relatively rapid development

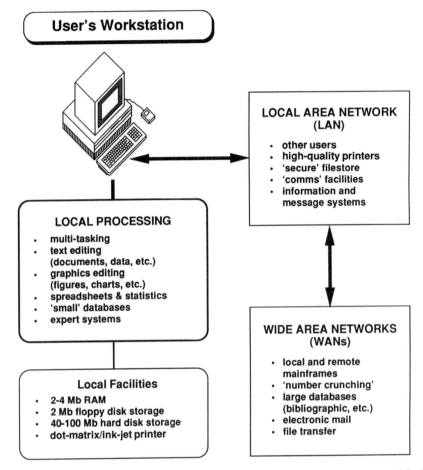

Figure 2.1 Some functions of a "personal workstation" and its networked links to other facilities.

of microcomputer and network technology promises to offer even greater "power" in the future. Figure 2.1 summarizes the relationship between the functions of a microcomputer, and the facilities accessible via both local area networks (LANs), which are generally restricted to, say, one department or a building, and wide area networks (WANs), which can attain global proportions.

A LAN enables work colleagues to share, quickly and easily, expensive computing resources (such as secure magnetic disk storage of documents and information, high-quality printers, devices for telephone and direct-line communications to other computers and networks), and to communicate with one another via "electronic mail" (Email) systems that do not depend on the synchronous presence of the communicators. I shall expand on the Email concept below. WANs enable and facilitate the use of computers at a considerable distance from the user where there might be software or databases that are not available locally. Essentially you run some software on your own microcomputer which allows it to talk directly to the remote computer and allows you to act as a user of that remote machine, sending it commands just as you would to the microcomputer on your desk. WANs also make national and global Email and file transfer systems possible, and a number of these exist already for the academic, industrial and commercial communities. Again these will be considered below. A very readable general account of computer networks can be found in a book prepared by Apple Computer Inc. (1989), and in Stokes (1984).

A detailed yet accessible discussion of the different types of LAN currently available can be found in Bridges (1986). It must be emphasized that setting up a LAN can be an expensive business, although some microcomputers (e.g. Apple Macintosh) do come with most of the necessary hardware and software for a simple low-speed network to be quickly and easily implemented. There are also some similar products available for IBM-compatible machines. Thus if you are considering the purchase of several computers, or connecting the machine you purchase to an existing or new network in your organization, this should be taken into account when selecting software and hardware.

Computer communications requirements

Inter-computer communication (usually referred to as "comms") requires that the microcomputer system you are using is equipped with either an appropriate network interface or the simpler serial interface to the RS-232-C or RS422/3/4 standards. Many microcomputers have these built-in now, although it is important to check this. In addition you will need either easy access to a LAN, or a direct line to your target computer system (be it a mainframe computer or simply a "larger" microcomputer), or a "modem"— a device to link your computer, via its serial interface, to your telephone (assuming that the target computer or WAN is also connected to a telephone). You will also need some communications software for your computer (again a few machines are supplied with such a package) which provides the facilities for controlling input and output via the serial interface, emulating particular standard forms of communications protocols (referred to as "terminal emulation") used by mainframe computers and WANs, and providing facilities for transferring files to or from other computers. Many such software packages have features which allow you to configure it for almost automatic contact with the distant machine—including, if you are using a modem that can act like a telephone, making the telephone call itself. It is worth noting that modems do not require a special (''dedicated'') telephone line, although poor line quality may necessitate the need for a more expensive type of modem that utilizes an error-correcting protocol. There are now some ''clever'' but expensive modems that allow you to both talk to a colleague, and send computer data over the telephone line at the same time!

Selecting a suitable modem is almost as complex as selecting the computer system software and hardware. You should seek expert advice with respect to your own particular circumstances before selecting equipment. More comprehensive details of how to connect your microcomputer to a mainframe computer via LANs, telephone, etc., can be found in Durr and Walker (1985).

Using wide area networks

Let us now turn to why you might wish to access other computers via your microcomputer in the context of clinical psychological practice. The main uses would probably be statistical analysis, literature searches, and file and mail transfers. There are other uses which could be valuable in the mental health context and may form a part of a research project or service, namely online information systems, the simpler forms of which are usually referred to as ''bulletin boards'' or ''computer conferencing systems''.

Literature searches

Literature searches will be familiar to all researchers, although their experience may be limited to enlisting the services of a librarian. Baker (1984) pointed out that most online bibliographic databases are not designed for use by individual researchers but by information specialists (librarians, etc.). Recently, however, accessibility to some of these online services has been made available to individual subscribers, thus opening them out to non-specialists in information science. There is an attempt by the corporations that run the databases to utilize some of the off-peak time when large educational, research, and business organizations are not active. Individual subscribers have access from late evening through to early morning. Savings over the usual rates are substantial, but this still does not make these services cheap. My own experience of using services like the various databases that exist on the giant DIALOG system (which contains several databases relevant to the behavioural, social and medical sciences) run by the Lockheed Corporation from their California base has tended to confirm Baker's point, although clearly one can learn how to make more successful searches with practice. Unfortunately, one can pay a heavy financial penalty for little return while acquiring such practice.

Thus, currently the best advice would seem to be to use available library services for your computer-based literature searches. The experienced librarian, who knows the databases being examined, can—following consultation on your requirements—extract what information is available quickly and easily. Even with an expert to guide you it is often best to do one or two test searches using areas where you know the literature well. Remember that many databases are not archival in the sense of containing information on sources older than the last ten years. Further details and examples of carrying out these types of bibliographic searches can be found in Madron, Tate and Brookshire (1985).

Online public access catalogues

Online public access catalogues (OPACs) in libraries offer a very useful facility for the busy researcher/practitioner. Using your desktop computer, you are able to check whether a particular book, periodical or issue of a periodical is in your or another institution's library, and if it is currently available or out on loan. This can save much time looking in physical catalogues and searching shelves in vain for the items that you require. While some OPACs seem to suffer from the design problems mentioned in connection with bibliographic databases (Miter, 1986), in general they are a boon to the busy professional.

Bulletin boards and conferencing systems

Other types of online information system are bulletin board systems (BBSs) and computer conferencing systems. These have proliferated in recent times and offer both large- and small-scale information and electronic-mail services often based around a particular theme. The commonest theme is still microcomputers themselves, and for users of particular machines this can offer a useful source of news, help, advice, even software (which can be transferred, or "downloaded", from a BBS directly into the user's machine).

BBSs often run on a microcomputer installed and connected to the telephone in a private individual's home. However, commercial organizations and local governments have also set up such services, primarily to offer information rather than mail facilties. Of interest in the context of mental health is the fact that some London boroughs have set up BBSs offering information on all the local health services, and have installed microcomputer-based terminals to this service in local libraries. Many such BBSs are based on similar software to that used by the national Prestel information service operated by British Telecom. This type of system, known as "viewdata" or "videotex", is based on a series of frames or screens of information containing up to 920 characters. Colourful text and relatively primitive graphics can be placed on the frames, which are often quite attractive and look very similar to the perhaps more familiar television-based "teletext" information services like Ceefax and Oracle in the UK. However, unlike the television services, viewdata systems are interactive, generally operate much faster, and have a larger number of frames or pages of information available (at least for the large national systems). Introductory descriptions of various types of BBSs can be found in Gold (1989), and McBride (1985) provides an in-depth account of viewdata systems, including a full description of how to set them up and run them.

Computer conferencing systems are generally much more substantial pieces of software that require the speed and capacity of multi-user computer systems to host them. They handle text only and were originally developed to provide an asynchronous communication medium for university-level teaching, particularly in distance education (see e.g. Mason and Kaye, 1989). However, they can also provide a useful forum for discussion between busy professionals. One advantage is that you can choose a suitable time to read other contributions to the "conference" and to "post back" replies; the other participants then read your contributions and comment, and so on. Again such systems have considerable potential and exist in a slightly different form on the global academic networks like BITNET, EARN, INTERNET, JANET and UUCP. I shall mention these again in the next section on electronic mail.

There are various advantages and disadvantages of the different types of online information system, and of the whole medium as a reference source, which are beyond the brief of this chapter. However, in the context of offering easily updated information on, say, local mental health services and facilities, including an electronic mail facility for contact between users of the system (be they mental health professionals or local residents), this use of microcomputers seems to have considerable potential.

File transfer and electronic mail (Email)

The important uses of file transfer between computers can be summarized as passing a file of research data to or from another computer for statistical or other analysis (including the sending of data from "field" locations to your home base), passing messages to an electronic mail facility on another computer, and passing computer software to or from another computer. In the context of clinical psychology these could all be important, but I should briefly like to pick out here two themes whose usefulness may not be apparent.

Firstly, in the cooperative writing of books or papers by individuals who are physically remote, the speedy transfer of text documents between them can greatly facilitate the process. Although floppy disks containing the text can be conveyed, this still depends on conventional carriage methods. Cotton (1984) pointed out that, on average, 70% of the life cycle of a document transmitted by conventional letter post is tied up in the actual mail. Electronic file transfer is easily achieved now in the academic and research community since the advent of electronic networks. In the UK the "joint academic network" (JANET) links all university and major research sites and is beginning to be made more widely accessible to other educational institutions, government agencies, and commercial organizations often through interlinking with other networks. Similar arrangements have long been established in North America and are now available in Europe, Asia and Australasia. In fact these national and geographically located networks are interlinked so that it is possible to send electronic mail between them. Thus from a desktop microcomputer you could send and receive chapter or paper drafts, read and make modifications to them on your microcomputer, and send them back.

Commercial Email services, which are often combined with information systems as described in the previous section, are expensive because users are charged for the time they are online to the system, for each message they send, and for any messages they store on the system. By contrast the use of academic Email systems is generally free, and the international links are often better than those in the commercial systems. However, they are not always as easy to use as one might like. Pliskin (1989) describes this aspect of academic Email systems and raises a number of other relevant issues regarding their use.

The main advantage of Email is its relative speed over conventional mail (i.e. messages are delivered almost immediately to the recipient's "electronic mailbox"), without the requirement of the recipient's physical presence as with the telephone, or the limitation on message space as with telephone answering machines, or the need for expensive dedicated equipment as with facsimile transmission (fax). Of course, you need to get used to looking in your electronic mailbox each morning when you come in, and this becomes just another part of using a microcomputer in your work. Email also forms the basis of many discussion groups that have grown up with the global networks. Particular university computers host what are called "listservers" to which users can send a simple Email message to join their name (and electronic address) to the list for a particular topic. Topics range across nearly all academic subjects, including psychology, and many other areas (especially anything and everything to do with computers!). An Email message sent to the list is redistributed by the host computer to all subscribers on that list. Questions, answers and information form the main traffic on such lists, and the traffic can be very heavy. However, it is easy to delete messages you are not interested in, and I have found Email a valuable method of obtaining advice rapidly from a very wide audience.

TRAINING AND SUPPORT IN COMPUTER USE

The issues discussed in this section could quickly become critical as your work becomes more dependent on the use of a microcomputer. Problems with either the hardware or the software could be very disruptive and some allowance for initial training in the use of the hardware and software is essential.

Training

One of the main problems with using computers is simply learning how to do it. This is probably more true for those whose education was completed before computers were introduced widely into the curriculum. Thus people who have not had a formal course on computer appreciation, usage or programming during their many years of training often feel at a disadvantage and somewhat wary of getting involved. This should not be the case at all.

There are various ways in which computer novices can acquaint themselves with *using* computers. Note my emphasis here on *use*, as opposed to programming, which can take considerable time to learn if you are going to produce useful pieces of software for yourself. This is not to discourage you but to forewarn you.

With respect to learning about computer use, I wish to draw your attention to two important points. Firstly, you need to feel that the time spent learning to use a computer is time well spent, because that time may not be especially productive in terms of your clinical work and/or research. However, the topics covered in this volume may convince you that computer use is worth looking into further, and if you have read this far you must have some interest in the possibilities. Secondly, you should realize that you do not need to know anything about how the hardware works in order to use the machine. A purely global functional knowledge of what the various components of a computer system do is sufficient (e.g. floppy or hard disks are for filing your data, text, programs). Some computer systems offer better features than others to help convey this message (O'Malley, 1986).

Short courses

Short intensive courses are run by many university computing centres, often in an inexpensive adult education programme. The intensive type of course (say two to five whole days) is usually found to be better than an hour or so a week over several weeks, especially for getting you going and using a machine. Avoid extremely expensive commercial courses which are rarely designed to give you the type of experience required in research or clinical applications. The dealer from whom one may purchase the microcomputer system often provides some training at no extra cost. However, the dealer may not be sufficiently experienced with the particular applications that you have chosen to be of much help with anything other than the general operation of the equipment.

Self teaching

You can, of course, simply sit down with the tutorial and reference manuals supplied with the system, and with any applications packages you have selected or intend to try, and work through them either on your own, with a colleague who also wishes to learn, or another colleague who knows a fair amount about the hardware and software (but preferably not a "computer buff"). Such colleagues will probably have been identified during your selection of appropriate software and hardware.

Many people prefer to come to grips with a machine on their own, and only consult others when they are really stuck. This can be very useful in allowing you to work at your own pace and with your own data, documents, etc., rather than simply using the examples supplied in the manuals. Mistakes are bound to be made, although remember that the computer will only do what you ask it to, and you are unable to damage it simply by typing on the keyboard. Your mistakes can be frustrating, especially when you erase a whole day's work. You may be unfortunate enough to come across a software bug (fortunately relatively rare in commercially produced software) which corrupts the data on your disk, making it unreadable. The lesson of making backup copies of important disks or files is soon learned.

A brief survey of academic and clinical psychologists who use computers has shown that most adopted self-teaching, largely because of time constraints. Unfortunately much hardware and software documentation has been rather poor, although some manufacturers and software producers have improved their standards tremendously in recent years. In addition there has been a very substantial publishing boom in guides to particular microcomputers and standard software packages which the potential user can find in many bookshops. Again, the level and helpfulness of these varies greatly and many do little more than re-work the manufacturer-supplied manuals, while others do a far better job than such manuals.

Keyboarding

Many potential users worry about their lack of familiarity with the standard QWERTY keyboard used on nearly all microcomputers. While the ability to touch-type can be useful, it is debatable whether it is a prerequisite for effective computer use. I find that, using just a few fingers, I can input text, data, etc., as fast as I can think about what I wish to do or write. If you are in the position of not being able to type, you will find that you quickly learn your way around the keyboard simply with practice in using the machine.

Increasingly computers with GUIs (see earlier) are appearing. These use a "mouse" device for some kinds of input. The device, about the size of a matchbox and attached to the computer by a lead, can be moved around the desk to control an on-screen pointer. By using this arrangement to point to command words or small pictures (called "icons") displayed on the screen, the computer can be made to execute various tasks. Many people find this system much simpler and quicker than typing command words all the time, although touch-typists may be less enthusiastic (see Martin, 1985, for an example of such a system).

While any system can be learned in time, busy clinicians may prefer the faster learning curve that usually seems to accompany training with computers employing a GUI, than with those utilizing the older command line mode of interaction with the machine.

Hardware support

Most hardware is very reliable these days, requires little, if any, regular maintenance, and most manufacturing faults show up very quickly, well within the warranty period. However, it is as well to consider what support is available should anything go wrong.

As your work becomes dependent on the use of the microcomputer you will not want to be without it for weeks on end if it breaks. Unfortunately, the insurance of an on-site maintenance contract whereby an engineer will visit you and repair your machine within a specified time period comes very expensive: an annual fee of 10–15% of the purchase price is common. All the alternatives involve a "back-to-base" arrangement whereby the faulty equipment has to be returned to the vendor and then possibly to the manufacturer. This can be very time consuming and frustrating but is often the only affordable solution, unless your organization invests heavily in one type or a limited range of hardware and trains staff in their repair and maintenance. The latter situation also means that there will probably be spare or under-utilized machines of the same type about that you can get access to, and thereby minimize the disruption to your work. From this you can see an advantage of purchasing equipment similar to that already used in your organization or by colleagues.

A final factor worth considering in this context is that purchasing your hardware from a local specialist dealer (and I would emphasize the local) rather than a discount retailer can often pay dividends in the long run despite a somewhat higher initial cost. A good relationship with a local dealer can often assist in getting problems sorted out quicker than if you have to be referred directly to the manufacturer by a discount retailer who sells on price alone and often knows relatively little about the equipment. The dealer may even be able to lend you a replacement machine temporarily or give you access to one.

Software support

You can afford to be less concerned about where you purchase software, since problems with these items often need to be referred to the producers, the larger ones of which commonly have a telephone-based technical enquiry service. The availability of such support may need to be a factor in your choice of suitable software if no other local source of help is available. Depending on assistance via bulletin boards and other electronic media can be somewhat precarious if you need to solve problems very quickly. While such sources can be valuable it must be remembered that the participants on such systems are mostly other users like yourself with little time to devote to the problems of others—unless it is one that they have encountered themselves and they can quickly describe the solution.

Major software packages are usually under constant development with regular updates that bring improvements, correction of subtle faults "bug fixes" and new facilities. You should find out what the producer's policy is with regard to supplying these updates. Most of them make a charge which depends on the extent of the update, but this is rarely more than 25–30% of the initial purchase price, and often less, especially if you only recently bought the software. Users are, of course, only informed of software upgrades if they register their purchase with the producer; so do send in those registration cards for all the software you buy.

Bannon (1986) noted that, despite the availability of online help facilities for many software packages, and detailed manuals, most users prefer to sort out any problems by asking a colleague who is familiar with the same software. Once again this has implications for your choice of software if there is a pool of local computer users.

SECURITY AND CONFIDENTIALITY ISSUES

There are two somewhat distinct and yet related sets of issues to be covered here. The first concerns the more general issue of maintaining the integrity of data stored on computer-readable media, which is relevant to all computer users and includes the need to make backup copies and avoid computer "viruses". The second set of issues concerns the need to protect and control access to sensitive data which relate to identifiable patients and other individuals. The latter issues also relate directly to the UK Data Protection Act and similar legislation in other countries which sets out rules for the processing, storage and accessibility of data describing identifiable living persons.

Secure storage

The data that you input to a microcomputer—the files of text, numbers, graphics, etc.—are precious since they took you time to create, and represent an investment for the future when you may wish to re-use them in whole or in part. They are most likely to be stored on magnetic media—floppy or hard disks—which, while reliable, do require some care in handling. Most microcomputers now have the 3.5 inch floppy disk drives which use the more robust plastic-encased disks. However, even these can be abused by careless handling and storage. Always keep the environment surrounding your computer and associated equipment clean and free from dust. Use dust covers when equipment is not in use, and store "floppies" away in purpose-designed boxes, or at least the cardboard boxes that the new ones come in. Avoid having food and drink near your computer equipment: a spilt cup of coffee can put a keyboard out of action and ruin a floppy disk containing a year's worth of data collection!

The security of data is clearly important, and it is advisable to have more than one copy of your files. Events outside your control can corrupt data on disks—software errors, or power failures for instance. It is possible to install an "uninterruptible power supply" (UPS). UPSs for microcomputers are commonly based on rechargeable batteries and cut in automatically when the power fails, providing you with sufficient time to close down your computer without losing any data. They also have the added advantage of smoothing out power surges and spikes that can sometimes corrupt data. However, UPSs are an expensive solution and are rarely justified in locations where disruption to the power supply is rare, except when an organization could hardly function without its computer systems. Thus backup procedures are an essential part of using computers. They provide a means of disaster recovery and of returning to an earlier state of a file that you have subsequently modified.

Making backups

There are a number of different methods of making backup copies of files and the choice depends largely on particular circumstances. Where very large amounts of data are being produced or edited each day, or many files are constantly being modified, all most likely on a hard disk, then the most efficient solution would be to backup to a tape streamer or even a WORM ("write once read many") drive. Tape streamers for microcomputers are essentially like a high-speed cassette tape recorder, not to be confused with the adapted audio cassette tape storage devices that came with the early "home" microcomputers. WORM drives are commonly based on optical disk technology, and although they are faster than tape and have vast amounts of storage space, the media costs are still high. Tape on the other hand is relatively cheap, although the actual drives in both cases are rather expensive items.

For the average user, backing up to a floppy disk is the best compromise in terms of efficiency and cost, since no extra equipment is required. It is important to have a clear routine, although it need not be as complex as some authorities advocate (e.g. Barden, 1988, pp. 73–7). Fortunately there are now a number of sophisticated software packages that make backups very simple. After the initial backup to a set of floppy disks, subsequent runs only backup the files that have been modified or added since the previous run. This saves the user the extra time and trouble of documenting backups. Many users will find it sufficient to carry out such backups weekly, although this might be supplemented by specific file backups on a daily basis, again depending on the quantity and importance of the relevant files. Users need to evolve their own routines, but it is important not to neglect them since the penalties can be substantial in terms of lost time getting back to where you were before some disaster.

A final important point with respect to backups is that you should occasionally check that the backup copy can be used to restore your files, at least by copying back a few samples and looking at them. It is better to discover any problems before a disaster rather than after!

Computer viruses

In recent years there has been much talk of computer viruses, and much anxiety raised amongst users as to what, if anything, they can and should do to protect their computer systems from such things.

The term "computer virus" has commonly been used to describe what are in fact three different types of surreptitiously distributed program. A virus itself is any program that spreads itself secretly whether the purpose is constructive or destructive. Many have merely put silly messages on the screen, or sometimes political slogans; others have damaged files either deliberately or because of bugs in the virus program itself. The second type of program is a "trojan" (after trojan horse) which appears to do something ostensibly useful while secretly doing something else. In the worst cases the secret action is to erase your hard disk! The third type is a "worm" which simply embeds itself within another program from where it may or may not spread and becomes disruptive by occupying space or processing time. Even non-destructive viruses are disruptive because they occupy memory and disk space and can thereby interfere with the running of the computer.

Fortunately, the threat from viruses has been met by a number of dedicated computer experts quickly analysing viruses as they appear and producing suitable detection and eradication software. Much of this software can be set up to run automatically on starting your microcomputer. Apart from this, adopt "safe computing" practices, like always checking disks that you receive from other people (including new software distribution disks—there have been some cases of viruses spread this way) and checking files downloaded into your microcomputer from other systems.

Owing to an ever changing scene, detailed information about computer viruses and their handling has been circulated as electronic documents on the global networks, as have many of the high-quality freeware and shareware programs to combat this menace. However, recently a major reference work on the subject has been published (Price Waterhouse, 1989).

Data protection

In the UK, the Data Protection Act 1984 was introduced to regulate the use of computerized data related to people, or "personal data" as the Act defines it. The nature, accuracy and length of time for which records on people are kept must necessarily be affected by this Act and it is essential for all such users to be registered. Often the institution or organization within which you work will have registered its staff and appointed a Data Protection Officer, who can advise on the implications of the Act for the way in which you use a computer to handle and process data about individuals. If this is not the case then useful free literature describing the Act and its implications (including who needs to register) is available from the national Data Protection Registrar or via the Post Office (see e.g. Data Protection Registrar, 1987). One problem seems to hinge on the access that individuals now have to computer-based information about themselves. While medical records and clinical case notes maintained as computer records are likely to be subject to the Act, it is unclear whether research data that often contains no direct personal references to individuals are also included. It is also unclear whether the information holder is obliged to explain what computer records mean in terms of exact codings, etc., and these often relate to difficult and uncertain concepts anyway. Unfortunately the Act is very complex and probably needs to be clarified via case law. It is also felt to be lacking adequate controls in some areas (see e.g. Campbell and Connor, 1987).

It is worth noting that, although this legislation relates only to the UK, it was designed to be consistent with the Council of Europe's Data Protection Convention, and many countries in Europe and North America have similar forms of legislation which you would need to be aware of when working with computers in such countries.

FINAL COMMENTS

This chapter has provided some guidelines for clinical psychologists who may be trying to reach some decision on the "hows" and "whats" of computerizing their work. The issues concerning support for microcomputers may have provided further insights to those who have already taken the plunge of utilizing computers in their work. Selecting and supporting microcomputers is a complex business and it is only when all the details are known that very specific advice can be given, so consider the comments here as general guidelines and discuss your particular case with colleagues, and others who have some expert knowledge of the topic. For larger scale computerization projects, it may even be worth using a specialist consultant; the service may not be cheap, but neither will be the acquisition of inappropriate software and hardware.

Acknowledgements

I would like to thank all the staff and students of the Psychology Department at Southampton University, and the clinical psychologists in the Wessex region, who have contributed to this chapter by the many questions they have asked me about computers over a number of years.

REFERENCES

Apple Computer Inc. (1989) *Understanding Computer Networks*, Addison-Wesley, Reading, Mass.

Baker, C. (1984) Human aspects of online information retrieval. In A. Burns (ed), *New Information Technology*, pp. 122–33, Ellis Horwood, Chichester.

Bannon, L.J. (1986) Helping users help each other. In D.A. Norman and S.W. Draper (eds), *User-Centred System Design: New Perspectives on Human–Computer Interaction*, pp. 399–410, Lawrence Erlbaum, Hillsdale, NJ.

Barden, R.A. (1988) *Personal Computers for the Business*, NCC Publications, Manchester.

Bridges, S.P.M. (1986) *Low Cost Local Area Networks*, Sigma Press/Wiley, Wilmslow, Cheshire.

Campbell, D. and Connor, S. (1987) Surveillance, computers and privacy. In R. Finnegan, G. Salaman and K. Thompson (eds), *Information Technology: Social Issues*, pp. 134–44, Hodder and Stoughton, London.

Capron, H.L. (1990) *Computers: Tools for an Information Age*, 2nd edn, Addison-Wesley, Reading, Mass.

Colbourn, C.J. (1989) Using computers. In G. Parry and F.N. Watts (eds), *Behavioural and Mental Health Research: A Handbook of Skills and Methods*, pp. 81–103, Lawrence Erlbaum, London.

Cotton, K. (1984) Electronic mail. In A. Burns (ed), *New Information Technology*, pp. 47–54, Ellis Horwood, Chichester.

Data Protection Registrar (1987) *Data Protection Act 1984. Guideline 1: Introduction to the Act*, Office of the Data Protection Registrar, Wilmslow, Cheshire.

Day, J.C. and Athey, T.H. (1989) *Microcomputers and Applications*, 2nd edn, Scott, Foresman & Co., Glenview, Illinois.

Durr, M. and Walker, D. (1985) *Micro to Mainframe: Creating an Integrated Environment*, Addison-Wesley, Reading, Mass.

Gold, S. (1989) *Hugo Cornwall's New Hacker's Handbook*, Century, London.

Hutchins, E.L., Hollan, J.D. and Norman, D.A. (1986) Direct manipulation interfaces. In D.A. Norman and S.W. Draper (eds), *User-Centred System Design: New Perspectives on Human–Computer Interaction*, pp. 87–124, Lawrence Erlbaum, Hillsdale, NJ.

Kapur, N. (1984) Using a microcomputer-based data management system for neuropsychological record filing, report generation, and as a clinical decision aid. *Bulletin of the British Psychological Society*, **37**, 413–15.

Madron, T.W.M., Tate C.N. and Brookshire, R.G. (1985) *Using Microcomputers in Research*, Sage University Paper Series on Quantitative Applications in the Social Sciences, no. 07-052, Sage, Beverly Hills and London.

Martin, J. and the Arben Group, Inc. (1985) *A Breakthrough in Making Computers Friendly: The Macintosh Computer*, Prentice-Hall, Englewood Cliffs, NJ.

Mason, R. and Kaye, A. (eds) (1989) *Mindweave: Communication, Computers and Distance Education*, Pergamon, Oxford.

McBride, J. (1985) *Instant Access: The Videotex Approach to Information Management*, Marathon Videotex, London.

Miter, N.N. (1986) Users and ease of use: online catalogues' raison d'etre. *Program*, **202**, 111–19.

Morris, R.G. (1985) Automated clinical assessment. In F.N. Watts (ed), *New Developments in Clinical Psychology*, pp. 121–38, the British Psychological Society/Wiley, Chichester.

Norman, D.A. (1988) *The Psychology of Everyday Things*, Basic Books, New York.

Norris, D.E., Skilbeck, C.E., Hayward, A.E. and Torpy, D.M. (1985) *Microcomputers in Clinical Practice*, John Wiley, Chichester.

O'Malley, C.E. (1986) Helping users help themselves. In D.A. Norman and S.W. Draper (eds), *User-Centred System Design: New Perspectives on Human–Computer Interaction*, pp. 377–98, Lawrence Erlbaum, Hillsdale, NJ.

Pliskin, N. (1989) Interacting with electronic mail can be a dream or a nightmare: a user's point of view. *Interacting with Computers*, **1**, 259–72.

Price Waterhouse (1989) *The Complete Computer Virus Handbook*, Pitman, London.

Stokes, A. (1984) Computer networks. In A. Burns (ed), *New Information Technology*, pp. 111–22, Ellis Horwood, Chichester.

Zorkoczy, P. (1990) *Information Technology: An Introduction*, 3rd edn, Pitman, London.

Chapter 3

Computer-Assisted Assessment of Psychological Problems

STEPHANIE B. LOCKSHIN AND KELLEY HARRISON

Interest in automated testing systems began in the 1960s and seems to have arisen out of a desire to provide more reliable, effective, and less costly psychological services to growing numbers of clients. This sentiment was expressed by Lanyon (1972) who advocated that mental health professionals utilize modern technology in an effort to make optimal use of the limited resources available so as to be able to provide services to as many people as possible.

Automated and computerized assessment was and continues to be seen as a possible solution to this problem. A large body of literature concerned with the efficacy of computer applications to clinical problems currently exists. To date, strong emphasis has been placed on assessing the reliability and validity of information obtained via computer-generated interviews and inventories as well as on the reliability and validity of automated administration of standardized psychological tests.

The speed with which tests can be administered and scored, the reduction of the psychologist's direct involvement in the testing process, and the resultant increase in the efficient use of skilled manpower are advantages which have historically been cited as strengths of computer-assisted assessment (Greist et al., 1973; Johnson and Williams, 1975). While proponents argue that computer utilization in the clinical process is cost-effective, there is some controversy even among those favorably disposed to computer assessment as to which aspects of assessment the computer is best suited. Others have questioned the logic of having the computer duplicate the functions of a skilled psychometrician and suggest, alternatively, that computer applications focus on the capabilities of the computer to create tests different from those currently available (Roid and Gorsuch, 1984).

Microcomputers and Clinical Psychology: Issues, Applications and Future Developments. Edited by A. Ager
©1991 John Wiley & Sons Ltd

Critics of computer-assisted assessment often allude to the impersonal and inhuman qualities of the computer. Another limiting factor is that computers have difficulty with information that deviates from a structured question and answer format (Erdman, Klein and Greist, 1985). It is argued that this shortcoming has direct bearing on the range and type of information which can be obtained via computer-administered interviews.

In an effort to determine the frequency, predominant uses, and attitudes towards computer applications by psychologists in professional practice, Farrell (1989) conducted a survey of 227 psychologists, the majority of whom were practitioners in clinical or counseling psychology. The psychologists included in the survey sample represented a variety of professional affiliations including private practice, academia, hospitals and outpatient clinics. The results of the survey indicated that, while over one-half of the respondents utilized computers in their practices, the majority of users restricted use to clerical applications such as wordprocessing, client billing, and administrative record keeping. Relatively few made use of clinically related applications. Concerning applications directly related to clinical assessment, respondents indicated that they used their computers most frequently for test scoring (41.3%) and test interpretation (29.4%) with test administration appearing as the next most frequent application (26.2%). Only a small percentage of respondents indicated that they used the computer to aid in client interviewing and generation of psychiatric diagnoses (5.1% and 5.9%, respectively).

Non-users were asked to rate the factors which were most responsible for the decision not to use computers. The factors most frequently rated in the top three concerns of non-users were the lack of time to learn how to use computers, inadequate training or experience with computers, and financial/practical concerns (i.e. having a practice that was too small to justify the expense involved in computerization). Two factors related to value conflicts were ranked in the top three concerns by more than 10% of non-users, namely preference for the use of a professional rather than a computer, and concerns related to the appropriateness of computer usage. Other apprehensions such as legal and ethical issues, anxiety about computer use, concerns about software quality and efficiency and concerns about negative client reactions were ranked in the top three by less than 10% of non-users. Regarding psychologists' attitudes towards specific computer applications, the trends revealed that nearly all of the respondents felt that computers were very appropriate for performing clerical tasks, maintaining records, and a number of applications involving direct client interaction with a computer (i.e. administration of standardized psychological tests, assisting with vocational and educational counseling, biofeedback, cognitive retraining, providing clients with didactic information, and collecting medical histories). The respondents were less enthusiastic about applications related to decision making such as generating test reports, psychiatric diagnoses and suggestions for treatment plans, interpreting psychological tests, and conducting psychosocial histories.

The present chapter aims to provide an overview of the literature in the area of computer-aided psychological assessment, addressing many of the concerns identified by the practitioners surveyed by Farrell (1989). The primary focus is on computer applications assisting the behavioral interview, behavior analysis, interpretive report writing and test administration. Since client reactions to computers are a critical component in assessing the efficacy of the role of computers in assessment, a portion of this chapter is also devoted to this topic. Finally, professional, ethical, and legal issues associated with computer utilization are discussed.

THE BEHAVIORAL INTERVIEW

The interview is extensively used in behavioral assessment as a method of obtaining self-report information about a client's behavior and his or her interactions with the environment. While various authors have outlined guidelines for conducting a behavioral assessment (Herbert, 1981; Kanfer and Saslow, 1969), there is some debate as to the extensiveness of the behaviors that should be examined; some argue for a broad-spectrum assessment (Kanfer and Saslow, 1969) while others recommend a narrow-band assessment that focuses on the client's presenting problem (Linehan, 1977).

Angle et al. (1977) identified two problems associated with conducting a broad-band assessment—the large amount of data that needs to be collected and the lack of specification of the information to be obtained from the client. The authors indicated that the latter has resulted in poor intra- and inter-rater reliability. Furthermore, Angle (1981) identified the following shortcomings of clinicians in the interview process: being unknowledgeable about asking certain clinical questions, forgetting to ask certain questions, and failure to record important facts. He and his colleagues (Angle, 1981; Angle et al., 1977; Angle et al., 1979) have developed a comprehensive computer interview and have tested the efficacy of computer interrogation as an alternative to traditional interviewing procedures.

A recent version of this computer interview (Angle, 1981) was designed to screen adult clients on 29 life problem areas which comprise the broad-band spectrum (e.g. sex, childrearing, employment, finances, assertion, phobias/fears, medical/physical status). Identification of problems is determined by client responses to more than 3500 multiple choice questions which are typically accompanied with a five-point frequency, intensity or duration scale. During the interview process, questions regarding client behavior are presented in a linear order. While only a minimum of conditional branching based on the client's previous responses occurs, the program will exclude problem areas that are contraindicated by client characteristics (e.g. no children) and will present additional questions to obtain more information when areas are identified as problematic. Upon completion of the interview, the computer provides the clinician with a printout of those responses designated as excess or deficit conditions based on predetermined criteria. In addition to a printout of the entire problem screen, a condensed version, the Problem Oriented Record (POR), is produced.

In an effort to investigate the efficacy of the computer as an interviewer, Angle et al. (1979) compared the results of the interviews conducted by the computer and by the clinician. The results indicated that the computer interview yielded considerably more information than did the clinicians'. Moreover, the clinicians failed to identify (as measured by lack of documentation) 76% of 20 critical problems that a group of 55 patients revealed in the computer interview and that experts believed were important patient findings. The results of investigations examining the ability of clinicians to obtain important clinical information via unstructured interviews are consistent with these findings (Carr, Ghosh and Ancill, 1983; Simmons and Miller, 1971; Weitzel, Morgan and Guyden, 1973).

In addition to the capabilities for obtaining initial screening information, Angle, Ellinwood and Carroll (1978) described the operation of their computer interview to measure treatment progress. This was accomplished by having patients periodically retake the interviews for those life problem areas on which treatment was focused. Evaluation of progress could be made by comparing scores obtained on subsequent administrations with scores obtained on the initial problem screen. Along these lines, it has also been proposed that the computer be used to gather follow-up data (Angle and Ellinwood, 1978; Johnson, Giannetti and Williams, 1976). Angle (1981) stressed the importance of outcome data for the development of a treatment science and suggested that the computer, used in the manner suggested above, could greatly facilitate outcome research.

Thus, the research conducted by Angle and his colleagues cited above not only provides support for the computer interview, but suggests that the computer may surpass the capabilities of the clinicians with respect to standardization of the interview and maintenance of accurate records.

Another hypothesized advantage of the computer-administered interview is that patients would be less inhibited about discussing problem areas of a sensitive nature and would provide more accurate information about these difficulties than they would during a face-to-face interview (Slack and Van Cura, 1968). Lending credence to this hypothesis are the findings reported by Evans and Miller (1969) who, in a between-group comparison in which subjects completed a questionnaire administered either by a computer or in a conventional paper-and-pencil format, found that subjects in the computer group admitted more symptoms of manifest anxiety, told fewer lies, and demonstrated a greater willingness to agree to socially undesirable statements than did subjects in the paper-and-pencil group.

The equivalence of computer and face-to-face assessment of alcohol-related problems has also been investigated in an effort to test the hypothesis that clients are more willing to provide information of a sensitive nature to a computer (i.e. an impartial, non-judgmental, and non-reactive interviewer) than to a human interviewer (Lucas et al., 1977). To date, a number of investigations have demonstrated that the computer is at least as accurate as mental health professionals (i.e. psychiatrists, nurses, and trained assessment technicians) in obtaining information about alcohol-related problems (Bernadt et al., 1989; Lucas et al., 1977; Skinner and Allen, 1983). However, the data regarding the issue of the disclosure of sensitive information are equivocal. Some investigators have found that patients reported higher estimates of alcohol consumption during computer interrogation as compared with face-to-face interrogation (Duffy and Waterton, 1984; Lucas et al., 1977) and others have failed to replicate this result (Bernadt et al., 1989; Skinner and Allen, 1983). Moreover, while some interpret the report of higher levels of alcohol consumption during computer-administered assessment as indicative of increased accuracy in self-report, others simply interpret this finding to mean that the two formats elicit different information (Bernadt et al., 1989).

Overall, the existing literature suggests that the computer's strengths lie in the areas of reliability, consistency, and recording of large amounts of data. However, to date it has not been determined that these factors are in any way related to treatment outcome. By way of contrast, the strengths of the clinician include elements of clinical intuition and clinical judgment. Perhaps, most importantly, the initial interview sets the stage for the interpersonal relationship between the client and the clinician. Before any definitive conclusions about the efficacy of the role of the computer as an interviewer can be reached, researchers must further investigate the effect of the computer on the therapeutic relationship, treatment outcome, and client reactions to computer-administered interviews.

BEHAVIOR ANALYSIS

The assessment of human behavior via direct observation has also been enhanced through computer technology. Repp et al. (1989) developed a computerized behavior recording system which is capable of collecting data for up to 43 behaviors. The program records the start and finish time for each behavior observed, the order in which the behaviors occurred and provides the number, rate, duration, and percentage of sessions in which responding occurred. Additionally, the program can be used to assess inter-observer agreement and to conduct a lag sequential analysis to address antecedent–response–consequence relationships. The authors cite two major advantages of computerized behavior observation assessment over the traditional paper-and-pencil method: the significant savings of time, and a real-time record of behaviors and events in their exact sequence of occurrence which allows for a complex behavior analysis (see Felce et al., 1987).

INTERPRETIVE REPORT WRITING

There are basically two approaches to the utilization of computers in the testing process. The first of these uses the computer to score and/or interpret psychological tests that have been administered in the traditional manner and produce a written report based on the test results. The second method employs the computer for test administration as well as for its scoring and interpretive report writing capabilities.

The types of outputs produced by various software programs can be differentiated by the level of analysis provided, with some programs providing only numerical or graphic summaries of the results obtained and others providing detailed narrative reports. The interpretive statements contained in the reports are typically developed via two different types of software programs: clinician-modeled programs and clinical–actuarial programs (Roid and Gorsuch, 1984). In the clinician-modeled programs, interpretive reports are generated either by a computer simulation of the interpretive logic of a renowned clinician or via a validated statistical model of the process used by expert clinicians. Clinical–actuarial programs are designed to produce extensive narrative descriptions and clinical hypotheses based on empirical evidence for particular patterns of scores. However, Butcher, Keller and Bacon (1985) have noted that there are currently no interpretive systems that produce purely actuarial reports since the limited number of empirically validated classifications identified to date cannot accommodate the diversity of profiles generated by examinees. As a result, the interpretive reports reflect a mixture of empirically derived relationships and other rules based on clinical expertise.

The few formal studies examining the validity of computer-based test interpretation have produced somewhat inconsistent findings. Evaluations of interpretive systems for the MMPI, for instance, have generally been positive when related to clinicians' ratings of the accuracy of computer outputs based on their knowledge of their clients (Moreland, 1987). Studies adopting rather more rigorous external criteria for accuracy, however, suggest that such systems may generate an unacceptably high level of false positives with regard to symptom detection (Hedlund, Morgan and Master, 1972). The issues that this sort of finding raises for professional practice are discussed subsequently.

TEST ADMINISTRATION

Proponents of computer-administered psychological tests have suggested that, in addition to providing the same function as their manually administered counterparts, the computerized versions may in fact be superior. Table 3.1 summarizes some of the advantages of computerized testing cited in the literature.

Numerous software programs are currently available which administer psychological tests that were originally standardized using traditional asessment procedures. However, a major concern regarding the utilization of computers in the administration of psychological tests involves the prevailing trend to transform traditional psychological tests into a computerized format. In translating these tests into computerized formats, software developers have made the assumption that the computerized versions are equivalent forms of tests which have been standardized in a traditional paper-and-pencil format (see the detailed discussion by Wilson and McMillan in this volume). Logically, this strategy makes sense in that traditional psychological tests that are commonly used in clinical practice have documented reliability and validity, provide normative data which facilitates computerized scoring, and have explicit rules for interpretation. While this assumption has been challenged by some experts who contend that the issue of equivalence has yet to be empirically established (Hofer and Green, 1985; Honaker, 1988), others have concluded that the majority of evidence suggests that non-equivalence between modalities is typically small enough to be considered inconsequential (Moreland, 1987).

CLIENT REACTIONS TO COMPUTERIZED ASSESSMENT

Central to the evaluation of the efficacy of computers in clinical assessment is client reaction. The study of client attitudes is not only important in

Table 3.1 Advantages of computer testing.

Advantages	Citations
1. Reduced costs	Butcher (1987); Byers (1981); Greist et al. (1973); Klinge and Rodziewicz (1976); Space (1981)
2. Decreased turn-around time from completion of test to results (i.e., summary report, narrative report) thereby expediting determination of the need for additional assessment or intervention	Butcher, Keller, and Bacon (1985); Byers (1981); Dunn, Lushene, and O'Neil (1972); Gedye and Miller (1969); Greist et al. (1973); Klinge and Rodziewicz (1976); Space (1981)
3. Interpretive and report writing capabilities	Buyers (1981); Johnson and Williams (1979)
4. Examiner free to observe patient's behavior as he is being tested	Klinge and Rodziewicz (1976)
5. Reduction of psychologist's direct involvement in testing and hence, more efficient use of skilled manpower	Allen and Skinner (1987); Burke and Normand (1987); Krug (1987)
6. Increased reliability and validity of results as a function of standardized presentation of test stimuli and decrease in examinee errors.	Butcher, Keller, and Bacon (1985); Gedye and Miller (1969); Krug (1987)
7. Increased potential to assess clients unable to complete assessments administered in conventional formats	Burke and Normand (1987); Gedye and Miller (1969); Wilson, Thompson, and Wylie (1982)
8. Ability to produce radically different types of test items than those currently used in standardized testing	Hofer and Green (1985); Johnson (1984); Krug (1987)
9. Provision of a data base for clinical and administrative decision-making	Angle (1981); Johnson and Williams (1976)
10. Reduction in problems associated with scheduling assessment	Burke and Normand (1987); Schmidt, Urry, and Gugel (1978)
11. Potential for eliminating examiner-examinee bias during test administration	Johnson and Mihal (1973)
12. Increased ease of administering test items based on previous response of examinee, i.e., adaptive or tailored testing and the concomitant decreases in testing time and the boredom and fatigue which may adversely effect test results	Burke and Normand (1987); Hofer and Green (1985)
13. Ability to obtain graphic presentations to aid in patient education	Allen and Skinner (1987)
14. Increased reliability of reports, i.e., given identical data, the computer will repeatedly produce the same report	Burke and Normand (1987)

determining the experiential equivalence of assessment devices standardized via traditional methods, but is also important as this area of research has the potential to identify subgroups of clients for whom computer-administered assessment may be contraindicated.

Whilst current literature suggests that clients generally respond favorably to computer-administered assessment, it is clear that some clients do not. Duffy and Waterton (1984), for example, reported that the refusal rate for the computer-administered interview was greater than for the face-to-face interview, and Skinner et al. (1985) found that 5% of the patients assigned to the computer modality refused to complete the assessment. Similarly, in an investigation by Elwood and Clark (1978), one subject refused to complete the second administration of the computer-administered Peabody Picture Vocabulary Test. Five other subjects in this investigation were excluded from the subject pool because their scores on at least one form of the test were below the extrapolated norms. Unfortunately, the authors did not elaborate on subject characteristics.

Both Skinner and Allen (1983) and Lucas (1977) report males giving more favorable ratings of computer assessment than females and younger subjects more favorable ratings than older clients. Cruickshank (1982; cited by Allen and Skinner, 1987) reported that studies have found that patients who were highly stressed or extremely nervous did not respond well to computerized assessments.

One seemingly obvious variable which had not been included in the studies conducted before 1985 was the client's experience with computers. To address this issue, Skinner et al. (1985) conducted a study in which patients were asked to rank order their preferences for human, paper-and-pencil, and computer-administered assessment prior to the completion of a lifestyle assessment administered in one of the three formats to which the patients were randomly assigned. At the time of the initial preference rating, the majority ranked face-to-face interview as their first choice and few patients ranked the computer as their first choice. However, post-assessment ratings of preferred assessment modality indicated that actual experience with computer-administered assessment resulted in an increased preference for the computer modality. Specifically, while only 13% ranked the computer as their first choice at pretest, 43% indicated a preference for the computer modality following completion of the assessment. In addition, it was found that the largest increase was seen among those who had never interacted with a computer.

While the data suggest that clients respond/react differentially to computer and face-to-face administration of psychological tests/interviews, only a limited amount of research has examined either individual differences or specific population differences which may interact with test modality. There is some empirical evidence which suggests that computer-administered tests may reduce examiner bias in the assessment of black students (Johnson and Mihal, 1973). There is also some evidence which suggests that older subjects perform more poorly on tests of intellectual functioning when the test is administered by computer (White and Johnson, 1975, cited in Johnson and White, 1980) and experience discomfort when questioned by computer (Carr et al, 1982). However, Johnson and White (1980) found that providing elderly subjects with preliminary training and practice with the computer resulted in a significantly greater number of correct responses for subjects in the pre-training group. This finding highlights the importance of instruction and practice for certain subgroups.

ISSUES INVOLVED IN COMPUTERIZED TESTING

Historically, traditional assessment procedures have been criticized for their focus on the identification of assumed underlying personality traits as a means for predicting behavior and their lack of utility in the design of treatment. Kanfer and Saslow (1969) and Goldfried and Kent (1972) provide an excellent review of these criticisms. The availability of computer software products which have the ability to administer and score personality inventories with little cost to the clinician, clearly brings this issue to the fore. Space (1981), for example, noted that: "Computerized approaches describe an individual as a point on a continuum in comparison with the rest of the population, but they are not geared to regularities and patterns unique to that single individual. Thus, the clinically more important *idiographic* information is lost in favor of nomothetic information" (p. 599). Similarly, Matarazzo (1986) has noted that, in clinical assessment, "variation is the rule rather than the exception" (p. 20) and has criticized computer-based interpretive reports for their failure to provide a "family of well-validated actuarially based interpretations" (p. 21) based on assessment data from more than one source.

Another related issue involves the question of whether or not the loss of observational data during computer-administered assessment is acceptable. The term observational data, as used in this context, includes information related to the client's mood, facial expression, tone of voice, body posture, and activity level as well as the specific processes that the examinee engages in to arrive at a response. Quite often, observation of the client's behavior provides the examiner with invaluable information which can be utilized in the interpretation of test data, generation of clinical hypotheses, and development of specific treatment recommendations. These observational data are not only central to the interpretation of projective tests, but also apply to ability tests and tests of intellectual functioning (i.e. objective tests).

Matarazzo (1986) has stated that the historical distinction between objective and projective tests is illusory and that the interpretation of test data "is a highly subjective art that requires a well-trained and experienced practitioner to give such scores predictive meaning in the life of any given human being" (Matarazzo, 1972, p. 11).

Several overviews of the issues and controversies involved in the use of computer-based testing and test interpretation are currently available in the professional literature (Hofer and Green, 1985; Groth-Marnat and Schumaker, 1989; Matarazzo, 1986; Zachary and Pope, 1984). Among these concerns are (a) the often unwarranted impression of accuracy created by computer-generated interpretive reports, (b) untested validity including the concern that computer-based interpretive reports are currently available for tests for which validity for conventional administration is non-existent (Groth-Marnat and Schumaker, 1989), and (c) the availability of products to unqualified users. With respect to the latter, it is interesting to note that, of the software products listed in Krug's (1987) *Psychware Sourcebook*, the sale of 57% of the software products is restricted by APA guidelines to individuals with formal training in the area of assessment. Another 22% are restricted to use by "qualified professionals" and seem to be produced for the user outside of psychology (e.g. social worker, psychiatrist, physician, etc.). Only 19% of the products are presumably sold to anyone.

Another potential misuse of computer-based interpretive reports noted by concerned psychologists is the utilization of the software as a low-cost, in-house clinical consultant (Groth-Marnat and Schumaker, 1989; Matarazzo, 1986). This issue is magnified by the fact that the large majority of the software produced by commercial companies yield interpretive reports that are unsigned by the authors. Additionally, while some computer-based interpretive software packages provide a time-released message informing the user to return the software package to the manufacturer for the purpose of updating the normative data on which the scoring and interpretation are based, users of obsolete software run the risk of perpetuating invalid interpretations (Groth-Marnat and Schumaker, 1989; Zachary and Pope, 1984).

Finally, others have criticized computer-based interpretive reports on the basis that they are sometimes authored by individuals who have little or no training and experience in clinical assessment (Groth-Marnat and Schumaker, 1989; Moreland, 1985) and that the software developers typically do not provide the user with the algorithms and decision rules upon which the reports are based. Zachary and Pope (1984) have stressed the need for test developers to integrate knowledge of appropriate computer programming, psychometrics, and the parameters associated with valid clinical use of a particular assessment device in the development of interpretive programs. These authors and others (Groth-Marnat and

Schumaker, 1989; Honaker, 1988; Matarazzo, 1986) have highlighted the need for test developers to document the rationale and decision rules upon which the interpretive programs are based to enable independent evaluation of the software. Hofer and Green (1985) have indicated that practitioners do not need to know all of the rules and algorithms incorporated into the software, but that minimally, they must be aware of the scale or combination of scales, the specific scale scores, and the relevant empirical or clinical evidence upon which each interpretation is based.

In response to the concerns related to computer usage in the area of psychological assessment, the American Psychological Association's Committee on Professional Standards and Committee on Psychological Tests and Assessment published "Guidelines for computer-based tests and interpretations" (APA, 1987). These guidelines represent an interpretation and extension of the "Standards for educational and psychological testing" (APA, 1985) as they apply to computer-based testing and interpretation. As such, the guidelines specifically outline the responsibilities of both the test user and the test developer.

On the issue of the credentials of qualified computer-based test users, the APA specifically states that the user "should be a qualified professional with (a) knowledge of psychological measurement; (b) background in the history of the tests or inventories being used; (c) experience in the use and familiarity with the research on tests or inventories, including gender, age, and cultural differences if applicable; and (d) knowledge of intended application" (p. 417). In addition, the guidelines state that practitioners must have knowledge of the methods utilized in the generation and interpretation of the scores, and be familiar enough with the specific assessment device to assess the applicability of the test for the intended purpose. Relevant here is the issue of professional competence; i.e. "Psychologists recognize the boundaries of their competence and limitations of their techniques. They only provide services for which they are qualified by training and experience. They maintain knowledge of current scientific and professional information related to the services they render" (p. 417). In addition, the practitioner is responsible for providing optimal conditions for test administration (i.e. eliminate distractions, ensuring that the computer screen is legible and free from glare, and that the testing area is comfortable and private). In cases where testing procedures deviate from the procedures outlined in the manual, the practitioner must be confident that these differences do not significantly affect test scores. In cases where deviations from standard administration procedures are expected to affect the resultant test scores, it is the responsibility of the practitioner to calibrate the test scores to account for these variables. The guidelines also specify that the practitioner is accountable for routine monitoring and maintenance of equipment, monitoring the examinee to provide assistance or detect irregularities in the testing procedure, training the examinee on proper use of the computer equipment, and for making reasonable accommodations for individuals who may be disadvantaged by computer-administered assessment.

The responsibilities of the test developer are enumerated in 21 guidelines and are outlined under four topical headings as follows: human factors, psychometric properties, classification, and review. While these are too numerous to list, those most relevant to the preceding discussion include:

- establishing the validity of computer versions of conventionally administered tests;
- providing sufficient information in the manual to enable reviewers and practitioners to determine how the interpretive statements were derived;
- providing information regarding the extent to which the interpretive statements were derived empirically or from clinical judgment as well as information to enable users to weigh the credibility of interpretive statements based on clinical judgment;
- providing information regarding common errors and the consistency of interpretations;
- ensuring that the interpretive reports are comprehensible and delimit the boundaries within which accurate conclusions can be drawn.

CONCLUSIONS

After reviewing the current literature, we concur with others that there is tremendous potential for the role of computers in the area of psychological assessment. Our enthusiasm, however, is mitigated by the status of the software products which are currently available to administer and score psychological tests/inventories which were originally developed and validated in their conventional, paper-and-pencil formats. Research on the equivalence of computer and conventional formats is limited and the findings are equivocal. As with conventionally administered tests, it is incumbent upon practitioners to be aware of the populations comprising the standardization samples and the degree to which individual clients differ from the normative sample. In order to ensure against the use of obsolete norms, practitioners must remain abreast of new developments in the standardization of psychological tests.

In the area of test interpretation, practitioners need to be aware of decision rules and algorithms used to produce interpretive reports. Furthermore, given the well-delineated legal and ethical responsibilities, psychologists need to be familiar with the history, purposes and limitations of specific tests administered as well as the relevant research; i.e. validity of measure for specific populations, and predictive validity of interpretive statements. In other words, the practitioner must have the ability to interpret assessment data without the aid of a computer.

It is also the responsibility of practitioners to be critical consumers of software. Suggestions for responsible evaluation of computer programs/ computer testing services include scoring and interpreting the same test protocol using different programs and comparing the outputs (Roid and Gorsuch, 1984). In addition, practitioners are encouraged to review technical manuals and users' guides to evaluate program rationales, empirical and decision rules and classification statistics and to seek out independent reviews of specific automated scoring and interpretive programs in professional literature (Buros, 1978, pp. 938–962; Lachar, 1974).

Perhaps most importantly, the results obtained via the administration of computer-generated assessments and interpretive reports must be viewed as tools as opposed to end-products. This sentiment was eloquently expressed by Matarazzo (1986) who stated that ''Basic science information, whether established or being generated, merely comprises the tools from which a practitioner will choose (according to her or his personal predilections) reliable and, to varying degrees, validated aids that will help him or her serve a client. The psychologist-practitioner is and may long remain an artisan'' (Matarazzo, 1986, p. 20). Hence, the assessment data and the various computer output and interpretive statements merely provide the raw materials for responsible clinical assessment.

REFERENCES

Allen, B. and Skinner, H.A. (1987) Lifestyle assessment using microcomputers. In: J.N. Butcher (ed), *Computerized Psychological Assessment: A Practitioner's Guide*, Basic Books, New York.

American Psychological Association (1985) *Standards for Educational and Psychological Testing*, APA, Washington, DC.

American Psychological Association (1987) Guidelines for computer-based tests and interpretations. In: J.N. Butcher (ed), *Computerized Psychological Assessment:A Practitioner's Guide*, Basic Books, New York (reprinted from *Guidelines for Computer-Based Tests and Interpretations*, 1986, APA, Washington, DC.

Angle, H.V. (1981) The interviewing computer: a technology for gathering comprehensive treatment information. *Behavior Reseach Methods and Instrumentation*, **13**, 607–12.

Angle, H.V. and Ellinwood, E.H. (1978) A psychiatric assessment–treatment–outcome information system: evaluation with computer simulation. In: F.H. Orthner (ed), *Proceedings of the Second Annual Symposium on Computer Application in Medical Care*, Institute of Electrical and Electronic Engineers, New York.

Angle, H.V., Ellinwood, E.H. and Carroll, J. (1978) Computer interview problem assessment of psychiatric patients. In: F.H. Orthner (ed), *Proceedings of the Second*

Annual Symposium on Computer Application in Medical Care, Institute of Electrical and Electronic Engineers, New York.

Angle, H.V., Ellinwood, E.H., Hay, W.M., Johnsen, T. and Hay, L.R. (1977) Computer-aided interviewing in comprehensive behavioral assessment. *Behavior Therapy*, **8**, 747–54.

Angle, H.V., Johnsen, T.J., Grebenkemper, N.S. and Ellinwood, C.H. (1979) Computer interview support for clinicians. *Professional Psychology*, **10**, 49–51.

Bernadt, M.W., Daniels, O.J., Blizard, R.A. and Murray, R.M. (1989) Can a computer reliably elicit an alcohol history? *British Journal of Addiction*, **84**, 405–11.

Burke, M.J. and Normand, J. (1987) Computerized psychological testing: overview and critique. *Professional Psychology: Research and Practice*, **18**, 42–51.

Buros, O.K. (1978) (ed) *The Eighth Mental Measurement Yearbook*, vol. 1, Gryphon Press, Highland Park, NJ.

Butcher, J.N. (1987) Computerized clinical and personality assessment using the MMPI. In: J.N. Butcher (ed), *Computerized Psychological Assessment: A Practitioner's Guide*, pp. 161–97, Basic Books, New York.

Butcher, J.N., Keller, L.S. and Bacon, S.F. (1985) Current developments and future directions in computerized personality assessment. *Journal of Consulting and Clinical Psychology*, **53**, 803–15.

Byers, A.P. (1981) Psychological evaluation by means of an on-line computer. *Behavior Research Methods and Instrumentation*, **13**, 585–7.

Carr, A.C., Ghosh, A. and Ancill, R.J. (1983). Can a computer take a psychiatric history? *Psychological Medicine*, **13**, 151–8.

Carr, A.C., Ghosh, A., Ancill, R.J. and Margo, A. (1981) Direct assessment of depression by microcomputer. *Acta Psychiatrica Scandinavica*, **64**, 415–22.

Carr, A.C., Wilson, S.L., Ghosh, A., Ancil, R.J. and Woods, R.T. (1982) Automated testing of geriatric patients using a micro-computer based system. *International Journal of Man–Machine Studies*, **28**, 297–300.

Cruickshank, P.J. (1982) Patient stress and the computer in the consulting room. *Social Science and Medicine*, **16**, 1271–6.

Duffy, J.C. and Waterton, J.J. (1984) Under-reporting of alcohol consumption in sample surveys: the effect of computer interviewing in fieldwork. *British Journal of Addiction*, **79**, 303–8.

Dunn, T.G., Lushene, R.E. and O'Neil, H.F. (1972) Complete automation of the MMPI and a study of response latencies. *Journal of Clinical and Consulting Psychology*, **39**, 381–7.

Elwood, D.L. and Clark, C.L. (1978) Computer administration of the Peabody Picture Vocabulary Test to young children. *Behavior Research Methods and Instrumentation*, **10**, 43–6.

Erdman, H.P., Klein, M.H. and Greist, J.H. (1985) Direct patient computer interviewing. *Journal of Consulting and Clinical Psychology*, **53**, 760–73.

Evans, W.M. and Miller, J.R. (1969) Differential effects on response bias of computer vs. conventional administration of a social science questionnaire. *Behavioral Science*, **14**, 216–27.

Farrell, A. D. (1989) Impact of computers on professional practice: a survey of current practices and attitudes. *Professional Psychology: Research and Practice*, **20**, 172–8.

Felce, D., Saxby, H., deKock, U., Repp, A., Ager, A and Blunden, R. (1987) To what behaviors do attending adults respond?: A replication. *American Journal of Mental Deficiency*, **91** (5), 496–504.

Gedye, J.L. and Miller, E. (1969) The automation of psychological assessment. *International Journal of Man–Machine Studies*, **1**, 237–62.

Goldfried, M.R. and Kent, R.N. (1972) Traditional versus behavioral personality assessment: a comparison of methodological and theoretical assumptions. *Psychological Bulletin*, **77**, 409–20.

Greist, J.H., Gustafson, D.H., Strauss, F.F., Rowse, G.L., Langren, T.P. and Chiles, J.A. (1973) A computer interview for suicide risk prevention. *American Journal of Psychiatry*, **130**, 1327–32.

Groth-Marnat, G. and Schumaker, J. (1989) Computer based psychological testing: issues and guidelines. *American Journal of Orthopsychiatry*, **59**, 257–63.

Hedlund, J.L., Morgan, D.W. and Master, F.D. (1972) The Mayo Clinic automated MMPI program: cross-validation with psychiatric patients in an army hospital. *Journal of Clinical Psychology*, **28**, 505–10.

Herbert, M. (1981) *Behavioral Treatment of Problem Children: A Practical Manual*, Academic Press, London.

Hofer, P.J. and Green, B.F. (1985) The challenge of competence and creativity in computerized psychological testing. *Journal of Consulting and Clinical Psychology*, **53**, 826–38.

Honaker, L.M. (1988) The equivalency of computerized and conventional MMPI administration: a critical review. *Clinical Psychology Review*, **8**, 561–77.

Johnson, D.F. and Mihal, W.L. (1973) The performance of blacks and whites in computerized vs. manual testing environments. *American Psychologist*, **28**, 694–9.

Johnson, D.F. and White, C.B. (1980) Effects of training on computer test performance in the elderly. *Journal of Applied Psychology*, **65**, 357–8.

Johnson, J.H., Giannetti, R.A. and Williams, T.A. (1976). Computers in mental health care delivery: a review of the evolution toward interventionally relevant on-line processing. *Behavior Research Methods and Instrumentation*, **8**, 83–91.

Johnson, J.H. and Williams, T.A. (1975) The use of on-line computer technology in a mental health admitting system. *American Psychologist*, **30**, 388–90.

Kanfer, F.H. and Saslow, G. (1969) Behavioral diagnosis. In: C.M. Franks (ed), *Behavior Therapy: Appraisal and Status*, McGraw-Hill, New York.

Klinge, V. and Rodziewicz, T. (1976) Automated and manual intelligence testing of the Peabody Picture Vocabulary Test on a psychiatric adolescent population. *International Journal of Man–Machine Studies*, **8**, 243–6.

Krug, S.E. (1987) *Psychware Sourcebook 1987–1988: A Reference Guide to Computer-Based Products for Assessment in Psychology, Education, and Business*, Metri Tech, Champaign, Ill.

Krug, S.E. (1987) Microtrends: An orientation to computerized assessment. In: J.N. Butcher (ed), *Computerized Psychological Assessment: A Practitioner's Guide*, pp. 15–25, Basic Books, New York.

Lachar, D. (1974) Accuracy and generalizability of an automated MMPI interpretation system. *Journal of Clinical and Consulting Psychology*, **42**, 267–73.

Lanyon, R.I. (1972) Technological approach to the improvement of decision making in mental health services. *Journal of Consulting and Clinical Psychology*, **39**, 43–8.

Linehan, M.M. (1977) Issues in behavioral interviewing. In: J.D. Cone and R.P. Hawkins (eds), *Behavioral Assessment: New Directions in Clinical Psychology*, pp. 30–51, Brunner/Mazel, New York.

Lucas, R.W. (1977) A study of patient's attitudes to computer interrogation. *International Journal of Man–Machine Studies*, **9**, 69–86.

Lucas, R.W., Mullin, P.J., Luna, C.D. and McInroy, D.C. (1977) Psychiatrists and a computer as interrogators of patients with alcohol related illnesses: a comparison. *British Journal of Psychiatry*, **131**, 160–7.

Matarazzo, R.P. (1972) *Wechsler's Measurement and Appraisal of Adult Intelligence*, 5th edn, pp. 137–255, Oxford University Press, New York

Matarazzo, R.P. (1986) Computerized clinical psychological test interpretation: unvalidated plus all mean and no sigma. *American Psychologist*, **41**, 14–24.

Moreland, K. (1985) Validation of computer-based test interpretations: problems and prospects. *Journal of Consulting and Clinical Psychology*, **53**, 816–25.

Moreland, K. (1987) Computerized psychological assessment: what's available. In: J.N. Butcher (ed), *Computerized Psychological Assessment: A Practitioner's Guide*, pp. 26–49, Basic Books, New York.

Repp, A.C., Harman, M.L., Felce, D., VanAcker, R. and Karsh, K.G. (1989) Conducting behavioral assessments on computer-collected data. *Behavioral Assessment*, **11**, 249–68.

Roid, G.H. and Gorsuch, R.L. (1984) Development and clinical use of test-interpretive programs on microcomputers. In M.D. Schwartz (ed), *Using Computers in Clinical Practice: Psychotherapy and Mental Health Applications*, pp. 141–9, Haworth Press, New York.

Schmidt, F.L., Urry, V.W. and Gugel, J.F. (1978) Computer assisted tailored testing: examinee reactions and evaluation. *Educational and Psychological Measurement*, **38**, 265–73.

Simmons, E.M. and Miller, O.W. (1971) Automated patient history-taking. *Hospitals*, **45**, 56–9.

Skinner, H.A. and Allen, B.A. (1983) Does the computer make a difference? Computerized vs. face-to-face self-report assessment of alcohol, drug and tobacco use. *Journal of Consulting and Clinical Psychology*, **51**, 267–75.

Skinner, H.A., Allen, B.A., McIntosh, M.D. and Palmer, W.H. (1985) Lifestyle assessment: applying microcomputers in family practice. *British Medical Journal*, **290**, 212–14.

Slack, W.V. and Van Cura, L.J. (1968) Patient reaction to computer-based medical interviewing. *Computers and Biomedical Research*, **1**, 527–31.

Space, L. (1981) The computer as psychometrician. *Behavior Research Methods & Instrumentation*, **13**, 595–606.

Weitzel, W.D., Morgan, D.W. and Guyden, T.E. (1973) Towards a more efficient mental status examination. *Archives of General Psychiatry*, **28**, 215–18.

Wilson, S.L., Thompson, J.A. and Wylie, G. (1982) Automated psychological testing for the severely physically handicapped. *International Journal of Man–Machine Studies*, **17**, 291–6.

Zachary, R.A. and Pope, K.S. (1984) Legal and ethical issues in the clinical use of computerized testing. In: M.D. Schwartz (ed), *Using Computers in Clinical Practice: Psychotherapy and Mental Health Applications*, pp. 151–64, Haworth Press, New York.

Chapter 4

Microcomputers and Psychological Treatment

TONY C. CARR

HARDWARE CONSIDERATIONS

Computers are well-equipped to "treat" certain conditions, but many patients encounter some difficulty in operating a traditional computer. The QWERTY keyboard is often unfamiliar, and reading printed displays on a TV screen requires considerable concentration and literacy. Until recently these handicaps have limited computerized treatment to an experimental basis.

Computers must be able to talk to their patients. Computer voice synthesis was pioneered by Colby (Colby, Christinaz and Graham, 1978), but until recently sound production was of poor quality, and therapists preferred computer-controlled audiotape. Early workers (Lang, Melamed and Hart, 1970) successfully relaxed and desensitized patients using tapes controlled by relays ("DAD"), and others (McFall and Twentyman, 1973) provided semi-automated social skills and assertiveness training, giving illustrative dramatized episodes with corrective feedback. Dramatized audio clips enlivened an alcohol self-help program (Carr and Ruzek, 1986) and provided a basis for further questioning by the computer. However, there have been tremendous advances in computer hardware and the last decade has seen the development of inexpensive, lifelike digitized speech, opening the way to much more ambitious uses of computers in health care.

For many years patients have operated computers by pressing keys or buttons. Three recent developments in response devices seem likely to monopolize the future of computer assessment and treatment. Schwartz (Lieff, 1987) was the first to develop a computer information system fully operated by *telephone*. A user calls the centre and the computer responds with a digitized voice recording which offers a menu of services, selected

Microcomputers and Clinical Psychology: Issues, Applications and Future Developments. Edited by A. Ager
©1991 John Wiley & Sons Ltd

by dialling a number. They can thus choose to hear information on anxiety, depression, suicide, etc.; ask for more information; return to the menu; request professional help; or even locate an empty hospital bed! This system presently responds only to touch-tone telephone signals.

One of the earliest *touch-screen devices* formed the heart of PLATO, an educational computer information system (Wagman, 1980). The display terminal has a TV screen surrounded by an array of hidden infrared photodiodes. When a finger touches the screen it interrupts the infrared beams, and the finger position is relayed at once to the computer. The user can thus indicate requests or responses by touching a menu, a small cartoon ("icon"), or a word from a list. Touching the screen is the simplest response available, and is readily acceptable to children, the elderly, the handicapped, etc. (see e.g. Carr, Woods and Moore, 1986) as no special response device has to be mastered.

However, the ultimate response device will use *voice recognition*, where the user simply speaks to the machine. Formidable investment in industrial research is yielding slow but steady progress. Currently available devices will recognize a limited range of words from any voice (e.g. numbers spoken into a telephone), or can be "trained" to recognize a larger vocabulary from one particular speaker. Coupled with digitized speech from the computer this method offers the most natural "conversation" between user and computer, and can accommodate the illiterate or visually impaired. It also drastically *increases* the program complexity, since the computer must cope with open-ended replies in plain English.

PROGRAM STRUCTURE

Early computer programs followed the familiar questionnaire format, presenting a sequence of questions, information or tests and awaiting a response to each item. Weizenbaum's original ELIZA program (Weizenbaum, 1966), for example, was intended to help college students locate wanted references in the literature. For use in treatment, many other approaches have now been developed.

The computer can keep a running tally of items or issues requiring further attention. For family therapy Mead (Lieff, 1987) produced a program to monitor the progress of psychotherapy, focusing the therapist's attention on key issues from session to session. Ghosh's phobia treatment program collected currently suitable tasks and printed out a custom-tailored worksheet for the patient near the end of each session (Ghosh, Marks and Carr, 1984) to serve as a daily reminder. Schneider's QUIT-BY-MAIL program used a similar technique, mailing "homework" sheets to smokers (Schneider, 1990).

Another imaginative technique uses the computer to simulate ongoing events, requiring the user to take appropriate decisions and then observe the consequences, receiving appropriate feedback. So far this approach has been confined to teaching applications. An early program (Penta and Kofman, 1973) simulated clinical situations, requiring the student to take management decisions and updating him on the patient's progress. The Upjohn Company (Kalamazoo, Michigan) has produced excellent case simulations (PSYCAL) encouraging the student to take decisions at various stages, with immediate feedback. These all present text, on-screen or voiced. Future developments include video-disk illustrative interview segments, pioneered by Schwartz (1984).

CLIENT ACCEPTABILITY

Early studies of patients operating computers encountered stiff opposition from doctors and other professionals. However, Lucas (1976) performed a careful, objective study of patients' feelings about his computerized symptom assessment, comparing patients' responses to attitude questions with established cutoff points (derived from independent judges). He found the vast majority of patients rated their computer experience about as good (or as bad) as seeing a physician, as regards enjoyment, understanding, accuracy, etc.

Carr and Ghosh (1983) used a similar technique on patients who had undergone a computerized behavioural assessment for phobias, prior to computer-supervised self-treatment. These patients had also seen a psychiatrist. Again the majority (75%) rated the computer experience as equally acceptable; none favoured the psychiatrist strongly, and a few patients much preferred the computer. These authors collected patients' comments: commonest reasons for preferring the computer were that they were more relaxed, had more time to formulate answers to the questions, and found it easier than talking to the clinician. These results should be interpreted with caution since their computer session was not a simple questionnaire but an interactive assessment dialogue, designed for acceptability.

Patients might be expected to confide more truthful information in the absence of a therapist, and many studies support this hypothesis. Two studies (Coddington and King, 1972; Greist, Gustafson and Strauss, 1973) found the computer-derived information more accurate than clinicians in sensitive areas such as sex, drugs and suicide. Predictions of future suicide attempts from the computer data proved more accurate than clinicians' guesses (Erdman et al., 1987). Smokers were more truthful to the computer

(Evans, Price and Wilson, 1973). Another study (Lucas et al., 1977) compared alcoholics' responses to a computer questionnaire with their responses to the same questions asked by a physician on the same day. Many reported drinking 50–100% more heavily at the computer interview: on verbal challenge, they often explained that the higher figure was accurate but they had been unwilling to disappoint the physician with their lack of progress!

TREATMENT APPLICATIONS

Historical developments

Cole noted the computer's limitations as a therapist (Cole, Johnson and Williams, 1976): a given program is designed to cope only with a specific problem; the computer must be reliable in operation; and a friendly, interactive approach is necessary. The first and most famous treatment program was invented unintentionally by Weizenbaum (1966, 1984). This computer scientist developed a program to allow a computer to converse with student library users in English, and called it ELIZA in view of its civilizing effect. As a humorous demonstration he produced a "psychotherapist" version which interrogated the user ("What is troubling you?" [MY MOTHER] "Tell me about your mother." [SHE DRIVES ME MAD] "Drives you mad?" etc.) To his chagrin this application was taken seriously, and various workers showed that computer psychotherapy is difficult to distinguish from the real thing (Colby, Watt and Gilbert, 1966; Colby and Enea, 1967; Meany, 1962; Starkweather, 1965).

The earliest *specific* treatment by computer was Colby's language development program for autistic and other children, who have difficulty relating to adults (Colby, 1968, 1973). For encouragement the child received audio and visual feedback when typing. Typing H, for example, displayed H on the computer screen and also produced a spoken "H" from a tape recorder. Successfully typing H-O-R-S-E resulted in the spoken word "horse" and a galloping horse displayed graphically. Eighty per cent of his subjects were "improved" after several months' treatment.

In a later study, retarded children progressed linguistically after being trained to use the LOGO programming language (Lehrer and de Bernard, 1987).

Treatment of anxiety disorders

Biofeedback can be a useful technique in relaxation therapy, useful in anxiety disorders and for some psychosomatic conditions (e.g. asthma, migraine).

The computer can monitor, display and record simultaneously the changes in various physiological parameters. One program links the subject's galvanic skin response (measured by a hand-held instrument) to a video game steering a spaceship! Automated relaxation feedback was successful in alleviating migraines (Pope and Gersten, 1977).

Computers have been used to administer systematic desensitization. In the earliest work (Lang, Melamed and Hart, 1970) patients with snake phobia were presented with a hierarchy of imagined situations described on audiotape. Each stimulus was presented twice and the patient indicated his discomfort level to the computer. If he remained comfortable the computer proceeded to a more difficult, more threatening narrative. If the patient was experiencing considerable anxiety the computer would switch to a tape of relaxation instructions, then return to the same stimulus again. The computer treatment worked just as well as treatment from a human therapist, with equally lasting benefit.

More recent work has shown that a computer can supervise *self*-treatment for phobic patients (Carr, Ghosh and Marks, 1988; Ghosh, Marks and Carr, 1988; Chandler, Burck and Sampson, 1988; Ghosh and Greist, 1988). One program assessed the particular phobia, excluded major depressive illness, explained the principles of desensitization and encouraged subjects to seek the assistance of a relative or friend. Drawing on a stored hierarchy of practice tasks for each type of phobia, the program discussed which tasks the patient could attempt, obtained his/her agreement and printed out a ''homework diary'' for the coming week, with space for the patient's comments and anxiety ratings. At successive weekly visits the patient was asked about compliance and success with the previous week's tasks, given sympathy and encouragement, and persuaded to graduate to tasks of increasing difficulty. The computer-supervised patients improved as much as others in conventional treatment.

In a novel approach (Baer et al., 1988) patients with obsessive–compulsive disorders were treated by a *portable* computer. Each patient carried a small hand-held computer and recorded whenever an obsessional checking urge was experienced. The computer then instructed them to resist the urge for three minutes, reassured them, and counted down the time. The computer provided daily feedback on the frequency of urges and level of coping success. Patients showed good improvement over two years, but only while persisting with the computer program.

Treatment of addictions

Habit retraining to treat addiction has been assessed by Schneider, who ran a QUIT-BY-MAIL program to stop smoking (Schneider, 1990). Clients receive regular printouts discussing their progress and giving behavioural homework based on self-control techniques, which emphasize patients' mastery of their behaviour and trains them to make smoking progressively more awkward and less rewarding (e.g. by using different fingers or setting different times of day). The patients then complete a questionnaire and mail it back to the computer. Later patients receive similar assistance entirely by telephone: smokers call the computer at their convenience, receive counselling from a natural-sounding digitized voice, and respond by pressing touch-tone telephone digits. This program attracts many more smokers than attend conventional programs and enjoys a comparable success rate.

For heavy drinkers, SAFEDRINK provides a series of "interviews" alone with the computer, which responds with screen messages interspersed with tape-recorded dramatizations. Early interviews assess the client's drinking habits and related problems, and explain the principles of controlled drinking ("paced" drinking, restricted hours, weekly goal-setting, record-keeping etc.). Drinking alcohol is seen not as abnormal but as a habit needing some retraining, just as an obese person has to cultivate new eating patterns. At each visit the computer reviews recent performance towards previously agreed goals, provides reassurance and encouragement, reviews underlying principles and strategies, and invites clients to comment on one or two audiotape dramatizations illustrating their current difficulties. Its effectiveness remains to be evaluated (Carr and Ruzek, 1986).

General health habits in teenagers were addressed by Burnett (Burnett et al., 1989). His subjects completed regular paper questionnaires concerning exercise, smoking and obesity, which were processed by computer to yield feedback reports. He also developed a hand-held computer program which obese patients carried with them. The computer "beeped' at intervals to remind the patient to "report", discussed their dietary goals for the day, and praised them if they were making progress (Burnett, Taylor and Agras, 1985). Their computer-assisted patients lost much more weight than control patients completing the same two-month obesity program. Furthermore, they continued to lose weight over the eight-month follow-up period, while the control group gradually regained weight.

Psychotherapy applications

An unusual approach was developed by Dewart, a professional musician who produced a do-it-yourself music recording studio run by a computer (Lieff, 1987). A patient psychotherapy group is assigned the joint task of producing a "hit", allowing the clinician opportunity to observe and highlight interactions. Working with a therapist who has received some prior training, the group is given a limited time (weeks or months) to complete the project. Members may succeed or fail in their allotted contribution, and are encouraged to learn the benefits of persistence, self-control and mutual cooperation. Precise evaluation is difficult but this technique appears effective with adolescents, in-patients and out-patients, substance abusers, and even in nursing homes.

Other programs have been designed to assist a human therapist by drawing together information about the couple or family in treatment. For example, Gerson's FAMILY DATABASE MANAGER (Gerson, 1985) generates a chronological history of the family and even draws genograms. MATESIM (Lehtinen and Smith, 1985) asks each partner to complete a series of questions on their attitudes and expectations (of themselves and of their partner), covering work, home life, sex, leisure interests, religious and political beliefs, etc. They also indicate how important they consider each item. The program then highlights the areas in which the couple differ the most, especially issues they consider important, so that these areas of weakness in the marriage can be explored, giving the therapist useful material to work through with the clients.

For individual psychotherapy, CASPER assists the therapist to monitor and record the severity of various symptoms as treatment proceeds, and will present graphs of the patient's progress. Some patients are much impressed and reinforced by this tangible evidence of success (McCullough, Farrel and Longabough, 1984; Friedman, 1985).

Selmi (1983) treated depressed patients with cognitive behaviour therapy administered by computer. His patients improved significantly on all depression ratings and retained their improvement at two-month follow-up, compared with controls. They showed as much improvement as matched patients receiving conventional cognitive therapy, and were just as satisfied with their treatment.

Counselling programs

A sex therapist (Reitman, 1984) has produced counselling programs for *home* use, intended to educate the patient and encourage suitable exercises. These are aimed at sufferers from erectile impotence, sexual difficulties, depressed feelings, marital problems, and life stress. In treating male erectile impotence, for example, the computer asks the patient about his difficulties and the embarrassment they have caused. Background information is given, together with reassurance that such problems are widespread and can be helped, and not to be taken as a personal failure by the patient. It then makes suggestions for the use of fantasies and various solo or couple exercises.

A more elaborate program is SEXPERT (Binik et al., 1988), a program designed to supervise self-administered couple treatment for sexual dysfunction, particularly premature ejaculation. The couple receive sessions to help them recognize and diagnose their sex problem, educate them about it, and suggest specific techniques for them to practise. Full evaluation of this program is not yet complete.

There is clearly a vast market for home self-treatment programs and some evaluation by a regulatory body will be needed. In the same category are programs designed to counsel healthy citizens in selecting careers, selecting school courses, etc.

One carefully evaluated counselling program is PLATO-DCS (Dilemma Counselling System), designed to cope with *any* life problem (Wagman and Kerber, 1980; Wagman, 1984, 1988). After some practice on sample problems provided by the program, the users type their own problem into the computer which then assists them step-by-step to reduce it to a standard dilemma paradigm ("I must do A or B. If I do A, I will suffer X. X is bad. If I do B, I will suffer Y. Y is bad."). The program then has the users explore each of the five statements in turn and invent ways of escaping from the dilemma. They then review each of these "solutions" and rank them for adequacy, thereby deciding how to handle the problem. If the users can find a problem like their own in the program database, the computer will suggest preformulated solutions (gathered from student counselling experience) at each stage to assist them. Most student volunteers found it helpful, although usually unable to find a problem similar to their own in the database. Counselled students reported somewhat more improvement than controls at one-month follow-up, although within chance levels.

ETHICAL PROBLEMS

Computers have met with opposition from many groups, some with a rational basis. Perhaps the foremost concern is confidentiality, the privacy of personal information. "Hackers" have broken into the British Royal Family's computer account, moved an American satellite by penetrating its control program, accessed patient records in a New York cancer centre, and manipulated telephone computer systems to obtain free calls. Are all computer files at risk?

This type of unauthorized access occurs only with multi-user (e.g. mainframe) systems. Patient assessment and treatment programs can be run on an isolated, desktop microcomputer having no links to any other system. Provided the computer and its disks are kept safely under lock and key between sessions, confidentiality is almost ensured. "Almost", because by advanced electronic espionage techniques it is now possible to pick up radio signals from a nearby computer or TV monitor as easily as one can "tap" a telephone line. However, patient treatment sessions are unlikely to excite this degree of interest.

Authorized access presents another problem. In Britain the Freedom of Information Act 1986 obliges all computer users to make any patient data available to the patient on request, with explanations where appropriate. This creates logistic problems, and the possibility of impersonators obtaining the information. There may also be times when revealing information to a patient is detrimental to his wellbeing. However, these problems already exist with written records in many countries.

Where treatment programs are computerized, there is a need to set professional standards. If patients are to undergo treatment with minimal supervision, at home or in a hospital, we may need legislative safeguards to ensure that unsuitable cases are screened out at entry; that an adequate standard of treatment is reached; and that subjects who deteriorate or develop other problems are detected immediately and referred back to the human supervisor for assistance. Human therapists require a licence to ensure they are competent, and the same should apply to computer programs. This problem is so pressing that for the moment the American Psychology Association has recommended that computer programs should be promoted only for use by health care professionals (APA, 1986).

THE FUTURE

Computers are poised to take over a great many human activities, and are currently waiting for two technical advances. The first is speech recognition. Without it computers are deaf and blind, requiring users to labour at a typewriter keyboard or to indicate their choices on numerous "menus". The 1980s saw worldwide industrial investment in speech recognition and major advances are occurring. Once a computer can take a history through verbal dialogue, directing and reassuring patients in their own language, the attraction of automated procedures will be greatly increased.

The second technological advance lies in the area of artificial intelligence (AI) (or "expert systems", "rule-based" or "knowledge-based systems"). These terms usually indicate the semantic analysis of language input (the computer encodes input sentences into constructs) and the more global concept of encoding and qualifying human feelings, drives, needs, etc. For example, PARRY was a computer program developed to simulate a paranoid patient (Colby, Faught and Parkison, 1975; Colby, 1977). In addition to a rudimentary vocabulary, PARRY kept mathematical scores representing feelings such as interest and irritation. PARRY could conduct a dialogue with a therapist, and if antagonized by aggressive questioning would "become" irritated and uncooperative.

Assessment and treatment programs developed so far have relied on the decision-tree strategy. The program "branches" to different lines according to a patient's responses, abilities and needs—but every separate line must be programmed in complete detail, a laborious effort. AI offers a much neater simulation of a human therapist. SEXPERT, for example, engages couples in a therapeutic (plain English) dialogue about their sexual interaction, "diagnoses" specific dysfunctions, and based on these decisions provides the couple with relevant information and advice, moves on to another topic, or terminates the interview (Binik et al., 1988).

What areas of psychology and psychiatry will be suitable for automation? There are few limits to the imagination. A simple example: "Contract" marital therapy (see e.g. Jacobson and Gurman, 1986) relies on extracting from the partners a list of behavioural goals to be practised at home, refining and clarifying the goals, motivating the partners and then assessing their success at regular intervals. A computer program able to monitor the clients' comprehension, cooperation, satisfaction, etc., and make suitable interventions as needed could conduct marital therapy, administering "homework" in much the same way as has been successful in densensitizing phobic patients (Carr, Ghosh and Marks, 1988). Such a program would be cheaper than a full-time clinician, could operate outside working hours, and might arouse less embarrassment among clients. It may go off sick, but is easier to repair than a clinician.

SOURCES OF PROGRAMS AND FURTHER INFORMATION

Lists of programs of interest to psychologists and psychiatrists are available. The American Association for Medical Systems and Information published the *Mental Health Systems Software Directory* (Green and Calderazzo, 1985). Sarah Wilson in Britain maintains an updated *Directory of Research in Automated Testing* (DRAT), available by mail for a small fee. Another directory is the *Psychware Sourcebook 1987–88* (Krug, 1987).

Marc Schwartz edits a monthly newsletter *Computers in Psychiatry/Psychology* with excellent reviews of new software. Dick Schoech produces a quarterly bulletin, *Computer Uses in Social Services Newsletter*, and also operates an electronic-mail bulletin service on FIDO-OPUS networks ("CUSS network"). Most of the above collect or review new programs, welcome enquiries, and offer programs for sale. They can also advise on local interest groups.

Writing books in this area is a formidable task, since program descriptions must be brief, detailed and up-to-date. Lieff (1987) has written an excellent book dealing with all aspects of computer-aided patient management. Wagman (1988) addresses computer counselling and psychotherapy. Schwartz (1984) collected a large number of brief articles from his newsletter, mostly reviewing specific programs in detail. Many of the programs are now obsolete but the book provides a good overview of possible applications. Sidowski (1980) collected chapters by various pioneers in the computer-patient field (Colby, Greist, Lang and others), and provides a fascinating introduction to the subject. Other publications cover special interests such as physical handicap, cognitive rehabilitation, family therapy, etc.

Several journals have devoted an issue to articles on computer testing and treatment, such as *Psychiatry Annals* (vol. 18, 1988), *Psychopharmacology Bulletin* (vol. 24, 1988), *Counseling Psychology* (vol. 11, 1983), *Journal of Counseling Developments* (vol. 63, 1984). Burnett gave a useful review of recent work (Burnett, 1989), as did Erdman (Erdman, Kline and Greist, 1985; Erdman, 1988). Maulucci reviewed cognitive testing and treatment (Maulucci and Eckhouse, 1988).

Finally, Professor Hedlund's department at the Missouri Institute of Psychiatry has specialized in the bibliography of psychiatric/psychological specialities. Their original listing (Hedlund, Vieweg and Wood, 1981) will no doubt see many revisions (e.g. Hedlund and Vieweg, 1988).

REFERENCES

American Psychological Association (1986) *Guidelines for Computer-Based Tests and Interpretations*, APA, Washington, DC.

Baer, L., Minichiello, W.E., Jenike, M. and Holland, A. (1988) Use of a portable computer program to assist behavioural treatment in a case of obsessive-compulsive disorder. *Journal of Behavior Therapy and Experimental Psychiatry*, **19**, 237–40.

Binik, Y.M., Servanschreiber, D., Freiwald, S. and Hall, K.S.K. (1988) Intelligent computer-based assessment psychotherapy—an expert system for sexual dysfunction. *Journal of Nervous and Mental Diseases*, **176**, 387–400.

Burnett, K.F. (1989) Computers for assessment and intervention in psychiatry and psychology. *Current Opinion in Psychiatry*, **2**, 780–6.

Burnett, K.F., Magel, P.M., Harrington, S. and Taylor, C.B. (1989) Computer-assisted behavioural health counseling for high school students. *Journal of Counseling Psychology*, **36**, 63–7.

Burnett, K.F., Taylor, C.B. and Agras, S.A. (1985) Ambulatory computer-assisted therapy for obesity: a new frontier for behaviour therapy. *Journal of Consulting and Clinical Psychology*, **53**, 698–703.

Carr, A.C. and Ghosh, A. (1983) Response of phobic patients to direct computer assessment. *British Journal of Psychiatry*, **142**, 60–5.

Carr, A.C., Ghosh, A. and Marks, I.M. (1988) Computer-supervised exposure treatment for phobias. *Canadian Journal of Psychiatry*, **33**, 112–17.

Carr, A.C. and Ruzek, J. (1986) Unpublished study.

Carr, A.C., Woods, R.T. and Moore, B.J. (1986) Developing a microcomputer based automated testing system for use with psychogeriatric patients. *Bulletin of the Royal College of Psychiatrists*, **10**, 309–12.

Chandler, G.M., Burck, H. and Sampson, J.P. (1988) The effectiveness of a generic program for systematic desensitization. *Computers in Human Behavior*, **4**, 339–46.

Coddington, R.D. and King, T.L. (1972) Automated history taking in child psychiatry. *American Journal of Psychiatry*, **129**, 276–82.

Colby, K.M. (1968) Computer-aided language development in nonspeaking children. *Archives of General Psychiatry*, **19**, 641–51.

Colby, K.M. (1973) The rationale for computer-based treatment of language difficulties in non-speaking autistic children. *Journal of Autism and Childhood Schizophrenia*, **3**, 254–60.

Colby, K.M. (1977) *Artificial Paranoia*, Pergamon, New York.

Colby, K.M., Christinaz, D. and Graham, S. (1978) A computer-driven, personal and portable speech prosthesis. *Computers and Biomedical Research*, **11**, 337–43.

Colby, K.M. and Enea, H. (1967) Heuristic methods for computer understanding of natural language in context-restricted on-line dialogues. *Mathematical Biosciences*, **1**, 1–25.

Colby, K.M., Faught, W.S. and Parkison, R.C. (1975) Cognitive therapy of paranoid conditions. Recommendations based on a computer model of paranoia. Memo ALHMF 11, Algorithmic Laboratory of Higher Mental Functions, Dept. of Psychiatry, UCLA.

Colby, K.M., Watt, J.B. and Gilbert, J.P. (1966) A computer method of psychotherapy; preliminary communication. *Journal of Nervous and Mental Diseases* , **142**, 148–52.

Cole, E.B., Johnson, J.H. and Williams, T.A. (1976) When psychiatric patients interact with computer terminals: problems and solutions. *Behavior Research Methods and Instrumentation*, **8** (2), 92–4.

DRAT (Directory of Research and Automated Tests) (postal service for references). Dr Sarah Wilson, Department of Psychology, University of Surrey, Guildford, Surrey GU2 5XH, England.

Erdman, H.P. (1988) Computer consultation in psychiatry. *Psychiatric Annals*, **18** (4), 209–16.

Erdman, H.P., Greist, J.H., Klein M.H. and Jefferson, J.W. (1987) A review of computer diagnosis in psychiatry with special emphasis on DSM-III. *Computers in Human Services*, **2**, 1–11.

Erdman, H.P., Klein, M.H. and Greist, J.H. (1985) Direct patient computer interviewing. *Journal of Consulting and Clinical Psychology*, **53**, 760–73.

Evans, C.R., Price, H.C. and Wilson, J. (1973) Computer interrogation of patients with respiratory complaints in a London hospital. *Computer Science*, **69**, National Physics Laboratories, Teddington, Middlesex, UK.

Friedman, P.H. (1985) The use of computers in marital and family therapy. In: C.R. Figley (ed), *Computers and Family Therapy*, Haworth Press, New York.

Gerson, R. (1985) Teaching systems psychotherapy with microcomputers: a creative approach. In: C.R. Figley (ed), *Computers and Family Therapy*, Haworth Press, New York.

Ghosh, A. and Greist, J.H. (1988) Computer treatment in psychiatry. *Psychiatric Annals*, **18**, 246–52.

Ghosh, A., Marks, I.M. and Carr, A.C. (1984) Self exposure treatment for phobias—a controlled study. *Journal of the Royal Society of Medicine*, **77**, 483–7.

Ghosh, A., Marks, I.M. and Carr, A.C. (1988) Therapist contact and outcome of self-exposure treatment for phobias: a controlled study. *British Journal of Psychiatry*, **152**, 234–8.

Green, R. and Calderazzo, C.M. (1985) *Mental Health Systems Software Directory*, American Association for Medical Systems and Informatics, Washington, DC.

Greist, J.H., Gustafson, D.H., and Stauss, F.F. (1973) A computer interview for suicide risk prediction. *American Journal of Psychiatry*, **130**, 1327–32.

Hedlund, J.L. and Vieweg, B.W. (1988) Automation in psychological testing. *Psychiatric Annals*, **18**, 217–27.

Hedlund, J.L., Vieweg, B.W. and Wood, J.B. (1981) *Computers in Mental Health: A Review and Annotated Bibliography*, National Institute of Mental Health, Washington, DC.

Jacobson, N.S. and Gurman, A.S. (eds) (1986) *Clinical Handbook of Marital Therapy*, Guilford Press, New York.

Krug, S.E. (ed) (1987) *Psychware Sourcebook 1987–88*. Test Corporation of America, Kansas City, Montana.

Lang, P.J., Melamed, B.J. and Hart, J. (1970) A psychophysiological analysis of fear modification using an automated desensitization procedure. *Journal of Abnormal Psychology*, **76**, 220.

Lehrer, R. and de Bernard, A. (1987) Language of learning and language of computing: the perceptual language model. *Journal of Educational Psychology*, **79**, 41–8.

Lehtinen, M.W. and Smith, G.W. (1985) MATESIM: Computer-Assisted Marriage Analysis for Family Therapists. In: C.R. Figley (ed), *Computers and Family Therapy*, Haworth Press, New York.

Lieff, J.D. (1987) *Computer Applications in Psychiatry*, American Psychiatric Press, Washington, DC.

Lucas, R. (1976) *Computerized Assessment of Alcohol Intake*. PhD thesis, University of London.

Lucas, R.W., Mullin, P.J., Luna, C.B.X. and McInroy, D.C. (1977) Psychiatrists and a computer as interrogators of patients with alcohol-related illness: a comparison. *British Journal of Psychiatry*, **131**, 160–7.

Maulucci, R.A. and Eckhouse, R.H. (1988) The use of computers in the assessment and treatment of cognitive disabilities in the elderly: a survey. *Psychopharmacological Bulletin*, **24**, 557–66.

McCullough, L., Farrel, A.D. and Longabough, R. (1984) The making of a computerized assessment system: problems, pitfalls and pleasures. In: M.D. Schwartz (ed), *Using Computers in Clinical Practice*, Haworth Press, New York.

McFall, R.M. and Twentyman, C.T. (1973) Further experiments in the relative contributions of rehearsal, modelling, and coaching to assertion drawing. *Journal of Abnormal Psychology*, **81**, 199–218.

Meany, J. (1962) *The Automation of Psychotherapy*, System Development Corporation (AD-294122), New York.

Penta, F.B., and Kofman, S. (1973) The effectiveness of simulation devices in teaching selected skills of physical diagnosis. *Journal of Medical Education*, **48**, 442–5.

Pope, A.T. and Gersten, C.D. (1977) Computer automation of biofeedback training. *Behavior Research Methods and Instrumentation*, **9**, 164–8.

Reitman, R. (1984) The use of small computers in self-help sex therapy. In: M.D. Schwartz (ed), *Using Computers in Clinical Practice*, Haworth Press, New York.

Schneider, S.J. (1990) Computerized communication as a medium for smoking cessation treatment. *Computers in Human Behaviour*, **6**, 141–51.

Schoech, Dick (ed) *Computer Uses in Social Services Newsletter*. CUSS Network Coordinator, University of Texas at Arlington, PO Box 19129, Arlington, Texas 76019–0129.

Schwartz, Marc (ed) *Computers in Psychiatry/Psychology Newsletter*. 26 Trumbull Street, New Haven, CT 06511.

Schwartz, M. (1984) *Using Computers in Clinical Practice*, Haworth Press, New York.

Selmi, P.M. (1983) *Computer-Assisted Cognitive Behavior Therapy in the Treatment of Depression*. Doctoral dissertation, Illinois Institute of Technology.

Sidowski, J.B., Johnson, J.H. and Williams, T.A. (eds) *Technology in Mental Health Care Delivery Systems*, Ablex Publishing Corporation, Norwood, NJ.

Starkweather, J.A. (1965) Computest: a computer language for individual testing, instruction, and interviewing. *Psychological Reports*, **17**, 227–37.

Wagman, M. (1980) PLATO-DCS: an interactive computer system for personal counseling. *Journal of Counseling Psychology*, **27** (1), 16–30.

Wagman, M. (1984) Using computers in personal counselling. *Journal of Counseling Developments*, **63** (3), 172–6.

Wagman, M. (1988) *Computer Psychotherapy Systems: Theory and Research Foundations*, Gordon and Breach Science Publishers, New York.

Wagman, M. and Kerber, K.W. (1980) PLATO-DCS, an interactive computer system for personal counseling: further development and evaluation. *Journal of Counseling Psychology*, **27** (1), 31–9.

Weizenbaum, J. (1966) ELIZA: a computer program for the study of natural language communication between man and machine. *Communications Association for Computing Machinery*, **9**, 36–45.

Weizenbaum, J. (1984) *Computer Power and Human Reason*, Penguin, Harmondsworth.

Chapter 5

Microcomputers in Psychometric and Neuropsychological Assessment

Sarah L. Wilson and Tom M. McMillan

Microcomputers have the potential to fulfil a number of useful functions for the clinical psychologist. In this chapter the use of the microcomputer as a medium for presentation of psychometric tests is discussed.

Interest in computer-based tests first began in the 1960s, but it was not until the arrival of the microcomputer, at a much lower cost than its predecessors, that work in computer-based testing proliferated. A number of test packages have been commercially available for several years; furthermore a quantity of good software is available on a non-commercial basis. The use of automated assessment can have a number of advantages and disadvantages; both will be considered in the next section.

ISSUES IN MICROCOMPUTER-BASED ASSESSMENT

General advantages

The ideal in test administration is to give the test in a standardized manner, without cues or prompts (except those permitted by the test protocol), and to be able to do so every time the test is administered. The microcomputer can do this perfectly. Microcomputers cannot consciously or unconsciously cue the client by changes in gesture and posture, as humans are prone to do when emotionally concerned about the client's performance, or bored or anxious about getting the client to complete the test in time for a subsequent appointment. Other human frailties are overcome, too, as response will be accurately recorded and no test item will be omitted.

Microcomputers and Clinical Psychology: Issues, Applications and Future Developments. Edited by A. Ager
©1991 John Wiley & Sons Ltd

Before the test commences, giving instructions to and gathering information from the client can be carried out by the microcomputer. The microcomputer can also score the test when completed, in a time substantially faster than the human can do it. This is particularly so if a complex scoring scheme, such as that used in Cattell's 16PF (IPAT, 1972), is used. If normative data are available in the software, an "interpretation" of the client's performance can be presented immediately. Features such as timing of response latencies, analysis of response patterns, transfer of results to a database for further analyses, collection of normative data or report writing can all be included in the automation. It is therefore possible to have tests administered and scored without the clinical psychologist being in the room. In some cases the client can be unsupervised (but preferably left with a means of summoning help). In other cases the client can be left under the supervision of less-skilled personnel. In either case the cost of assessment can be reduced and the psychologist can be relieved of some of the more routine and sometimes tedious aspects of practice. The time required for testing can actually be reduced. Beaumont and French (1987) estimated savings of up to 60% of total assessment time in their study of the use of microcomputer-based cognitive tests with adult psychiatric patients. Another time-saving possibility is the use of tailored or adaptive testing techniques where testing is concentrated on those items that the client finds difficulty with, the easy ones being skipped through (Watts, Baddeley and Williams, 1982; Weiss and Vale 1987).

Features such as colour, animation and sound can be incorporated in the instruction phase of the program, if not always in the actual test material itself, and can make the assessment more interesting and enjoyable for the client. Initially, it was thought that some groups, such as the elderly, would find microcomputer technology awesome and would comply poorly with automated methods of testing. The work of a number of authors has not supported this view: with the elderly (Carr et al., 1982; Simpson and Linney, 1984), with psychiatric patients (French and Beaumont, 1987) and with the adult physically disabled (Wilson, 1990). Microcomputers, unlike many aids provided for groups such as the neurologically impaired and the elderly, carry no stigma; on the contrary their use may subjectively carry prestige.

General disadvantages

At this time, the greatest disadvantage is the limitation on the types of test material that can be presented by the computer. If the test is to be scored as well as administered, then test material has to be restricted, either to multiple-choice format or to having answers such as spellings or numbers that can be precisely defined. If it is sufficient simply to record the answer of a client for later scoring by hand, then open-ended questions can be used, as long as the client is competent to use a QWERTY keyboard. When systems that use natural language become available it should be possible to have the answers to open-ended questions—such as those in the Comprehension section of the WAIS—scored by the computer; although, as Wilson (1988) points out, the idiomatic nature of the English language may make this a difficult proposition in practice. Geographical variations in usage can even lead to words and expressions having widely differing meanings; the expression "to knock up" has widely differing meanings in the UK and the USA, for example.

If the test requires graphics, and the use of interactive video is not feasible, care should be taken to ensure the adequacy of the computer system for presentation of pictorial material. In their recommendations for the design of software for computer-based assessment, Bartram et al. (1987) recommend that for simple graphics which require only vertical and horizontal lines a system with the resolution of about 256×256 should suffice. For well-defined oblique lines a minimum resolution of 512×512 is likely to be needed. For complex graphics involving fine detail and curved lines a resolution of 1024×1024 would be the minimum necessary to achieve a quality of representation comparable with pen-and-paper tests. Graphic material can only be two-dimensional, although the third dimension can be indicated by the use of perspective; perhaps future developments in holography may overcome this problem.

Moving microcomputers between sites can cause problems. Individual items such as monitors can be very heavy and awkward to carry. Systems can be susceptible to extremes of temperature and to vibration. The use of "laptop" computers may dispose of some of the transport problems, but the adequacy of the display unit for test presentation should be ensured.

Special considerations

Hardware

In setting up a testing system, one of the first considerations is hardware. The professional may be constrained to the use of hardware acquired for other purposes and will therefore have to look for test software that can be run on that system. Software can be converted for use on different computer systems, but care must be taken particularly when graphics are involved, since the test material may actually look different, necessitating evaluation studies before use. On the other hand, if the prime function of the microcomputer is assessment then a machine can be chosen which can run the desired software; use for other functions such as word processing will have secondary importance.

An important factor which must be considered is the means of communication between client and computer. The use of the QWERTY keyboard may not be possible or desirable (Bartram et al., 1987), for a variety of reasons:

- The keyboard itself may be at risk of damage from those with poor motor or behavioural control.
- Clients with poor motor control or impaired sensory ability may not be able to operate a standard keyboard.
- In most assessment situations, much of the keyboard will be redundant and this excess of information could have a detrimental effect on performance—for example, in an individual with an attention deficit.
- In tests where speed is required, the keyboard layout can convey a disadvantage. Imagine the difficulties for a non-typist of having to locate the keys *a*, *b*, *c*, and *d* at speed, for example. The client should concentrate on the screen and not the keyboard, but the large number of relatively small keys in close proximity significantly increases the likelihood of errors.

Bartram and colleagues recommended the use of a special response medium for use with clients, the QWERTY keyboard being retained, of course, for the professional's own interaction with the machine. If the use of the QWERTY keyboard is unavoidable, Beaumont (1982) described the use of a "software lock" to disable all those keys which were not required, thereby avoiding accidental or other disruption of the software. An alternative is to use a keyboard guard which exposes only the necessary keys.

In addition, there are many alternative response media available. These include mice, joysticks and trackerballs; in using these, movements of the hand are translated to movements on screen. Touch-pads include devices such as the Concept Keyboard, in which areas to be used for specific functions are delineated by overlays. Bit-pads are similar in concept but require a stylus for operation. There are non-QWERTY keyboards, usually with a specific use in mind—such as that designed for use with the Bexley–Maudsley Automated Psychological Screening Battery (Acker and Acker, 1982). Such keyboards can have keys dedicated to specific functions such as "yes" and "no" or have their layout specifically matched to the layout of material on screen. Devices such as light-pens and touch-screens allow the client to point directly to the answer of their choice, rather than having to locate a keypad. Carr, Woods and Moore (1986a) evaluated the usefulness of the touch-screen against a board with illuminated response buttons in the assessment of cognitively impaired elderly patients. The touch-screen not only produced lower response latencies and higher scores, but was also preferred. A study on the performance of stroke victims compared scores from, and subjective preference of, the following response devices: mouse, trackerball, touch-pad and touch-screen (Petheram, 1988). The trackerball produced the best scores and was also most popular with this group.

Modified versions of the QWERTY keyboard have been developed for use by the physically disabled and are commercially available. These include expanded keyboards with sunken keys, which are especially suitable for those who may have a full range of gross movement but who lack fine coordination (such as individuals with athetoid spasticity). Another alternative requires only two switches for operation. Alphanumeric elements are arranged in a matrix, and selection of the row containing the desired element is made by operating one switch and selection of an element within that row with the other switch. Such devices are of great value to people with severe communication difficulties and can be put to use in assessment as well as in activities of daily living.

Software

In acquiring test software, similar considerations apply to those for acquiring a conventional test. It is appropriate to question whether the test provides useful information, if it is in a form suitable for use with the client population, if the form of presentation of results and quality of normative data are adequate, the ease of its use by the professional, whether any additional equipment is required, and the cost per administration: some test software is available with unlimited use, in other cases a fixed number of test administrations is offered.

Test purchasers should also enquire about the availability of user support and, if required, whether the software offers any form of data storage facility. If an automated version of a conventional test is to be acquired, it is advisable to consider the validity of non-automated evaluative data carefully since automation may change the nature of the test.

Clients

There are certain circumstances in testing in which scores or information such as response latencies may not be sufficient. In neuropsychological assessment, for example, the professional may need to have the flexibility to formulate hypotheses about the nature of the client's deficits during the process of assessment and then test them out. The use of computer-based tests may constrain the behaviour of both the psychologist and the client and make this process difficult.

On the other hand there is one client group for whom computer-based tests may be the only approach which allows objective assessment. That group is the severely physically disabled (Wilson, Thompson and Wylie, 1982; Wilson and McMillan, 1986; Wilson, 1990). Most conventional tests have been developed for use with able-bodied clients who comprise the majority of the population. They can require the client to speak, write or use a writing implement, draw, manoeuvre objects in response to test items and sometimes to do so at speed. Some or all of these modes of response may be difficult or impossible for the client. The psychologist may often have the problem of dissociating cognitive deficits from physical disabilities. Some conventional tests in multiple-choice form can be applied using eye-pointing or a "yes or no" responses approach, but these require the examiner to be certain that they are interpreting the client's responses correctly. Furthermore, when working with an individual for whom communication is physically effortful, the tendency to unconsciously prompt the client with changes in posture and tone of voice tends to be greater than it is for more able clients.

For physically disabled people, microcomputers can be of use in assessment for communication purposes or environmental control. Regardless of severity of disability it should be possible to provide some form of control or response device, if the client is willing to use it. If expertise in electronic engineering is available, then the construction of purpose-designed response devices can usually be easily accomplished and often at less cost than off-the-shelf response media (Wilson, 1990). The microcomputer will, of course, give a body-language-free presentation of the test and the client will not be dependent on the professional, whose beliefs about that individual may be biased. A well-chosen response device should allow the client to be able to respond at a reasonable speed. If this is not possible it is probably less stressful to keep a computer waiting rather than a professional. Some disabled clients may only be able to operate one or two switches at most; this problem can be overcome by using software that includes a moving cursor. If aural presentation of material is required then a computer-controlled audiotape system can be incorporated (Wilson, Wylie and Wedgwood, 1984) or synthetic speech can be used. In cases where frequent repetition of items is required this can save a lot of strain on the examiner's voice!

In computer-based tests, as a rule, items are presented one at a time. This is an advantage particularly for clients with attentional problems and can avoid responses being incorrectly placed or items omitted because of visual scanning difficulties. It is also important to have response media containing as little distracting information as possible for a number of groups, including the neurologically impaired, psychiatric patients and the elderly.

The method of response used for a particular test may have an interactive effect on performance on that test. It appears that automated versions of some tests produce significantly different results from the standard version whilst others do not (Beaumont and French, 1987). This phenomenon is, of course, not a problem if evaluative studies are carried out on the tests before they are put to general use. In some cases the type of response medium used with the microcomputer can also have an interactive effect on performance. A study comparing performance by severely physically disabled adults on an automated version of the Mill Hill Vocabulary Scale, using either a six-keyed board for response or a single switch with a software-based moving cursor, showed that in this case the means of response did not have any effect on results (S. L. Wilson, unpublished). Beaumont and French (1987) found no significant difference in score sizes for the Mill Hill Vocabulary Scale, Raven's Progressive Matrices, the Money Road Map Test or the Eysenck Personality Questionnaire when a QWERTY keyboard and touch-screen were compared as response media with adult psychiatric patients. In contrast, Beaumont (1985) looked at the effect of response media on digit span performance, using a QWERTY keyboard, numeric keypad and light-pen. The best performance was obtained with the QWERTY keyboard and the worst with the light-pen; these significant effects were present for forward span only. Wilson (1987) evaluated a microcomputer-based digit span test against that from the WAIS with physically disabled adults. The study also found a significant difference between the results for the two test forms for the forward span measure but not for backward span. Wilson attributed these differences to the greater processing requirements for backward span. Acquisition of the data for a satisfactory response was more difficult than for forward span, but once achieved was less liable to disruption by having to concentrate on activities such as key-pressing.

ETHICAL CONSIDERATIONS

Many of the ethical considerations that apply to the use of microcomputer-based tests also apply to standard forms of tests. The client should be emotionally, physically and cognitively able to deal with the test material and able to comprehend the instructions. The professional should also be responsible for the feedback that is given to the client during and/or after testing, and for the interpretation of the client's scores and the dissemination of this information to other parties when necessary. In short, the use of the microcomputer in psychological assessment is as a tool and is not in any way to be considered as a substitute for a professional. The computer may be able to present a test perfectly, score it and even present the score in terms of the normative data, but only the professional with detailed knowledge of the client's history and present condition can properly put the test performance in its true context.

Finally, as software can be easily copied and because computers can be regarded as being infallible, there is a danger that the control of administration and interpretation of the results of psychological tests may pass to individuals who do not have a proper understanding of the task in hand. Such concerns have been expressed by Matarazzo (1983) and by the British Psychological Society (1984). There are also no safeguards to the public against the sale of spurious tests and questionnaires in software form.

COMPUTER-BASED TEST INTERPRETATION

Computer-based test interpretation (CBTI) systems are available for a number of tests in the USA but do not appear to have attracted much interest in the UK. Initially, professionals had to send off test data by post for scoring and interpretation by computer. Now, however, a number of microcomputer-based packages are on sale. CBTI systems are available for tests such as the MMPI, Cattell's 16PF, the Rorschach Test, the Halstead–Reitan Battery and the Luria–Nebraska Neuropsychological Battery. Several CBTI systems may be available for each test; for example, Fowler (1985) in his review lists six systems available for interpretation of the MMPI. There are a number of reviews on the problems and benefits of the use of CBTIs, including Fowler (1985), Adams and Heaton (1985), Harris (1987), Moreland (1987) and Eyde and Kowal (1987). There is concern amongst these authors that computer-based test interpretations should not be used as a substitute for interpretation by a skilled professional.

AUTOMATION OF PSYCHOMETRIC TESTS

It is not our intention to give a fully comprehensive review of the work in this field, a task that is impossible in the space available. Our intention is rather to give an indication of the sort of work that has been done, to help readers decide what may be practicable for themselves. The automation of standard tests is reviewed, first considering psychometric procedures of general interest, then procedures that are of particular interest to the neuropsychologist. Whenever available, the automated-standard test reliabilities found by different authors will be reported. In the last section we look at novel psychometric procedures.

General psychometric tests

Although a few of the subtests are amenable to presentation in computer-based form, the WAIS, because of the open-ended format of a number of its items, is not available in its entirety as a microcomputer-based test at the present state of technology. Other intelligence tests are amenable to automation, particularly those in multiple-choice format. Wilson, Thompson and Wylie (1982) reported on the evaluation of computer-based presentation of the Mill Hill Vocabulary Scale (Synonyms section) and AH4 Part 1 with physically disabled adults using a system based on an Apple II microcomputer. They reported automated-standard correlations of 0.87 and 0.81 respectively for the two tests and no significant differences between the size of scores. Beaumont and French (1987) evaluated automated versions of the Mill Hill Vocabulary Scale and Raven's Standard Progressive Matrices, also using an Apple II-based system, on a large sample of psychiatric patients. They reported the reliability between forms for the Mill Hill Vocabulary Scale as being 0.90 with no significant differences in score sizes. For the Standard Progressive Matrices, the reliability between forms was 0.84, but scores on the automated version were significantly smaller.

Ridgway, MacCulloch and Mills (1982) described an automated version of the Eysenck Personality Inventory based on a Commodore Pet computer. In a study using nurses as subjects, they found overall correlations between machine and paper forms of the tests of 0.96 for "extraversion", 0.95 for "neuroticism" and 0.91 for the "lie" scale. Beaumont and French (1987) in their study using psychiatric patients found automated-standard reliabilities of 0.68 for "psychoticism", 0.82 for "extraversion", 0.87 for "neuroticism" and 0.88 for the "lie" scale. No significant differences were reported in score sizes. Wilson (1990) briefly reported the evaluation of a BBC-based version of Cattell's 16PF on a group of physically disabled adults. Although the correlations between standard and automated versions for each of the 16 factor scores were positive and significant, and ranged from 0.47 to 0.79, the correlations were lower than the retest reliabilities given in the test manual (0.68–0.86). A subsequent study of the retest reliability of this group of subjects on the standard form of the test has shown them to be less reliable on this test than the norm (S.L. Wilson, unpublished).

Memory and attention

Memory and attention tests are as a rule more amenable to automation if they involve a recognition rather than a recall paradigm. As has already been mentioned, a number of published studies have investigated automated Digit Span. Beaumont and French (1987) found correlations of 0.56 for forward span, 0.71 for backward span and 0.73 for total span in comparison with scores from the Digit Span subtest of the WAIS. The score sizes were significantly smaller for all three measures on the automated version of the test. Wilson (1987) also compared automated Digit Span, using an Apple II microcomputer, with performance on the WAIS Digit Span subtest, with physically disabled adults. Correlations were found of 0.57 for forward span, 0.50 for backward span and 0.65 for total span. Forward and total span scores were significantly smaller for the automated test, but there were no significant differences in backward span scores. For this group the test–retest reliability for the automated test was better than that from the WAIS scores. A test analogous to Digit Span, for assessing spatial memory, is the Corsi Block Span Test. An automated version of this test based on an Acorn BBC microcomputer with a touch-sensitive screen is described by Morris et al. (1988). This test was part of a battery used in a study of planning and spatial working memory in Parkinson's disease.

Morris et al. (1987) described a delayed matching-to-sample test for assessments of short-term memory, again using an Acorn BBC machine with a touch-screen. The test paradigm was developed from animal work. In the test, the subject is shown an abstract pattern which is the target stimulus; this disappears and is followed by the presentation of four abstract patterns, one of which matches the target stimulus which the subject has to touch. A correct match is rewarded by a red tick and a "bleep" from the computer. The test starts with simultaneous presentation of target and choice stimuli but the inter-stimulus interval is gradually increased. Performance on the test is expressed in terms of the percentage of items correctly recognized at the different inter-stimulus intervals. Data are presented for Parkinson's disease, Alzheimer-type dementia and matched controls. The Visual Spatial Memory test in the Bexley–Maudsley Automated Psychological Screening (BMAPS) battery (Acker, 1982) is similar to this except that three choice stimuli are used. Carr, Woods and Moore (1986b) also use this paradigm, using as stimuli the outlines of common objects (e.g. a teapot) made up of coloured blocks. The arrangement of the blocks was varied in the choice stimuli. Item difficulty could be varied by altering the size of the blocks and two, three or four options were provided per trial. This is part of a test battery for assessment of the dementing elderly, and uses a Commodore 64 with a touch-sensitive screen.

Also included in BMAPS (Acker, 1982) is a symbol–digit coding task, a test similar to the Digit Symbol subtest of the WAIS except that, instead of having to draw the symbol that is a code for a number, subjects have to press the keyboard number that goes with the symbol. As in the WAIS, subjects are asked to proceed as fast as possible in this test which requires attention, visuomotor coordination, motor speed and learning. The BMAPS battery was originally written for the Commodore Pet computer, but a version for the Apple II has subsequently been produced (NFER–Nelson, 1989).

Perception and orientation

The BMAPS battery also includes a test of spatial orientation known as the "Little Man Test" of which non-computerized versions were reported by Benson and Gedye (1963) and Ratcliff (1979). This test requires the ability to carry out visuospatial transformations mentally.

Money's Standardized Road-Map Test of Direction Sense has been automated by Beaumont and French (1987) using an Apple II-based system, evaluated against the standard version using psychiatric patients. The correlation between automated and standard form scores was 0.74 and the error scores did not differ significantly between the two forms. The standard version of the test was found to be completed more quickly.

The Perceptual Maze Test (Elithorn et al., 1964) has been described as a "visual search test" (Lezak, 1983). An automated version of this task was produced using a DEC-based system (Elithorn, Mornington and Stavrou, 1982), but subsequently a version for the Apple II has been produced (DRAT, 1988). The advantages of the computer-based version were summarized by Weinman (1982) as including the ability to make accurately timed responses, the ease of analysis of response pathways, the ease with which new test mazes can be generated and their mirror-images produced, and the facility for adopting a "tailored testing approach".

Line bisection tasks can be automated. Wilson (1990) reported an Acorn BBC-based test evaluated against the standard form of the test described by Schenkenberg, Bradford and Ajax (1980). The tests were scored in terms of percentage deviations from the centre of the line. For horizontal lines the correlations between forms were 0.38 for left centred lines, 0.41 for middle centred and 0.51 for right centred lines. All correlations were significant. The test was evaluated on physically disabled adults, most of whom were neurologically impaired, and this might account for the variability in the scores. Halligan and Marshall (1989a, b) describe two single cases assessed using an automated line-bisection task, also using an Acorn BBC system.

Executive functions

Morris et al. (1987) also described a computerized version of the Tower of London Test (Shallice, 1982). In the original version a set of three different coloured beads is threaded on three upright sticks of unequal length. The beads have to be moved one at a time from one stick to another and form, in as few moves as possible, a precise colour sequence. The test is presented using a touch-screen. Automation has allowed a more detailed analysis of performance, including recording of move sequences and initiation and execution times for moves. Data are presented from Parkinson's disease patients and normal control subjects.

A variation on the Stroop Test was reported by Iregren et al. (1986). In their Colour–Word Vigilance Test, the Swedish words for red, yellow, white or blue (all of which are three-lettered words in Swedish) were presented on screen one at a time in any one of the colours. The subject had to press a button as fast as possible when there was congruence between the meaning and the colour of the text. There was a two-second interval between stimuli. An ABC 800 machine was originally used, but software is now being developed for IBM compatible machines (DRAT, 1988).

With regard to tests of concept formation, the Wisconsin Card Sorting Test has been commonly used for development of automated analogues (Grant and Berg, 1948; Nelson, 1976). One version described by Acker (1982) is the Bexley–Maudsley Category Sorting Test. A direct analogue of the Wisconsin Card Sorting Test is described by Davidson et al. (1987) for the Apple II microcomputer. Beaumont and French (1987) evaluated their software for this test against the standard form and found that subjects were more likely to complete the standard version of this test; the standard version also took significantly less time to complete.

Novel psychometric tests

It may be argued that there is no such thing as an entirely novel psychometric procedure and that in any test established paradigms can be recognized. It can also be said that in the automated forms of standard tests that have just been described, there is much that is novel, in some cases automation having significantly changed the nature of the test. The novel procedures to be described utilize microcomputers' facilities for animation, sound and colour or rapid analysis of data in ways that would not have been feasible using conventional test technology. With such potential for development, the aim of this brief review is to whet the appetite.

Tiplady (1988) has developed a Continuous Attention Test (CAT) using non-verbal material which he has used in the assessment of the acute behavioural effects of drugs. The test stimuli consist of shapes built up from a random pattern of four light and five dark squares arranged in a 3×3 grid. Each pattern is flashed on to the screen for one-tenth of a second with a variable interval between presentations. The subject has to respond whenever two consecutive patterns are the same and measures are of correct and incorrect responses. Tiplady has found the CAT sensitive to the effects of several commonly used psychoactive drugs including caffeine.

Davidson et al. (1987) describe an animated tracking task in which a winding road is scrolled down the screen. The subject has to keep a small "car" within road boundaries by movement of a joystick. Scrolling begins at the rate of 3.0 cm/s and becomes faster as the test progresses, dependent on the subject's success. Outcome in this tailored test is measured by distance travelled on the road in a fixed time. Data are presented comparing traumatically head-injured adults and control subjects.

Draper et al. (1983) developed a novel computer-based test of cognitive function for the purpose of detecting alcoholic brain impairment. During the test a maze is presented on the screen using graphic characters in a grid formation. The characters at the edge are labelled with letters. A track through the maze, formed according to simple logical rules, stops half-way across the grid. The subject has to determine the principle behind the pattern and then enter the grid reference which will continue the track. The computer signals whether this is correct or not. After two consecutive correct responses, a new and more difficult pattern is presented. If a subject fails to respond correctly up to five more attempts are allowed at the same pattern, each starting at a different point. Draper and Larraghy (1986) present data from alcoholic and control subjects. There are versions of the test software for both Apple and IBM compatible machines (DRAT, 1988).

The problems of getting early warning of shunt blockage in hydrocephalic children were described by Grant (1986), who developed a battery with a view to monitoring functions vulnerable to increases in CSF pressure. The battery is designed for self-administration on a repeated serial basis, so that it could be used, for example, in schools. One test assesses spatial imagery. The child has to "take a cat on a journey" through a maze on the screen. A path is shown through the maze which then disappears and the child has to trace it through the maze from memory. In the "day" condition, the reference markers of the maze are visible, in the "night" condition they are not. Validation data are being collected (DRAT, 1988).

CONCLUDING REMARKS

Microcomputer-based testing conveys a number of benefits and disadvantages. The onus is on the professionals concerned to consider the implications of using or not using particular applications in their own working situations, and to decide what will be of most benefit to their clients, their colleagues and themselves. It is also appropriate for professional bodies to take a leading advisory role, publishing readily available guidelines on the use of microcomputers in assessment and updating these regularly in view of the rapid developments in this technology.

REFERENCES

Acker, W. (1982) A computerized approach to psychological screening: the Bexley–Maudsley Automated Psychological Screening and the Bexley–Maudsley Category Sorting Test. *International Journal of Man–Machine Studies*, **17**(3), 361–9.

Acker, W. and Acker, C.F. (1982) *Bexley–Maudsley Automated Psychological Screening*, NFER-Nelson, London.

Adams, K.A. and Heaton, R.K. (1985) Automated interpretation of neuropsychological test data. *Journal of Consulting and Clinical Psychology*, **53**(6), 790–802.

Bartram, D., Beaumont, J.G., Cornford, T., Dann, P.L. and Wilson, S.L. (1987) Recommendations for the design of software for computer-based assessment (CBA). *Bulletin of the British Psychological Society*, **40**, 86–7.

Beaumont, J.G. (1985) The effect of microcomputer presentation and response medium on digit span performance. *International Journal of Man–Machine Studies*, **22**, 11–18.

Beaumont, J.G. and French, C.C. (1987) A clinical field study of eight automated psychometric procedures: the Leicester/DHSS Project. *International Journal of Man–Machine Studies*, **26**, 661–82.

Benson, A.J. and Gedye, J.L. (1963) Logical process in the resolution of orientation conflict. RAF Institute of Aviation Medicine, report 259, Ministry of Defence, London.

British Psychological Society (1984) Notes on the computerization of printed psychological tests and questionnaires. *Bulletin of the British Psychological Society*, **37**, 416–17.

Carr, A.C., Wilson, S.L., Ancill, R.J., Ghosh, A. and Woods, R.T. (1982) Automated testing of geriatric patients using a microcomputer-based system. *International Journal of Man–Machine Studies*, **17**(3), 297–300.

Carr, A.C., Woods, R.T. and Moore, B.J. (1986a) Automated cognitive assessment of elderly patients: a comparison of two types of response device. *British Journal of Clinical Psychology*, **25**, 305–6.

Carr, A.C., Woods, R.T. and Moore, B.J. (1986b) Developing a microcomputer-based automated testing system for use with psychogeriatric patients. *Bulletin of the Royal College of Psychiatrists*, **10**, 309–12.

Davidson, O.R., Stevens, D.E., Goddard, G.V., Bilkey, D.K. and Bishara, S.N. (1987) The performance of a sample of traumatic head-injured patients on some novel computer-assisted neuropsychological tests. *Applied Psychology: An International Review*, **36**, 329–42.

Draper, R. and Larraghy, J. (1986) Specificity in the measurement of cognitive impairment in man using a novel automated procedure. Paper presented at the 36th Annual Meeting of the Canadian Psychiatric Association, Vancouver, BC, September.

Draper, R., Manning, A., Daly, M. and Larraghy, J. (1983) A novel cognitive function test for the detection of alcoholic brain damage. *Neuropharmacology*, **22**, 567–9.

DRAT (Directory of Research into Automated Testing) (1988) S.L. Wilson (compiler). London: Royal Hospital and Home, Putney.

Elithorn, A., Jones, D., Kerr, M. and Lee, D. (1964) The effects of the variation of two physical parameters on empirical difficulty in a perceptual maze test. *British Journal of Psychology*, **55**, 31–7.

Elithorn, A., Mornington, S. and Stavrou, A. (1982) Automated psychological testing: some principles and practice. *International Journal of Man–Machine Studies*, **17**(3), 247–64.

Eyde, L.D. and Kowal, D.M. (1987) Computerised test interpretation services: ethical and professional concerns regarding U.S. producers and users. *Applied Psychology: An International Review*, 36(3/4), 401–18.

Fowler, R.D. (1985) Landmarks in computer-assisted psychological assessment. *Journal of Consulting and Clinical Psychology*, 53(6), 748–59.

French, C.C. and Beaumont, J.G. (1987) The reaction of psychiatric patients to computerised assessment. *British Journal of Clinical Psychology*, 26, 267–78.

Grant, D.A. and Berg, E.A. (1948) A behavioural analysis of the degree of reinforcement and ease of shifting to new responses in a Wiegl-type card sorting problem. *Journal of Experimental Psychology*, 38, 401–11.

Grant, D.W. (1986) Cats and fishes: an automated neurological, self-administered program for hydrocephalic children. Presented at Innovations in the Application of Microcomputers to Psychological Assessment and Therapy, Royal Hospital and Home, Putney, May.

Halligan, P.W. and Marshall, J.C. (1989a) Perceptual cueing and perceptuo-motor compatibility in visuo-spatial neglect: a single case study. *Cognitive Neuropsychology*, 6(4), 423–35.

Halligan, P.W. and Marshall, J.C. (1989b) Two techniques for the assessment of line bisection in visuo-spatial neglect: a single case study. *Journal of Neurology, Neurosurgery and Psychiatry*, 52, 1300–2.

Harris, W.G. (1987) Computer-based test interpretations: some development and application issues. *Applied Psychology: An International Review*, 36(3/4), 237–48.

IPAT staff (1972) *Administrator's Manual for the 16PF*. Institute for Personality and Ability Testing, Champaign, Illinois.

Iregren, A., Akerstedt, T., Anshelm Olson, B. and Gamberale, F. (1986) Experimental exposure to toluene in combination with ethanol intake. *Scandinavian Journal Work Environmental Health*, 12, 469–75.

Lezak, M.D. (1983) *Neuropsychological Assessment*. Oxford University Press, New York.

Matarazzo, J.D. (1983) Computerised psychological testing. *Science*, 221, 323–68.

Moreland, K.L. (1987) Computer-based test interpretations: advice to the consumer. *Applied Psychology: An International Review*, 36(3/4), 385–400.

Morris, R.G., Downes, J.J., Sahakian, B.J., Evenden, J.L., Heald, A. and Robbins, T.W. (1988) Planning and spatial working memory in Parkinson's disease. *Journal of Neurology, Neurosurgery and Psychiatry*, 51, 757–66.

Morris, R.G., Eveden, J.L., Sahakian, B.J. and Robbins, T.W. (1987) Computer-aided assessment of dementia: comparative studies of neuropsychological deficits in Alzheimer-type dementia and Parkinson's disease. In: S. Stahl, S. Iversen and E. Goodman (eds), *Cognitive Neurochemistry*, pp. 31–36, Oxford University Press, Oxford.

Nelson, H.E. (1976) A modified card sorting test sensitive to frontal lobe deficits. *Cortex*, 12, 313–24.

NFER–Nelson (1989) *1989 Catalogue*, p. 18, NFER–Nelson, Windsor.

Petheram, B. (1988) Enabling stroke victims to interact with a microcomputer—a comparison of input devices. *International Disability Studies*, 10, 73–80.

Ratcliff, G. (1979) Spatial thought, mental rotation, and the right cerebral hemisphere. *Neuropsychologia*, 17, 49–54.

Ridgway, J., MacCulloch, M.J. and Mills, H.E. (1982). Some experiences in administering a psychometric test with a light pen and a microcomputer. *International Journal of Man–Machine Studies*, 17, 265–78.

Schenkenberg, T., Bradford, D.C. and Ajax, E.T. (1980) Line bisection and unilateral visual neglect in patients with neurologic impairment, *Neurology*, 30, 509–17.

Shallice, T. (1982) Specific impairments in planning. *Philosophical Transactions of the Royal Society*, **B298**, 199–209.

Simpson, J. and Linney, A. (1984) Use of computer-automated psychological tests to assess mentally impaired old people. In: F.C. Rose (ed), *Modern Approaches to Dementia. Part 2: Clinical and Therapeutic Aspects. Interdisciplinary Topics in Gerontology*, vol. 20, pp. 43–51, Karger, Basel.

Tiplady, B. (1988) A continuous attention test for the assessment of the acute behavioural effects of drugs. *Psychopharmacology Bulletin*, **24**(2), 213–16.

Watts, K., Baddeley, A. and Williams, M. (1982) Automated tailored testing using Raven's Matrices and the Mill Hill Vocabulary Tests: a comparison with manual administration. *International Journal of Man–Machine Studies*, **17**(3), 279–90.

Weinman, J.A. (1982) Detailed computer analysis of performance on a single psychological test. *International Journal of Man–Machine Studies*, **17**, 321–30.

Weiss, D.J. and Vale, C.D. (1987) Adaptive testing. *Applied Psychology: An International Review*, **36**, 249–62.

Wilson, S.L. The evaluation of a BBC microcomputer-based psychological test battery for use with physically disabled adults. Unpublished report.

Wilson, S.L. (1987) The development of an automated test of immediate memory and its evaluation on severely physically disabled adults. *Applied Psychology: An International Review*, **36**, 311–28.

Wilson, S.L. (1988) Direct use with clients: automated assessment, treatment and decision making. In: B. Glastonbury, W. LaMendola and S. Toole (eds), *Information Technology and the Human Services*, pp. 63–7, John Wiley, Chichester.

Wilson, S.L. (1990) Psychological assessment and severe physical disability. In: R. West, M. Christie and J. Weinman (eds), *Microcomputers, Psychology and Medicine*, pp. 121–30, John Wiley, Chichester.

Wilson, S.L. and McMillan, T.M. (1986) Finding able minds in disabled bodies. *Lancet*, **8521/22**, 1444–6.

Wilson, S.L., Thompson, J.A. and Wylie, G. (1982) Automated psychological testing for the severely physically handicapped. *International Journal of Man–Machine Studies*, **17**(3), 291–6.

Wylie, G.A., Wilson S.L. and Wedgwood, J. (1984) The use of microcomputers for the psychological assessment of physically disabled adults. *Journal of Medical Engineering and Technology*, **8**, 224–9.

Chapter 6

Microcomputer-Based Cognitive Rehabilitation

CLIVE SKILBECK

Microcomputers have become widely available in clinical psychology departments only within the last ten years. Although they have a range of general uses, there is increasing interest in their specific application to cognitive/neuropsychological areas. Much of this interest has been centred upon psychometric/cognitive assessment (see Chapter 5), although in recent years research in clinical practice with microcomputers has also focused upon the rehabilitation or retraining of cognitive deficits arising from acquired brain damage. Work has addressed deficits in a wide range of functions, including perceptual–spatial abilities, perceptual–motor (eye–hand) coordination, conceptual reasoning abilities, memory, attention/concentration, information processing, maths and language.

The role of a microcomputer in neuropsychological/neurological retraining has three aspects: assessment of cognitive functions and deficits prior to rehabilitation, assessment of the effectiveness of some cognitive treatment (e.g. medication), and delivery of cognitive rehabilitation. The first of these is covered within the chapter by Wilson and McMillan relating to psychometric/neuropsychological assessment. This chapter concentrates upon the third aspect and includes a brief review of the literature, offers some illustrations of software applications, and points to the very practical possibility of home-based microcomputer use in cognitive rehabilitation. The chapter also considers classification of software and design, as well as suggesting some sources. Possible future developments are briefly outlined.

Microcomputers and Clinical Psychology: Issues, Applications and Future Developments. Edited by A. Ager
©1991 John Wiley & Sons Ltd

MECHANISMS OF RECOVERY

There is a continuing debate in the literature regarding both the mechanism and the extent of cognitive recovery following acquired brain damage, and the processes involved are not yet fully understood. These processes may relate to:

- restitution of cognitive function;
- reorganization of brain functioning leading to improved cognitive functioning;
- compensation for cognitive deficits.

Restitution of cognitive functioning implies that temporarily dysfunctional brain tissue has regained adequate operation, either by neuronal recovery following damage or the dissipation of diaschsis ("cerebral shock" to brain tissue outside the immediate lesion site). *Reorganization* refers to the taking over by one brain area of a cognitive function previously associated with another area. Both restitution and reorganization are contentious issues in terms of the extent and time course of cognitive recovery associated with their operation. Functional *compensation* refers to a person achieving the same cognitive result as would have been achieved prior to the brain damage, using some functional restructuring. In the case of memory for a specific set of information, such as a list of people's names, following brain injury a person may compensate for their deficit by introducing internal memory aids (e.g. visual imagery, or mnemonics). Alternatively, the compensation may draw upon external aids, such as an electronic memory system. For example, Naugle et al. (1988), using a case report, discussed the use of the Casio module 563 (or "databank") digital wristwatch as a sophisticated cueing device. The Casio allows the programming of up to 50 alarms/cue signals over a period of weeks, including a five-letter verbal reminder with each cue so that the person has only to respond to the alarm by reading the cue to receive an appropriate reminder.

Whatever the particular processes involved in the improvement of cognitive functions following brain injury, evidence continues to accrue that microcomputers can play an important part in their rehabilitation and retraining. The microcomputer may be employed to provide extended practice in the area of cognitive loss, drawing either upon its capacity to repeat stimulus material endlessly without becoming bored, or its flexibility to vary the nature and specific features of the stimulus material being practised in retraining the patient. The microcomputer can also be used to build skills, working on individual components prior to synthesis. One step further is to use the machine as a "learning manager", in which the microcomputer offers suggestions (based upon patients' past and current performance) for cognitive projects of an appropriate level and type. This should facilitate the user in acquiring a skill in the most effective manner (Rizza, 1981). Obviously, the computer initially needs to be programmed with relevant decision rules and normative data on which to base its suggestions.

IS COMPUTER-BASED COGNITIVE TREATMENT EFFECTIVE?

There are now a number of reviews of the use of microcomputers in cognitive rehabilitation (see e.g. Robertson, 1990; Skilbeck, 1991a; Bradley, Welch and Skilbeck, 1991). As the field has existed for less than ten years, and research studies have only emerged in any number over the last five years, a definitive answer to the question of whether micro-based cognitive retraining works is not yet possible. Much of the published research is based on case study methodology. This, coupled with a host of variables which have not been controlled across studies, makes it difficult to evaluate the results obtained.

Variations in hardware, software, and clinical features (e.g. diagnosis, severity, time since acquired brain damage) complicate the evaluation. Consistency in type of response device and in program characteristics (number of trials, level of difficulty, cognitive bases of retraining routines) has not yet been achieved.

One major variable is the type of cognitive deficit. All of the areas mentioned in the introduction to this chapter have been investigated to some degree. Owing to limitations of space, the areas of maths and language functioning are not covered in any detail here (see Robertson, 1990, and Bradley, Welch and Skilbeck, 1991, for relevant reviews).

Given the facilities offered by microcomputers it might be expected that cognitive deficits involving visual–perceptual, spatial and visual memory problems might be the most appropriate for remediation. However, there have been relatively few outcome studies investigating visual–perceptual retraining. Robertson, Gray and McKenzie (1988) studied three patients (two with stroke, one with head injury) who showed left-sided visual neglect. They utilized a maximum of seven 45-minute training sessions over a 3–8 day period, employing a visual search computer program in which the patient had to locate a target stimulus. The patient was offered visual and auditory cues to assist the search process. These authors' findings were impressive: improvement occurred on the search task, and on related objective measures, but not on cognitive indices which were irrelevant to the training process. In their larger study of 23 patients receiving micro-based cognitive rehabilitation, Bradley, Welch and Skilbeck (1991) also included a visual search program (VISCAN) as well as one designed to improve right–left orientation (ROADRIGHT). Significant improvement in visual–perceptual performance during training was noted using these routines, with some generalization to other visual–spatial tasks being observed. So far, the evidence is good that visual–perceptual deficits can be treated using micro-based visuospatial retraining programs.

A larger number of outcome studies are available on attention/concentration and information processing performance. Sohlberg and Mateer (1987) studied four patients (two with closed head injury, one with penetrating head injury, one with an aneurysm), attempting to remediate attentional deficits. The retraining centred on the components of focused, selective, divided, alternating, and sustained attention, and included a number of computerized tasks (e.g. "REACT" from Life Science Associates). Patients received between seven and nine sessions per week for ten weeks. Sohlberg and Mateer found that PASAT scores improved for all four subjects as a result of attention training, the value of their findings being enhanced by the design adopted; i.e. single-case, multiple baseline across function (see Barlow and Hersen, 1984).

Gray and Robertson (1989) also employed the same single-case methodology in their research on three severely head-injured patients with attentional deficits. Retraining tasks were individually chosen to suit the type of attentional deficit displayed by each patient. Two of the patients received a computer version of the WAIS digit symbol subtest as a training routine, and two patients worked with a computerized version of the Stroop (Dyer, 1973). RAPID NUMBER COMPARISONS (Braun, Bartolini and Bouchard, 1985) was used in the training of one of the three patients; the task involves the simultaneous display of four strings of numbers (each of between one and six digits), the patient being required to identify the digit which is repeated. Exposure time can be varied, and results are considered in terms of percentage correct for each exposure condition. An arcade game, BREAKOUT, was also used with one patient. Gray and Robertson's findings indicated significant improvement in attentional functioning during the training phase, with no attendant gains during the pretraining baseline phase.

One problem in comparing different studies and their outcomes is the variation in the amount and intensity of microcomputer training provided for patients. As indicated above, Sohlberg and Mateer (1987) used between 70 and 90 sessions over a 10-week period, whereas Wood and Fussey (1987) used 20 one-hour training sessions, across 20 days, to deliver an attentional retraining program which targeted information-processing ability. Their results with a group of ten patients reflected gains over the first week's training, and generalization to other tasks where attentional performance was a major component. Some consistency across studies in terms of rate and amount of microcomputer retraining offered would be welcome.

One of the largest studies to include examination of attentional and information processing retraining using microcomputers was carried out by

Bradley, Welch and Skilbeck (1991). Their ATTENTION program (described in detail subsequently) addressed alertness, sustained attention, and selective attention (discrimination). SPEED exercises encouraged speed of information processing. The patient's task was, for example, to identify as soon as possible the second cheapest car, when provided with the prices of five cars on the monitor screen. Five levels of difficulty were included by using one-digit to five-digit prices, and both number correct and response time were recorded by the microcomputer. The results indicated that significant improvement in performance, in each of the three information conditions, occurred for the group in terms of number correct using the ATTENTION routines. These authors also noted significant gains in accuracy, but not in response time, from using SPEED. Bradley and her co-workers included a number of objective measures of information processing ability which are often employed in routine clinical neuropsychological assessment: the WAIS digit symbol subtest, and Coughlin information processing tasks (Coughlin and Hollows, 1985). Whilst no significant changes in these indices were observed during the pretraining baseline phase, the patient group showed significant improvement on these measures at post-training follow-up assessment. Good evidence of generalization was thus provided by Bradley and her colleagues.

Overall, the evidence available from the limited research strongly suggests that providing patients with micro-based training exercises directed towards attentional deficits has a significant remediating effect on these deficits.

The field where most studies of cognitive rehabilitation using microcomputers have been carried out is that of memory dysfunction. A number of different aspects of memory have been investigated. Skilbeck (1991a) reported on a program, RE-ORIENTATE, designed to assist a patient's level of orientation following acquired brain damage. The program allowed for the repeated, frequent, presentation of relevant personal and general information questions to the disorientated patient in a multiple-choice format. Following the patient's response, corrective or confirmatory feedback was provided. Results obtained with the program indicated significant improvement in orientation level on the information items used as exercises, thereby confirming that, even for severely damaged patients, a systematic relearning program can be planned soon after injury.

In an earlier study, Kerner and Acker (1985) studied 24 head-injured patients, employing memory treatment software devised by Gianutsos and Klitzner (1983). This software was based on the "Cogrehab" exercises. "Cogrehab 1" includes some memory training programs: FREEREC and TRIPREC both focus upon free-recall performance in the areas of short- and long-term memory, with SPAN concentrating on short-term memory capacity. As its name suggests, SEQREC provides exercises for visual sequential memory. "Cogrehab 3" has two memory programs designed for neurological patients who are functioning at a relatively high level: PAIRMEM provides training in developing associative strategies for verbal material, and WORDMEM assists in developing verbal immediate memory span. Kerner and Acker used these programs to deliver twelve 45-minute sessions to each patient, over the course of approximately four weeks. Assessment of outcome was judged by a change in task scores during therapy, and via pre- and post-training Randt memory test scores (Randt, Browne and Osborne, 1980). These authors not only noticed significant improvement on the training tasks over the 12 sessions, but also observed significant gains on the Randt scores following training, thereby pointing to a strong generalization effect. In addition, Kerner and Acker found that the computer training group's gains on Randt scores were significantly higher than those noted in the two control groups (one of which was a "no exposure" group, the other controlling for exposure by subjects receiving recreational computer use only).

Bradley, Welch and Skilbeck (1991) included a number of memory training tasks in their study. These tasks provided a range of indices to judge improvement during training, amongst which were level of information to be remembered, immediate recall and short/long delayed recall. The results obtained by Bradley and her colleagues in relation to the memory training tasks themselves generally indicated significant improvement in functioning, although the lack of evidence of wide-ranging generalization to objective memory tests was disappointing.

A small number of studies investigating micro-based memory training have used mastery of the computer system itself as the index of successful treatment. For example, Glisky et al. (1986) used this approach with four patients, all of whom were at least two years post-damage (three with closed head injury, one with viral encephalitis). The patients' task was the learning of computer terminology, including commands, the training being based on vanishing cues. Although these patients learned more slowly than undamaged control subjects, strong evidence of learning and generalization was noted across the eight sessions, delivered approximately twice-weekly. A couple of other memory treatment studies are discussed subsequently in the context of home-based rehabilitation. Taking all these studies together suggests a clear role for microcomputers in the rehabilitation of memory dysfunction.

Katz and Nagly (1984) offered an example of a study whereby a microcomputer was used in the cognitive rehabilitation of patients who were aphasic. These authors used the Apple equipment to deliver diagnostic reading tests, five training tasks for reading deficits, and the maths program, as well as to allow the clinician to monitor patient performance over time. The diagnostic tests were:

- matching identical letters, numbers, and words;
- identifying the function of objects (words);
- identifying associated words;
- identifying synonyms;
- identifying words and rhymes;
- understanding sentences;
- understanding paragraphs—immediate;
- understanding paragraphs from memory;
- identifying correct grammatical structures;
- solving simple arithmetic problems.

The therapy tasks were:

(1) *Functions*—identifying the functions of objects
(2) *Question words*—identifying the meanings of "who", "what", etc., in context
(3) *Hangman*—spelling words correctly
(4) *Sentences*—identifying correct grammatical structures
(5) *Short stories*—understanding short paragraphs
(6) *Maths drill*—adding/subtracting numbers.

Their CATS system (Computerized Aphasia Treatment System) requires a clinician to read some instructions to the patient concerning the rehabilitation programs during initial training. Katz and Nagly reported on the value of the software with three chronic aphasic patients who received two, three or four sessions of 20–60 minutes of computer training, these sessions being distributed across an 8–12 week period. The three patients were moderately impaired non-fluent aphasic subjects, and each showed post-training gains on reading tests compared with their pre-treatment level.

Overall, the results of outcome studies across a range of cognitive areas tend to confirm the hypothesis that microcomputers can be of assistance in the rehabilitation of acquired cognitive deficits. As might be expected, the evidence of improvement is stronger from the micro-training tasks themselves than from objective tests used to assess generalization of learning effects. The exception to this general statement seems to be the area of attention and information processing, where not only the results from the training tasks themselves, but also those from objective assessment, point to the success of micro-based cognitive rehabilitation. Research in the field has reached the point where some general statements on the classification and design of cognitive retraining programs can be made. These are provided later in the chapter, along with some sources of relevant software.

EXAMPLES OF SOFTWARE APPLICATIONS

Although the field has a short history, the use of microcomputers in cognitive rehabilitation has been attempted across a wide range of areas. A complete review of the software literature is beyond the scope of this chapter, though a number of illustrative examples are provided below. Many of the programs outlined have been written by Bracy, and are designed to run on Apple, IBM-compatible and Atari computers.

Perceptual–spatial abilities

As might be expected, given the modern microcomputer's capability in terms of displaying visual information—including presentation of fine detail, colour, 3-D simulation and movement—there are more programs available in this category of software than in any other. Bracy has offered a number of illustrations of this type of program. ALPHAREAC (Bracy, 1987) visually presents an alphabet letter to the patient, initially for 1–3 milliseconds. With repetition the exposure time is gradually increased, the patient's task being to identify the letter as soon as possible. Bracy (1988a) extended this type of visual recognition training task in a development (ALPHABIT) where the patient receives a random presentation of parts of a letter on the screen, one at a time. The patient has to draw upon visual integration and closure skills to recognize the letter. ALPHABIT records both response time and number of errors. In an earlier development, LINES, Bracy (1986a) produced a program to exercise patients' spatial integration ability by asking them to match (from a multiple-choice array) a stimulus design consisting of between one and five lines. The program offers auditory feedback following error responses, and an accuracy score is produced. Bracy has also written other programs to practise shape and size recognition (e.g. CIRCLEMATCH; Bracy 1985a).

For a neuropsychologist wishing to employ the most appropriate visuospatial retraining tasks with patients, published research data on the use of particular tasks would be very helpful, although this is often not available. In their study, Bradley, Welch and Skilbeck (1991) included a program, VISCAN, designed to improve visual scanning and search competence, and aspects of their ROADRIGHT program encouraged right–left orientation. The former program runs on the BBC microcomputer, and the latter on the Commodore 64. In VISCAN a bank of 64 keys can be sequentially illuminated in a random order. The patient's task is to press each key as it illuminates, as rapidly as possible. If not depressed, the key will remain illuminated for a length of time preset by the therapist. At the end of the session the number of keys pressed within the time allowed, and response time for each key, are shown on the screen. Response times are also represented graphically, using different colours for the various timebands, allowing patient and therapist to check the results easily. The ROADRIGHT program involves spatial orientation learning of a route between two "houses" depicted on the screen. The authors provided data pointing to the potential cognitive rehabilitation value of the programs. In the commercial sector, "Cogrehab 1" software (Life Science Associates) includes a number of exercises aimed at remediating visuoperceptual deficits.

Attention/concentration and information processing

Perceptual–spatial tasks often include elements of immediate attention, sustaining concentration, or speed of information processing. A program devised by Katz (1988), RECOGNISE, requires the patient to sustain attention over time and produce a reaction-time response. A randomly chosen target digit is briefly displayed on the screen, followed by a series of digits. The patient must respond as quickly as possible when a match with the target appears. Feedback is provided to the patient on commission and omission errors. Bradley, Welch and Skilbeck's (1991) ATTENTION program utilizes elements of alertness, sustained attention and selective attention. It has proved useful in redeveloping the attentional skills of patients and was based upon Yigal Gross's idea of a "patch" to hide a changing subset of digits in a continuous moving stream of digits. The patient has to predict which digit will next re-emerge from the patch (see Figure 6.1). To be successful the patient must keep monitoring a continuously changing subset of digits disappearing behind the patch, in order correctly to identify the order of re-emergence from the patch.

Various analogues of WAIS digit symbol tasks are available (see e.g. Acker, 1980). These may be used in training attention and the maintenance of information processing speed.

A number of microcomputer versions of traditional games can also offer appropriate practice/training materials for patients with attentional/

Figure 6.1 Gross's information processing exercise.

concentrational difficulties who are operating at a relatively high level. For example, most systems have commercially available versions of draughts, Othello and backgammon. Also within the commercial sector, the "Cogrehab 4" package contains a program (ATTEND) designed to improve attentional deficits using a number of vigilance tasks.

Conceptual/reasoning abilities

As with traditional board games and attentional performance, micro-versions of games may be used to assist in the reacquisition of reasoning skills. Meyers (1986) developed an equivalent of the board game Mastermind, which employs five levels of difficulty. Bracy (1985b) offered PATTERNS & SEQUENCES to help improve logical-reasoning/problem-solving abilities. This program displays a four-number sequence, and the patient's task is to complete the series by supplying the fifth number. The program CONCEPTOR (Psychological Software Services Inc.) offers training exercises to develop problem-solving ability. The program includes 122 concepts, and for each the patient's task is to work out the concept from separate pieces of information.

Memory functions

The number and variety of memory training programs is second only to those in the field of perceptual–spatial performance. In their EASY STREET program Nagler and Nagler (1989) provided exercises in immediate and delayed recall, based on remembering directions to specific locations. The ROADRIGHT program of Bradley, Welch and Skilbeck (1991) is similar in being based on the remembering of a route. Some programs have been devised to examine spatial memory using geometric shapes, rather than sequential visual orientation. For instance, Bracy (1985c) developed a program, SEQUENCED MEMORY, which begins with the exposure of a single geometric shape for the patients to identify from an array of six. After each successful recognition an additional stimulus shape is added, so that the task becomes one of sequential memory. Some programs address the area of spatial memory, without sequential aspects. For example, COLOURMATCH is a micro-version of the board game Concentration, in which colours are hidden behind 48 grid boxes; the patient's task is to discover the 24 colour matches in the smallest number of attempts.

Auditory memory has less often been the subject of retraining in this way. Bracy (1988b) wrote a basic program, NUMBER RECOGNITION, in which the microcomputer generates a number (1–10) of "beeps", following which the patient has to indicate the number produced. Auditory and visual feedback are offered by the computer.

One of the aspects of micro-based cognitive rehabilitation which is often neglected is the degree to which the training task parallels the real life situation. Most programs specifically written for patient rehabilitation focus on relevant functional areas which show deficit (e.g. attention, memory) though the material employed, and the nature of the training program, do not generally represent a real, everyday task for the patient. In their memory rehabilitation programs (MEMCHAT, PROMEM), Bradley, Welch and Skilbeck (1991) tried to address this issue. MEMCHAT presents visual–verbal information on the screen designed to closely parallel the type of material which might be encountered in conversation with a recent, or casual, acquaintance. The program includes three levels of difficulty beginning with a basic level in which a single idea is offered in one sentence; e.g. "Jan lives in London", "Fred used to be a painter". Difficulty level is manipulated via the amount of information to be remembered, and at level-3 a short story is presented which might be heard in casual conversation (three or four sentences long). The information to be learned is retained on the screen until the patient indicates that he/she has memorized it by pressing a key. Following this, a question and multiple-choice array of six possible answers is displayed for the patient to select the correct response. A delayed recall phase is also included in the program, and at the end of the session the number of correct responses for both immediate and delayed recall are displayed.

PROMEM displays a digital clock in one corner of the monitor screen and in the centre is presented the statement of a task and when it is to be carried out; e.g. "At 5 p.m. I must remember to take my tablets". The statement is displayed for a predetermined time, chosen by the therapist. After offset, immediate recall for the information is examined via a multiple-choice format, followed by a "filled delay", during which the patient watches moving patterns on the screen. The patient is then required to stop the clock at the time designated for the task. Stopping the clock leads to the patient having to identify what the task entailed using a multiple-choice array. The number of correct responses for each condition is presented on the screen at the end of the session.

Some of the above illustrations employed commercially prepared programs. A range of such software for cognitive rehabilitation is now available (see section on software classification, design and sources, below). An early study of microcomputer cognitive retraining in general, and of a specific software package in particular, was offered by Kerner and Acker (1985). These authors researched 24 patients who had suffered a head injury, using Gianutsos's software (Gianutsos and Klitzner, 1983). Their major findings were summarized in an earlier section.

Lynch (1985) reviewed a suite of cognitive retraining programs called CAPTAIN, which runs on Apple machines and offers *attention skills* (including auditory discrimination-rhythm and tones, colour discrimination, and scanning, *visual motor skills* (e.g. finger tapping, maze learning, spatial orientation, and visual tracking), and *conceptual skills* (e.g. size discrimination, symbolic display matching). Lynch concluded that the suite of programs has good clinical utility: the programs' content should have a high interest value to patients and shows considerable variety in terms of both stimulus and response characteristics. He felt that the programs would have applications to a wide range of patients.

HOME USE OF MICROCOMPUTERS IN REHABILITATION

Given the rapid spread of home computers, the potential savings in therapists' time (using relatives as monitors in their place), and the great increase in the number of supervised microcomputer therapy exercises which can be achieved, cognitive rehabilitation at home is becoming popular. Although much of the treatment can be carried out at home, provision of programs and direction of the rehabilitation still lies with the neuropsychologist. Bracey (1983) reported on a study of home-based memory retraining, in which patients received an intensive 25 hours per week, for up to two years. The study demonstrated that delivery of a micro-based cognitive rehabilitation system in patients' homes was practical, the results also suggesting some generalization into intellectual functioning.

In their rehabilitation unit, Purdy and Neri (1989) noted that patients whose traditional therapy was supplemented by cognitive retraining through computer programs showed improved concentration and motivation beyond the deficits targeted by therapy. These positive features were also observed by relatives who were keen to purchase a microcomputer for home use with their patient/relative. This family enthusiasm was supported by Purdy and Neri, given that it would thereby be possible to significantly increase the amount of rehabilitation time for the patient. Purdy and Neri's resultant study aimed to investigate appropriate criteria upon which to select patients for home computer rehabilitation, and establish guidelines for the use of microcomputers with patients in their own homes. Their results, obtained via questionnaire, indicated that all ten patients studied rated home use of "micros" in their rehabilitation as helpful, although there was a strong suggestion that such use should be formally monitored. Purdy and Neri pointed out that selected patients should be able to work independently with a computer, but such subjects should have:

- a capacity to sustain task attention;
- an ability to learn computer routines;
- adequate motivation;
- sufficient motor competence for response generation; and
- adequate auditory and visual perceptual attention to use the VDU and/ or speech synthesizer.

Alternatively, patients should have a helper available at home (for a minimum of three sessions per week) to assist with the home programs. In terms of hardware and software requirements, Purdy and Neri recommended a psychologist or other appropriate rehabilitation professional to advise the patient and family on appropriate software (taking into account the nature of a patient's specific deficits and his or her current level of cognitive disability in relation to these). The software must have especially good documentation, provision of backup disks can be helpful, and the availability of some support service from a software supplier can be very useful in answering specific queries. The software should also be as "friendly" as possible in terms of task/response instructions, and amount and nature of response input (including any requirements with regard to amount of available computer memory and additional peripherals). In terms of the most suitable hardware, given software focused on the areas of education and cognition, in the USA the most appropriate machines would be Apple or IBM-compatible (see Kreutzer and Morrison, 1986, for a software review), though in the UK the BBC computers are also often employed. Patients and their relatives also need to be advised in relation to the selection of appropriate peripheral response devices, such as type of joystick, mouse, or specifically adapted equipment.

Once hardware and software considerations have been dealt with, Purdy and Neri advocated that a "shadowing" training period for patient and assistant should be undertaken within the rehabilitation unit. This training should cover basic operations with a computer and the specific software to be used, the cognitive targets of the microcomputer's home use, and the record-keeping system for monitoring use of the programs and the patient's progress. Following this period, the home use can commence in association with continued monitoring by a member of the rehabilitation team. Purdy and Neri were optimistic regarding the development of home use and pointed to the potential value of commercially available video games in addition to specific cognitive rehabilitation software. This aspect was considered by Lynch (1983), and is discussed below.

In an important study, Marks, Parenté and Anderson (1986) investigated both the use of micro-based cognitive rehabilitation in patients' homes, and the question of whether any gains achieved persist after cognitive retraining is discontinued. Their study included a sample of 10 experimental subjects (E), and a sample of 10 control subjects (C). The E group had a microcomputer system in their homes with rehabilitation software covering training of perceptual grouping, mental imagery, verbal mediation, and other memory strategies, as well as having available games for training the maintenance of attention. Patients in the E group used the computer for 2–4 hours per day, over a 6–12 month period, and received visits from a rehabilitation therapist every two weeks, who assessed improvement and delivered additional software. The control group received no cognitive retraining. The E group received pretreatment memory assessment using the Wechsler Memory Scale, and were also administered this scale at termination of training, and at subsequent follow-up. The control group was tested on the Wechsler Memory Scale only once, at a time interval after discharge from hospital which approximated the "discharge to follow-up" period of E group subjects.

The results demonstrated no differences between control group memory quotients and pretreatment E group memory quotients, with E group subjects showing significant gains during cognitive rehabilitation in terms of memory quotient ($p < 0.05$). Memory quotient scores also showed a significant rise between pretreatment and follow-up ($p < 0.05$), there being no evidence of a significant drop in MQs between post-treatment and follow-up assessment.

Some units' home-based rehabilitation is becoming routine. For example, the Burden Neurological Institute in Bristol, UK, has built up a network of patient users for whom appropriate software is developed and provided for their use at home. Their cognitive rehabilitation suite of 56 programs runs on BBC machines and is designed to address a number of cognitive systems damaged by head injury.

VIDEO GAMES

Lynch (1983) reviewed the development and availability of video games, charting their progression to microcomputer systems. Writing in 1983, Lynch could find no reference to the use of video games in cognitive rehabilitation. He described his own experiences, and judgement of which games are potentially helpful to cognitive rehabilitation, categorizing them into:

● *verbal* (e.g. "hangman") or *mathematical* (e.g. arithmetic operations, blackjack);

- *memory* (e.g. Simon, counting sequences, "concentration");
- *spatial* or *perceptual–motor* (e.g. Breakout, Space Invaders, driving simulations, flying simulations);
- *table games* (e.g. chess, backgammon, Othello).

Lynch pointed out that patients' scores on video games must be fully recorded to assess progress (e.g. name of program and game, level of difficulty, number of trials undertaken, total and subset scores). He viewed video games as being useful in diagnosis, treatment, and in leisure/recreation.

Malec et al. (1984) produced one of the few formal investigations of the use of video games in cognitive rehabilitation, employing groups of patients rather than single case studies. Malec and colleagues examined 10 head-injured patients, gaining pretreatment Stroop, letter cancellation, symbol cancellation, and reaction-time data. They employed a video game based on the shooting of moving targets (with or without the presence of interfering non-target stimuli), using the "novice" level of difficulty. Subjects were reassessed after each of the four weeks of the study.

Interpretation of the study's findings, however, is not straightforward. Some subjects received ABAB or BABA designs although, given the presumed permanent learning changes associated with the therapy, "reversals" in performance should not be expected. In fact, Malec et al.'s findings tend to bear out a cumulative, non-reversing, benefit from video game exposure. The authors also employed an unusual, complex method of examining changes in test scores. In addition, it should be noted that, although Malec et al.'s results provided evidence of improvement in patients' ability to sustain attention, on entry into the study all patients were within six months of their head injury (mean: 80 days). Improvement may have resulted, therefore, partly from spontaneous post-traumatic recovery (Skilbeck, 1991b).

RESPONSE DEVICES

For many patients, using a keyboard as a response device should be avoided—its use requires too much information to be processed, and the risk of error input is high. A number of alternatives are now available, some of which were not specifically developed to assist patients to respond through the computer but to simplify inputing for undamaged people. A "mouse" (a remote pointing device to indicate/select from options displayed on the screen) facilitates interaction with a microcomputer because it is a single hand-held response device. Information from research studies is accruing on a variety of response devices in terms of their acceptability for patient use and their effects upon performance. Important amongst these was the work of Beaumont (1985) who investigated differences in response speed using a QWERTY keyboard, numeric pad, touch-sensitive screen, and light-pen. He found the touch-sensitive screen to be superior. However, in their research Smart and Richards (1986) pointed out that if the variety of touch screen used is a membrane placed immediately in front of the VDU, then one disadvantage is the possible loss of clarity of displayed information (through light diffusion). This drawback, however, only applies to "membrane" screens; if the VDU screen is itself touch-sensitive, then clarity of display is not compromised. Although standard, relatively inexpensive, alternatives to the microcomputer's own keyboard are now available, some workers prefer to produce a specific, customized response device to suit individual patient requirements. These can usually be produced cheaply by a hospital medical physics or electronics department (Norris et al., 1985).

SOFTWARE CLASSIFICATION AND DESIGN

Illustrations of available programs for specific cognitive deficits were provided earlier. The amount and range of new software can be confusing for the neuropsychologist.

Although Goldojarb (1985) introduced her software classification scheme to keep track of her personal library, the method can be usefully extended to all available cognitive rehabilitation software. She suggested the following classification areas:

Level of difficulty:	5-point scale
Type of program:	Teaches new skill
	Drill
	Game
Skill analysis:	Hand–eye coordination
	Spelling
	Mathematics
	Reading-words
	Sequencing
	Visual discrimination
	Logic and reasoning
Format:	Multilevel
	Gives instructions
	Timed
	Large type
	Multiple players
	Requires few keys

Therapist control:	Number of items
	Timing
	Starting point
Feedback:	Provides correct answer
	Keeps score
	Gives reinforcement
Access:	Keyboard
	Joystick
	Mouse
	Voice

Use of a similar classification scheme by software producers which allows potential purchasers to better judge the clinical utility and specific application value of software for their patients would be welcome.

Rehabilitation computer programs need to be designed to meet the requirements for optimal cognitive rehabilitation. The rehabilitation might be planned to develop the underlying processes associated with the particular cognitive deficit under study, or might focus on the particular functional deficit which is to be remediated (Kurlychek and Levin, 1987). Kurlychek and Levin hypothesized that the latter approach is less likely to be suitable for severe deficits, where the cognitive skill can be best addressed by breaking it down into the small elements which together constitute it. These elements can then receive remedial attention separately. Kurlychek and Levin offered suggestions as to the features which should be taken into account when providing cognitive retraining:

- Work from simple tasks to more complex ones.
- Select a difficulty level of the task which allows the patient to have a high rate of success.
- Ensure mastery at one level of difficulty before moving the patient to the next, higher, level of task.
- Work on rate/speed of response of the patient, not just accuracy.
- Provide frequent feedback, both corrective and confirmatory.
- Gradually reduce fading prompts.
- Encourage initiative and endurance in the patient.

Software for treating cognitive deficits needs to be specialist: simply employing or adapting commercial video games is usually inappropriate, owing to the high demands generally made on the patient in terms of speed of response (e.g. Space Invaders) and the amount of information to be processed (e.g. Flight Simulators). Devices which slow down the pace of such commercial programs are available but seldom provide a comprehensive solution. Development of specialist cognitive software, along the lines of programs described earlier in this chapter, allows the aspects outlined by Kurlychek and Levin to be incorporated into the programs. It is to be recommended, also, that if possible the computer task should parallel the real-life situation, as advocated by the work of Bradley, Welch and Skilbeck (1990).

The guidelines offered by the latter are complimentary to Kurlychek and Levin's suggestions:

(1) First they suggest, identify areas of cognitive functioning to be targeted by the computer training exercises. Problem areas should be agreed between therapist, patient and carer. An analysis of the underlying cognitive deficit(s) and involved system(s) can then be made. A formal neuropsychological assessment of deficits can then be carried out, using clinical tests: this helps to confirm the presence of the putative deficit and its severity, and offers a baseline against which to judge change. If a number of cognitive systems appear affected, then a decision needs to be made regarding the hierarchy of retraining, to target more basic functions (such as attention) early within the retraining period. Bradley and her colleagues discussed this issue in greater detail.

(2) The second step is to design a computer task, which ideally should be a good analogy of the real-life reported cognitive difficulty. At the very least, the training task needs to tap the cognitive attributes which underly the real-life problem.

(3) Write the program which fits point (2), or identify a suitable commercial alternative.

(4) Decide on the length of computer training session and frequency of delivery. Generally recommended are short (30–60 minute) daily training sessions. The period over which computer exercises are provided varies enormously in the literature, from a matter of days to over two years.

SOURCES

Training exercise programs for use in cognitive rehabilitation can be obtained from commercial suppliers and, often, direct from psychologists working in rehabilitation units. The largest supplier of specialist cognitive rehabilitation software is: Psychological Software Services Inc., 6555 Carrollton Avenue, Indianapolis, IN46220, USA. This organization publishes a range of programs.

Hill (1989) provided a very useful catalogue of programs in the public domain for use with the Apple microcomputer in the area of mathematics and language skills. Kreutzer, Hill and Morrison (1987) compiled information on the use of microcomputers in cognitive retraining, and included a comprehensive list of available training software for the Apple II. This was published by Neuroscience Publishers (their address is the same as that for Psychological Software Services Inc.), who also publish the central journal in the field—*Cognitive Rehabilitation*. Many of the programs devised by Bracy (described earlier) are listed in this journal and are then annually collated on to disk (suitable for Apple, Atari, and IBM-compatible computers). To date, seven such disks (called "Soft Tools") have been made available. Each disk currently costs between $35 and $50. Bracy has also made available (via Psychological Software Services Inc.) a range of programs that have been developed in the clinical environment. For example, VISUOSPATIAL II, marketed in 1988, contains ten programs relating to basic visual perceptual processes and perceptual–motor performance. It runs on Apple and IBM-compatible machines. Forthcoming software from Bracy will include problem-solving and conceptual skills. Other software developed by Bracy is outlined in Skilbeck (1991a).

Another large supplier of cognitive rehabilitation program is: Life Science Associates, Fenimore Road, Bayport, New York 11705, USA. Their "Cogrehab" series, based on the research of Gianutsos (see e.g. Gianutsos and Klitzner, 1983), is particularly popular. Some of these programs were described earlier.

Bradley, Welch and Skilbeck (1991) have developed a range of software which is available from: John Welch, Department of Clinical Psychology, Regional Neurological Centre, Newcastle General Hospital, Newcastle NE4 6BE, England. A number of their programs have been employed and evaluated in the clinical environment, and others are under development to meet therapists' needs. This group can develop programs to run on Apple, Apple Macintosh, IBM-compatibles, Commodore 64, Commodore PET, and BBC machines. Currie, from the Burden Neurological Institute, Bristol, England, will supply a wide range of software suitable for BBC machines.

A large-scale project, funded by the Scottish Home and Health Department, has evaluated cognitive rehabilitation software in the areas of attention and visual neglect. Details of this, and some of the programs employed which are marketed by Locheesoft, are available from: Ian Robertson, Department of Clinical Psychology, Astley-Ainslie Hospital, Grange Loan, Edinburgh E9 2HL, Scotland. Other software developed at the Astley-Ainslie Hospital, which runs on BBC machines and was devised to address visual neglect, is available at an approximate cost of $300 from: Microvitec, Futures Way, Bolling Road, Bradford BD4 7TU, England.

The St Andrews Attention Assessment and Retraining Package was developed by Mark Cook for use with head-injured people at St Andrew's Hospital, Northampton, England. Roger Johnson, working in the Psychology Department at Addenbrooke's Hospital, Cambridge, England, can supply a disk to encourage the use of mnemonic strategies in patients with profound memory deficits. Bradley, Welch and Skilbeck (1991) produced a more comprehensive list of software sources than is offered above.

SUMMARY AND FUTURE DEVELOPMENTS

The overall conclusion to be drawn from the foregoing review must be that computers can be usefully employed in the rehabilitation of cognitive deficits. Interpretation of outcome studies is made difficult by the relative newness of the field, and by variations across studies of a host of potentially relevant factors, such as the amount and intensity of retraining, the neurological diagnosis, time since damage, checks for generalization, and the nature of retraining exercises. Nonetheless, most areas of cognitive deficit investigated have produced at least two or three outcome studies suggesting the effectiveness of micro-based rehabilitation. The clearest evidence of its value, both in terms of improvement on training tasks and in terms of generalization effects, has been noted in the area of attention/information processing ability. The evidence is also good that using computers in the rehabilitation of memory dysfunction can produce significant improvement.

Although employing microcomputers reduces the amount of direct therapist–patient rehabilitation time, there is still a practical limit to the amount of cognitive retraining that can be provided at a rehabilitation unit. This has led to the investigation of home-based retraining systems which, given the availability of a carer as helper and of a microcomputer in the home, can significantly increase the amount and intensity of the cognitive retraining effort. Early results from this area are very promising.

The amount of available software which is relevant to the rehabilitation of cognitive impairment has rapidly increased over the last ten years. The speed of this development has been unguided, which is reflected in a very wide range of idiosyncratic programs. Notable exceptions are the "Cogrehab" series, and other programs marketed by Psychological Software Services Inc., and the "Soft Tools" from Neuroscience Publishers which comprise individual programs listed in each issue of the journal *Cognitive Rehabilitation*. Goldojarb's classification system for cognitive rehabilitation software would, if generally adopted, assist the neuropsychologist to identify the most appropriate programs for individual patients.

Parenté and Anderson-Parenté (1988) concluded that one of the most important features of cognitive rehabilitation will be the routine, frequent use of micro-administered programs. Although these authors appeared very optimistic about future developments, Long and Wagner (1986) counselled caution: they pointed out that the main purpose of this use is to gain for patient and neuropsychologist a cost-effective addition to traditional assessment in therapy. This being the case, then rigorous scientific evaluation of the use of micro-based cognitive rehabilitation, including validity and reliability studies, need to be carried out. Perhaps to date users have shown a tendency to be seduced by impressive graphics, rather than therapeutic outcome. A major risk is that the rapid proliferation of "cognitive rehabilitation" software, across rehabilitation disciplines, will lead to the uncritical use of computers in cognitive rehabilitation, in the areas of both assessment and retraining. At the moment, an appraisal of micro-based cognitive rehabilitation would have to conclude that the general case was supported but not yet proved. There are, however, a growing number of studies which suggest areas where computers can be particularly therapeutically effective, but considerably more research needs to be undertaken before we can feel satisfied that adequate formal evaluation of such systems has been achieved.

An important paper by Chute et al. (1988) challenges our too-limited assumptions regarding the use of microcomputers in the support of patients with acquired brain damage. These authors argued that virtually all of the clinical research time so far invested in computer assistance in rehabilitation has been directed towards the "tutorial" or computer-aided-learning function of these machines. Neglected has been the area of help from computers in terms of the rehabilitation of patients' interaction with and/or control of their environment. Chute and his colleagues felt that the potential tutorial role of microcomputers with rehabilitation patients may have been overstated, particularly as demonstrated retraining gains are sometimes not very high, and questions of generalization to real life have yet to be answered satisfactorily. They argued that the prosthetic value of microcomputers for activities of daily living should be investigated. As a prosthetic tool, the machine can focus on ecologically relevant issues for each patient. Such customization might be interpreted as necessarily implying large software costs, but the authors argued that the introduction of advanced machines such as the Apple Macintosh (a user-friendly, large-capacity microcomputer with high-resolution graphics) has opened the way for more flexible software to be developed. Chute and colleagues, it should be said, do have a University Software Development Group to support their rehabilitation activities. However, Chute's group felt that the introduction of a new generation of programs for the Apple, such as Hypercard, both facilitates and makes more cost-efficient the funding of applications programmers, who can easily modify the generic software to produce programs tailored to the individual patient's needs. Chute et al.'s prosthetic approach does not require any theoretical position to be taken regarding the damaged brain's ability to restore/recover its functioning. To illustrate this approach, these authors give a case study to demonstrate the evolution of a piece of language-related software according to the patient's needs and capacities. This evolution was based on Hypercard's facility to allow customization, which entailed only brief program modification time. The development and modification of software in line with an individual patient's environment and their ideal needs promises to be an important focus of future work.

REFERENCES

Acker, W. (1980) In support of the microcomputer-based automated testing: a description of the Maudsley Automated Psychological Screening tests (MAPS). *British Journal of Alcohol & Alcoholism*, **15**, 144–7.

Barlow, D.H. and Hersen, M. (1984) *Single Case Experimental Designs*, 2nd edn, Pergamon Press, New York.

Beaumont, J.G. (1985) Speed of response using keyboard and screen-based microcomputer response media. *International Journal of Man–Machine Studies*, **23**, 61–70.

Bracy, O.L. (1983) Computer based cognitive rehabilitation. *Cognitive Rehabilitation*, **1** (1), 7.

Bracy, O.L. (1985a) CIRCLEMATCH. *Cognitive Rehabilitation*, **3** (1), 50–4.

Bracy, O.L. (1985b) Patterns and sequences. *Cognitive Rehabilitation*, **3** (5), 33–9.

Bracy, O.L. (1985c) Sequenced memory. *Cognitive Rehabilitation*, **3** (6), 38–46.

Bracy, O.L. (1986a) LINES. *Cognitive Rehabilitation*, **4** (3), 32–8.

Bracy, O.L. (1986b) Cognitive rehabilitation: a process approach. *Cognitive Rehabilitation*, **4** (2), 10–17.

Bracy, O.L. (1987) ALPHAREAC. *Cognitive Rehabilitation*, **5** (5), 44–50.

Bracy, O.L. (1988a) ALPHABIT. *Cognitive Rehabilitation*, **6** (3), 62–7.

Bracy, O.L. (1988b) Number recognition. *Cognitive Rehabilitation*, **6** (1), 55–8.

Bradley, V. Welch, J.L. and Skilbeck, C.E. (1991) *Cognitive Retraining Using Microcomputers*, Taylor & Francis, London.

Braun, C., Bartolini, G. and Bouchard, A. (1985) *Cognitive Rehabilitation Software*, Université de Quebec Montreal.

Braun, C.M.J., Ethier, M. and Baribeau, J.M.C. (1987) Initiation and termination criteria and comparison of performance by gender for the psychological software services cognitive-perceptual rehabilitation package. *Cognitive Rehabilitation*, **5** (4), 44–8.

Chute, D.L., Conn, G., Dipasquale, M.C. and Hoag, M. (1988) Prosthesisware: a new class of supporting the activities of daily living. *Neuropsychology*, **2**, 41–57.

Coughlan, A.K. and Hollows, S.E. (1985) *The Adult Memory & Information Processing Battery: Test Manual*, Coughlan, St James' Hospital, Leeds.

Dyer, F.N. (1973) The Stroop phenomenon and its use in the study of perceptual, cognitive and response processes. *Memory & Cognition*, **1**, 106–20.

Gianutsos, R. and Klitzner, C. (1983) *Cogrehab I: Perceptual & Memory Programs*, Life Science Association, New York.

Glisky, E.L., Schacter, D.L., and Tulving, E. (1986) Computer learning by memory-impaired patients: acquisition and retention of complex knowledge. *Neuropsychologia*, **24**, 313–18.

Goldojarb, M.F. (1985) The Goldojarb Software Classification Form: organising computer software. *Cognitive Rehabilitation*, **3** (5), 24–7.

Gray, J.M. and Robertson, I. (1989) Remediation of attentional difficulties following brain injury: three experimental single case studies. *Brain Injury*, **3**, 163–70.

Hill, M. (1989) *Public Domain, Volume I*, Neuroscience Publishers, Indianapolis.

Katz, R. (1988) RECOGNISE. *Cognitive Rehabilitation*, **6** (5), 61–3.

Katz, R. and Nagly, V.T. (1984) Cats: Computerised Aphasia Treatment System. *Cognitive Rehabilitation*, **2** (4), 8–14.

Kerner, M.J. and Acker, M. (1985) Computer delivery of memory retraining with head-injured patients. *Cognitive Rehabilitation*, **3** (6), 26–31.

Kreutzer, J.S., Hill, M.R. and Morrison, C. (1987) *Cognitive Rehabilitation Resources for the Apple II Computer*, Neuroscience Publishers, Indianapolis.

Kreutzer, J.S. and Morrison, C. (1986) A guide to cognitive rehabilitation software. *Cognitive Rehabilitation*, **4** (1), 6–17.

Kurlychek, R.T. and Levin, W. (1987) Computers in the cognitive rehabilitation of brain-injured persons. *CRC Critical Reviews in Medical Informatics*, **1**, 241–57.

Long, C.J. and Wagner, M. (1986) Computer applications in neuropsychology. In D. Wedding, A. Horton and J. Webster (eds) *The Neuropsychology Handbook*, Springer, New York.

Lynch, W.J. (1983) The use of electronic games in cognitive rehabilitation. In: L.E. Trexler (ed), *Cognitive Rehabilitation*, Plenum Press.

Lynch, W. (1985) Hardware/software review: Captain: cognitive training series. *Cognitive Rehabilitation*, **3** (6), 32–4.

Lynch, W. (1986) An update on software in cognitive rehabilitation. *Cognitive Rehabilitation*, **4** (3), 14–18.

Malec, J., Jones, R., Rao, N. and Stubbs, K. (1984) Video game practice effects on sustained attention in patients with craniocerebral trauma. *Cognitive Rehabilitation*, **2** (4), 18–23.

Marks, C., Parenté, F. and Anderson, J. (1986) Retention of gains in outpatient cognitive rehabilitation therapy. *Cognitive Rehabilitation*, **4** (3), 20–23.

Meyers, E. (1986) Logic Master. *Cognitive Rehabilitation*, **4**, 55–61.

Nagler, R. and Nagler, M.P. (1989) EASY STREET. *Cognitive Rehabilitation*, **7** (6), 49–59.

Naugle, R., Naugle, C., Prevey, M. and Delaney, R. (1988) New digital watch as a compensatory device for memory dysfunction. *Cognitive Rehabilitation*, **6** (4), 22–3.

Norris, D., Skilbeck, C.E., Haywood, A.E. and Torpy, D. (1985) *Microcomputers in Clinical Practice*, Wiley, Chichester.

Parenté, R. and Anderson-Parenté, J.K. (1988) A forecast of the future for cognitive rehabilitation. *Cognitive Rehabilitation*, **6** (2), 42–6.

Purdy, M. and Neri, L. (1989) Computer-assisted cognitive rehabilitation in the home. *Cognitive Rehabilitation*, **7** (1), 34–8.

Randt, C.T., Brown, E.R. and Osborne, D.R. (1980) A memory test for longitudinal measurement of mild to moderate deficits. *Clinical Neuropsychology*, **2**, 184–94.

Rizza, P.J. (1981) Computer-based education (CBE): tomorrow's traditional system. *Journal of Children in Contemporary Society*, **14**, 29–42.

Robertson, I. (1990) Does computerized cognitive rehabilitation work? A review. *Aphasiology*, **4**, 381–405.

Robertson, I., Gray, J. and McKenzie, S. (1988) Microcomputer-based cognitive rehabilitation of visual neglect: three multiple-baseline single-case studies. *Brain Injury*, **2**, 151–63.

Skilbeck, C.E. (1991a) Computer assistance in the management of memory and cognitive impairment. In: *Clinical Management of Memory Problems*, B. Wilson and N. Moffat (eds), Croom-Helm.

Skilbeck, C.E. (1991b) *An Information-Processing Approach to Cognitive Recovery Following Head Injury*. Unpublished PhD thesis.

Smart, S. and Richards, D. (1986) The use of touch-sensitive screens in rehabilitation therapy. *Occupational Therapy*, October, 335–8.

Sohlberg, M. and Mateer, M. (1987) Effectiveness of an attention-training program. *Journal of Clinical and Experimental Neuropsychology*, **9**, 117–30.

Wechsler, D. (1981) *Wechsler Adult Intelligence Scale—Revised*, Psychology Corporation, New York.

Wood, R.L. and Fussey, I. (1987) Computer-based cognitive retraining: a controlled study. *International Journal of Disability Studies*, **9**, 149–53.

Chapter 7

Clinical Applications of Microcomputers with Children

JO DOUGLAS

The 1980s saw a revolution in the use of personal computers with children in homes and in schools, owing to advances in technology and price reductions. Most of the programs available for home use by children are games for amusement that require high reaction speeds in shooting down monsters or fighting battles in the air, on land or sea. More recent developments have expanded into traditional strategic and planning games like chess, and into problem-solving exploratory games based on branching story lines.

As soon as computer game playing in arcades and at home became such a widespread phenomenon, psychologists were being asked about the effect on children of their long-term use. Issues were raised such as the addictive quality of several of the games, the problem of children stealing money to play in arcades, and the complete preoccupation of some children with interacting with a machine rather than with other children of the same age. Can they be of benefit to children? Do they help children learn to concentrate? Do they really increase reaction time, and if so how can this be used to best effect?

As the home market expanded, psychologists also started to consider how computers could be used in clinical practice. Can the highly motivating nature of some computer activities be utilized in developing treatment or learning strategies for children with difficulties (Malouf, 1988)? Are there any advantages in using computers over traditional remedial techniques? In what ways can they be used in treatment and therapy?

Developmental and child psychologists have been able to work both in the health and education services to examine the uses and benefits of computer

Microcomputers and Clinical Psychology: Issues, Applications and Future Developments. Edited by A. Ager
©1991 John Wiley & Sons Ltd

applications with children in several areas. This has included work with:

- physically disabled children (Butler, 1988; Douglas, Ryan and Reeson, 1988; Shell et al., 1988);
- children with mild learning difficulties (Howell et al., 1987; Williams, 1987; Woodward et al., 1988);
- children with severe learning difficulties (Bull, Cochran and Snell, 1988; Elf, 1988);
- children with sensory deficits, i.e. the partially sighted, blind and deaf (McGregor and Thomas, 1988, St Pe and Darby, 1987; Wischkin, 1987);
- neurologically impaired children (Story and Sbordone, 1988);
- socially, emotionally and behaviourally disturbed children (Fitzgerald, Fick and Milich, 1986); and
- children with speech and language disorders (Bridwell-Bowles, 1987; O'Connor and Schery, 1986; Shane, 1988).

PHYSICALLY DISABLED CHILDREN

Disabled children have to cope with often complete dependence on others to help them interact with their environment and even at times interpret their desires to the outside world. The immense frustration and lack of autonomy that this creates can undermine a child's self-confidence, self-esteem and motivation. Having to wait for others to help with even the simplest tasks perpetuates dependency long after appropriate developmental periods.

A child with cerebral palsy may never have the opportunity to go off alone and play or experiment or be naughty. The normal developmental patterns become distorted. Protest may only be possible by self-destructive acts like refusing to eat. Attempted non-cooperation may be interpreted as part of the child's disability rather than an expression of feelings and anger. Efforts to control his body and not do what is being asked can be seen as muscle spasms. If he becomes agitated he may be told to calm down, and adults start to control the child rather than trying to understand what is the matter. The increasing lack of communication exacerbates the physical frustration of not being able to control his own body. All too often the child's willpower is gradually eroded by impotence at being able to affect events. Passivity becomes easier and the child loses motivation and interest.

The immense importance of maintaining a child's desire to struggle and assert his own personality means that help is required at a very early age. Methods of enabling the child to exert some direct control in his environment is a necessity in order for him to realize that he is a separate and independent person. Activities that stimulate the child's intellect and engage his creative drive and need for learning are essential to maximize the child's potential. Opportunity for interaction and play with other children of the same age will enable the child to learn how to give and take in social settings rather than always fighting for control with adults and carers. Also time to have fun and amusement—plus a chance to be naughty—are all part of the young child's world. Enhancing the child's ability to communicate adequately is often the key to developments in these other areas (Brinker and Lewis, 1982).

Some disabled children have parents who are so dedicated to their needs that many of these developmental requirements are met with very astute attention and patience on the part of the adult. But this is a full-time and very wearing occupation that requires a selflessness that is not common. Trying to balance a child's emotional and social needs against his daily physical care can seem like walking a tightrope. Once the demands of schooling and educational progress start, then life can suddenly seem too crowded to take the time to manage the feelings and emotions of the situation.

Computer technology has seemed like a lifeline to some of these children. It has offered the chance to be independent in some part of their lives for the first time. A two-year-old disabled child can be fascinated and delighted by a simple cause and effect program on a computer where any noise he makes is translated into patterns on the screen. He is able for the first time to affect his environment without the intervention of an adult. He can be creative and experiment with noise, he can have fun, he can see that he has some mastery over another object. A feeling of competence, that is so essential to healthy psychological growth, can start to emerge with a simple opportunity such as this. The child can carry on doing the activity without an adult getting bored or trying to alter the activity in any way (Behrman and Lahm, 1983).

Cause and effect learning is an essential conceptual building block for understanding events and how they happen. Most children are able to try this out with toys and objects, but a disabled child is often unable to do this. He learns more by observation rather than experimentation. A combination of the two is the optimum learning environment for the child. A child who has full opportunity to experiment but no guidance will take a long time to find out simple scientific rules, while a child who is only told and shown may develop limited understanding of what is being taught. Attention to inappropriate aspects of the demonstration can disrupt the expected learning pattern. So for efficient learning to occur children needs some help and guidance, but also the opportunity to try it out for themselves. Computers can now offer this possibility to disabled children (Goldenburg, 1979).

A very young child with cerebral palsy can draw independently on the screen using switch control of cursors. He can have direct control over programs that involve simple hide and seek games. He can make choices in activities and carry out simple problem-solving. He can build up pictures by simple switch press. He can play or choose tunes and nursery rhymes or select stories that he wants to hear. Importantly, he can also make deliberately wrong choices so as to see the results (Douglas, Ryan and Reeson, 1988).

As the child grows older the computer can become a memory store and an access to information in many different ways. The communication function will be discussed in detail in a later section, but the child may use it as a store of words or phrases that are used regularly, or as a store of symbols that are used in communication. It functions as a wordprocessor, allowing the child to write and store his own work, correct it, alter it and access it at a later point. It can contain files of information that the child needs to refer to, avoiding the need for coping with textbooks and turning pages. It is a tool that can be used for all parts of a child's developing learning needs at school, at home and socially.

In summary, when able to use a computer a disabled child has:

- increased control over environmental events;
- more independence;
- opportunities for cause and effect learning;
- opportunities for creativity and experimentation;
- a powerful learning tool for all basic skills of reading, writing and maths;
- a usable information source for academic material, general knowledge, current affairs and events;
- a communication aid for language and writing;
- a memory store;
- a source of amusement and fun and a competitor in games.

Problems in using computers with disabled children

A computer can never compensate for the loss of the child's normal physical function and so it will always seem inadequate and frustrating in its limitations. Although the possibilities are enormous the question is whether computers will ever live up to the expectations.

The first hurdle is the interface between the child and the computer. Many children are held up at first base because of difficulties in matching their physical needs to switches and interfaces. The problem rests with the ingenuity of professionals in choosing the most appropriate voluntary movement that the child shows, and the range of reliable switches that can be used by the child. This is a lengthy and expensive process in time, effort and training. Specialists are needed to assess the child's physical functioning and engineers are needed to tailor-make switches to the child's particular needs. There are vast arrays of switches that can be used and they can be sited in many different ways. Switches can be proximity types touch- or pressure-sensitive, infrared, electrically sensitive or sound-sensitive. They can be positioned for hands, fingers, elbows, feet, toes, head-pointing, eye-pointing, head-turning, chins, tongues or teeth. But they need to be durable and totally reliable.

This development can take a long time and can be frustrating and irritating to parents, therapists and teachers, as well as the child. Lost opportunities only compound the disadvantages that the child is already enduring, and having to wait months or even years to be assessed for switch use is using up valuable developmental time.

The second hurdle is gaining access to a computer. Many parents cannot afford to purchase one and often schools do not have sufficient for every child to have one. For the child to feel confident in the use and control of a computer it is important for it to be available at all times. Unfortunately many children find themselves having access to one at school, but then go home and are not able to use one there. If the computer is being used as a memory store, a communication aid or a tool for creativity and fun, these uses need to be available at all times. A child cannot just stop wanting to play when he goes home from school; he does not stop wanting to communicate or feel independent. Making the child leave his computer is like taking away a lifeline and reinforces feelings of impotence and incompetence. If a child needs to wear glasses or a hearing aid do we take them away from him at certain times of the day so that he cannot see or hear clearly?

The third hurdle is finding appropriate software for the child's develop-mental needs. Software has lagged behind the hardware developments and it is often difficult to find suitable software that matches the child's growing needs and abilities (Sandals and Hughes, 1988). Professionals need time to survey the programs that are on offer and determine how best they can be used by children. Parents need guidance so that money is not spent on inappropriate software. Unlike with books, it is often not possible to look at a program before it is bought and so parents and professionals have to rely on advertising descriptions. The need for software to be accessible via other interfaces apart from the keyboard is essential. It may also be useful to be able to extend the required response times. It is not generally possible to buy commercially produced software that permits access to the program to alter it to the needs of the disabled child; so this may restrict the range of suitable programs to software specifically designed for this group of children.

Most of Britain's special-needs software has either been developed on specially funded projects or been designed and written by teachers and parents.

It is a new and developing field and the networks for dissemination of information across agencies and professionals is gradually developing. In the UK there are Communication Aid Centres, voluntary bodies like the Spastics Society, and a range of microelectronic Resource Centres that will provide detailed information and assessment of software. Also, many education authorities have advisors in computers for children with special needs. In the USA there are many resource groups, organizations and networks that can provide this information as well as a number of regular publications that keep people up-to-date with new information (Green, 1988; Moore, 1988; Pressman, 1987).

CHILDREN WITH IMPAIRED COMMUNICATION

Communication impairments cover a wide range of disorders, from disabilities that just affect vocalization to those which include bodily handicap. Children with cerebral palsy are often unable to voluntarily use speech or vocalization for communication, while children who have brain damage or sustained head injuries may have basic cognitive deficits that have affected their communication skills. Neurological impairments can manifest themselves as problems in sustaining attention, discriminating between stimuli, analysing presented information, and integrating new information with previously learned knowledge. In some instances this is demonstrated by children being able to talk, but only about present concrete objects and events—recall and retention of past experiences is not possible. Others may be able to read but not attribute meaning to the words—their comprehension of written text is non-existent but their pattern recognition of words is excellent.

Satisfactory communication involves not only speech but also the skills of listening, reading, writing, gestures and body language. It can also include drawing, design, music, maths and art (Ridgway and McKears, 1985). The ability to communicate is an essential feature of our lives as social beings and so impairments in a child's ability to communicate have wide implications across many areas of development.

The role of technology with these children is varied. For some the computer acts as a communication aid where generation of speech is of primary consideration. With others computers are used as remediation tools using programs designed to enhance the child's deficits and to practise and learn the required skills (Murdock, 1985; Story and Sbordone, 1988).

The computer as a communication aid

The possibility of a computer as a replacement for a child's voice is still a long way off, but access to computers has certainly opened some new doors for early communication. The particular problem faced by clinicians with young children is the fact that they do not read. How is it possible for a non-reading or writing child to communicate through a non-speech system?

Picture/pointer boards were the original solution to this dilemma, but they were very limited in the number and choice of pictures from which the child could select. The child also had to be able to recognize the picture and be able to match it with the object it represented. (This first step in symbolic representation being essential for language development). Pictures of objects also have severe limitations for a more developed communication system because of the difficulty in demonstrating verbs, pronouns, adjectives and other aspects of speech, like questions.

The next stage was to develop a pictorial language that could represent these other forms of speech and be usable by children at a pre-reading level. Bliss-symbolics has performed this function for many children very adequately. It is a flexible system that can be adopted to the child's level of functioning and grows with the child's rate of learning. Many disabled children have their Bliss board showing the words they regularly use attached to their wheelchair in front of them. Pointing with eyes or hands is usually the prime mode of communication. The difficulty is that the child needs time to learn the new language and must have voluntary movement precise enough to select a particular square on the board. It is also a closed communication system limited to the people who know it and use it regularly. It cannot be used to interact with other disabled children very easily as they cannot see each others' boards, and it cannot be used with able-bodied children who do not know the language.

Optimally a child needs a communication aid that is easily usable at its own developmental stage, contains a suitably wide range of words, allows developmental progression in the use of grammar, and is easily understood by others.

Computers have offered an increased flexibility and range of pictures for communication needs. Graphics have improved on 16-bit machines, and is has been possible to draw recognizable pictures without using up too much memory space. The prospect of greatly enhanced memory means that pictorial screen representation will be much easier in the future, with the possibility of, for example, demonstrating verbs via movement in picures on the screen. It is to be hoped that communication aids based on pictorial software will allow children to access a communication aid at an earlier age. The difficulty still faced, though, is the access of the program by the child. Reliable switch use is still a paramount consideration and remains the major restrictive factor in enabling very young children to use such aids.

Once the child is able to read then the world of adult aids comes within reach. Adult stroke or accident victims who have retained full mental capacities, but who have been adversely affected physically, now provide a strong pressure group to improve the technology and software required for easy and rapid communication systems.Once the child has mastered input via switches there is a range of words, phrases and letters that can be rapidly selected to construct sentences. The whole of the computer's memory is at the child's disposal. Individuals can build up a library of their own commonly used words and phrases, only relying on letter selection for building up new individual words.

The output of a communication aid can be written on the screen display or as a printout. Alternatively, speech synthesis involves the provision of a substitute "electronic" voice, which says the selected words. The development of good speech synthesis is a very complex and costly process which is still in its infancy. Some systems generate speech from the combination of selected phonemes (Murdoch, 1985), while others use prerecorded words in a human voice (Mirenda and Beukelman, 1987). Problems of inflection and intonation have created immense headaches for programmers. The difficulty faced is that it is not enough just for words to be reproduced. The expectation of the user increases as the ease of use increases, and frustration can build up as the communication aid does not reflect adequately the user's intentions (Mahaffey, 1985). Concerns about whether a child should have a voice of the appropriate sex and whether it should be an adult or a child's voice have introduced interesting psychological issues.

The accessibility of improved communication is a vital component of child development. It allows the child to learn and find out about the world, control others in the environment and express feelings and emotions. The social and emotional needs of communication-impaired children are often overlooked because they cannot be expressed. Sometimes from the adult's point of view it is easier not to know the immense feelings of frustration and anger these children have, as it may only enhance feelings of impotence, guilt or anger.

The computer as a remediation tool

Using the computer as a therapist or trainer emphasizes its ability to present material consistently, non-judgmentally, and with immediate feedback. It allows a form of repetitive drill and practice in order for children to overlearn skills. Programs designed to develop perceptual, memory and cognitive skills should, theoretically, improve language processing (Mahaffey, 1985).

The use of computers for this form of work can be seen as greatly expanding the treatment time with little ongoing cost (there is the initial outlay on hardware and software). But the clinician still needs to design the total rehabilitation programme, of which the computer training may only be a small part. The clinician has to identify the individual's deficits that require remediation, and to have a good and detailed knowledge of relevant software so that clear goals can be established for treatment. The computer is a tool to be used within an overall treatment plan.

The decision to use a computer in therapy must involve clear identification of its intended role. Its purpose should be different from exercises that can be provided through books, puzzles or other commonly available equipment. If a child needs to practise sequencing skills, then is a computer needed or can cards be used? What is the advantage of automating such a simple task? In some instances it is important to use a computer to avoid dependence on adult contact time. Also, a parent may be more inclined to set up a computer to take a child through several repetitive exercises than to spend a hour working through these with the child. The question then arises whether parent contact time is a necessary part of the treatment programme.

Arguments have been put forward that the computer should be used as a facilitator of communication skills rather than as a tool for drill and practice. It can be used as an alternative to traditional therapy material rather than as an alternative to an instructor (Bull et al., 1988). Using it as an engaging context for conversations between the child and clinician or parent creates another sphere in which it can be therapeutic. The content of the software is not then so critical. It should be designed not to train the child but to be open-ended, allowing the child to control the computer to accomplish a goal like drawing a picture, watching an animated sequence or listening to a song (Miller and Mariner, 1986). One study that compared the amount of vocalization and social play stimulated by toy play or a computer activity found that the computer was slightly more stimulating of vocalizations in two pre-schoolers who had social and language deficits (McCormick, 1987).

In order to facilitate this type of function, computer programs need to be easy to use so that control of the computer can be shared between the adult and child or between two or more children. There should also be a flexible outcome which can vary during the session or from session to session. This retains the children's interest and makes the process of using the computer investigative and creative. The program also needs to be flexible in its content and linguistic level. This approach considers software as being 'learner based': the child rather than the computer is determining the course of the activity (Mokros and Russell, 1986).

CHILDREN WITH SEVERE LEARNING DISABILITIES

Applications in this area have spanned from shaping and reinforcing hand movements in profoundly handicapped children to teaching basic concept formation and elementary academic skills (Lovett, 1985). Three- and four-month-old babies can be taught to increase their rates of hand or leg movements to control available consequences. They can also discriminate between different contingencies and will alter their behaviour to explore these different contingencies (Brinker and Lewis, 1982). The use of the computer to analyse the child's rate of movements and to provide immediate reinforcement creates a simple learning environment that is under the baby's control. The development of progressively more refined movements by such methods can be seen as one way of starting the assessment of appropriate switch use for the young handicapped child.

As their speed of learning is much slower, these children require more repeated opportunities to practise new skills, and so the 'drill and practice' component of computer use is very important (Lovett, 1985). The fact that computer-based work can be very predictable and repetitive means that these children have an extended opportunity to learn. Stages of learning can be broken down into very small steps, and as the child reaches a preset criterion of success the program can increase in complexity or demand a finer discrimination. The program can gradually shape the child's attention to the appropriate dimension of the concept being taught.

Teaching awareness of basic concepts like size or colour can occur without language. Children can simply be reinforced for always choosing the preset concept, such as ''the biggest'' or ''the red one''. Differences between the target concept and comparisons can initially be made very large or noticeable, with gradual refinements as the child becomes more accurate at the differentiation. Prolonged opportunities to learn in this manner at the child's own speed can allow individually tailored learning to occur. The use of special visual effects, music, movement, noise and colours can all be used to make the screen display interesting and motivating.

Sharing the analysis of the individual computer recorded results is also one way of helping parents recognize that their child is changing and learning. Convincing parents that their child is capable of learning can help them become atuned to subtle developmental changes and encourage them to take a more positive attitude to teaching (Brinker and Lewis, 1982).

Computer-assisted instruction (CAI) may be fine when teaching specific skills like concept matching, object sorting or simple number work, but is it of use for the more complex tasks that these children need to learn? Because of the severity of the learning problems, some argue that the skills the children should be taught should be functional ones that they will use regularly (Bull, Cochran and Snell, 1988). Repeated use ensures retention, so why should these children be taught information that is redundant and rarely used or which requires too much generalization to other situations? Is it a waste of time to emphasize more traditional curriculum-based concepts of learning rather than practical and useful skills? The priority of teaching should be chosen by examining the child's daily routine and by anticipating his future needs as they are important in relation to domestic, leisure and social activities. Learning to make a cup of tea, get dressed and undressed unaided or butter bread are necessary and important aspects of independent living, but it is not appropriate to limit a child's experience and learning just to this type of functional activity. Each of these activities uses a developed repertoire of behaviour that depends on understanding cause and effect, sequences of activities, time relations, place relations and memory. Computer-based work can help with all of these areas of understanding.

At a simple level, basic hide-and-seek games on the screen will help teach the child how to look for objects and how to remember where they were. How will a child be able to learn how to make a cup of tea if he cannot remember where the tea is? It is equally possible to teach specifically the principles involved in basic life skills through computer use. A program designed to teach tea-making or dressing could identify the sequences required and help the child practise and rehearse. The issue of generalizing this learning to the real life setting then needs to be addressed. Visual and auditory prompts from the computer could be used in the school or at home to help the child remember and cope with the sequence of activities that needs to be completed. It can be a memory prosthesis for a child with difficulties in retaining sequences in the correct order.

Again we come back to the issue, not of how the computer can be used—as this depends on ingenuity and programming—but more basically *why* it should be used. What does computer work offer above normal teaching and experience? In answer to this, computer work can provide:

- a systematic and consistent presentation of information to the child;
- a means of detecting incremental changes in a child's response;
- a means of releasing teachers to work with individual children for periods;
- a method of detecting how children with learning difficulties learn;
- extensive periods of repetitive practice with effective reinforcers to maintain motivation;
- a chance for creative activity with minimal physical and manipulative dexterity;
- an opportunity to learn and practice life and self-help skills in an unthreatening and safe environment.

The constellation of difficulties of children in this group may be very different. Noise and bright visual screen displays may be very motivating to one child but send another into seizures. Rates of learning vary dramatically, as does the ability to maintain concentration. Sensory handicaps, emotional and behavioural disturbance also play a part. Lack of reading and typing skills mean that programs need to be simple to administer and open to individual variation.

Many questions are still unanswered about the clinical applications of computers with these children. Could autistic children learn language concepts better from a computer than from a person? Are the direct and immediate reinforcers available on the computer more effective in maintaining motivation than intermittent social reinforcers from a teacher? How should tasks be broken down into easier steps? What are the future possibilities for errorless learning? In fact, a whole spectrum of children's delayed and deviant patterns of learning is open to investigation.

CHILDREN WITH MILD AND SPECIFIC LEARNING DISABILITIES

CAI for this group of disabled children has focused mostly on academic needs. The children may show general learning difficulties and need extended opportunities to practise new concepts, or they may show specific learning difficulties and need a specialized approach to remediation. Computers are frequently available in special schools but may not be so in ordinary schools, where a child may have to share one computer with a class of 35 others.

The special needs of these children require careful and detailed assessment. General curriculum demands can be held up by difficulties in reading and writing as so much of the basic work centres on these skills. Children with learning difficulties often need a more highly structured teaching approach and more motivating materials to maintain their interest in difficult areas of learning. Many different opportunities for practising the same level of skill are required. Remedial teachers are specialists in providing this range of material in small groups, and the use of CAI can be a valuable adjunct to this armoury.

The children often have a poor self-image and may never have paid attention to the correct cues to enhance their learning skills. Their interest and motivation is often very low because of repeated failure, and behaviour problems can often arise because a child is bored and starts to make amusement by being distracting and disruptive. Unfortunately many such children may not receive the specialist help they need on a regular basis. Computer-based work can help ameliorate the lack of specialist help as long as it is monitored and changed to meet the developing requirements of the child.

A psychologist is usually asked to aid parents and teachers in identifying the learning difficulties of a child and in recommending a remedial approach that will enable the child to function better in mainstream school. Writing, reading and maths are the skills that cause the most concern, and computers have a role in helping children with these difficulties.

Handwriting

Handwriting skills have traditionally been taught by tracing or copying. Tracing provides accuracy in the pattern produced but requires little thought or active decision-making in the letter formation, unlike copying. The child needs help in enabling the skill to become largely unconscious and a faster muscular process. Teachers and parents cannot help this directly as children have themselves to make the connection between the processes. Computer-based handwriting exercises can aid this by helping a child to be both an active and an accurate writer. Computer programs can vary the amount of guidance offered to the child and inform the child rapidly when incorrect movements are made.

Lally and Macleod (1983) have described a system of teaching handwriting with a light-pen on a computer screen. Children are presented with incomplete outlines of lower-case letters; if the letter shape is traced accurately it appears on the screen, but if the light-pen deviates from the letter outline nothing appears. This immediate feedback means that the child is always self-correcting and only ever sees the correct letter formation on the screen. As the child improves in accuracy the width of the tracing line and the size of the letter can be reduced. In a study evaluating the effects of this type of computer-based practice with children between the ages of 9 and 16 years with a mean IQ of 61, all children improved their handwriting skills over the course of one month (Lally, 1982).

The keyboard may instead be used as an alternative to writing. This approach seems particularly applicable with children who have minor eye–hand coordination difficulty and poor fine motor control. The frustration they experience as a result of their brains working faster than their fingers can start to cause considerable difficulties for them at school. Behaviour problems arise because the children feel that the content of their work is not recognized and that they are penalized because of the poor quantity of their written work. Using a wordprocessor to complete written work can also be one way out of a frustrating situation where the child gets bored by handwriting exercises. The opportunity to produce a well-presented piece of work can be a great incentive to these children to learn to type quickly and to extend the amount that they write. Using a wordprocessor at home can also avoid some of the fights around homework that parents report.

Reading

Reading is another critical area of learning that is demanding of a teacher's time. Computer-based programs can be used as an adjunct in the teaching of reading (Warren and Roseberry, 1988). Speech synthesis means that a flash-card approach can be used with individual children for the start of a basic sight vocabulary. The use of flexible interfaces has meant that a child can press a word on a touch-sensitive board in front of him to match it to the one on the screen. If the child makes an error the computer can remind the child which one was pressed, encourage a second try, and if that is inaccurate then show the correct word. Touch-sensitive screens can be used in much the same way (Lally and Macleod 1983).

Other aspects of teaching reading can be enhanced by building sentences with a library of words in the computer in much the same way as traditional sentence building with word cards is used in primary schools. The words chosen by the child can be written in sentence form across the top of the screen and then read out by the voice synthesizer.

Some children have particular difficulties in attributing meanings to words that they can read very accurately. Their comprehension skills lag far behind their reading accuracy and they need particular help in learning to think about the meanings of words. The "Cloze" procedure is a clinical tool that has been used with such children: sentences are presented with words missing and the child has to fill in the appropriate words (Jongsma, 1971). The child has to read the sentences to obtain contextual clues for both semantically and syntactically correct words.

Mathematics

Maths learning is another area with which many disabled children in this group have particular difficulty. A poor memory often means that the child is kept at the level of basic computation skills without progressing on to problem-solving. Remembering the basic arithmetic facts and being able to perform arithmetical operations may be two distinct phenomena (Brainerd, 1983). Using calculators to aid poor memory skills is a simple way in which technology can supplement normal learning and allow a child to progress to higher levels of learning. Programs are then required that address not just computational skills but the actual application of mathematical concepts.

Maths is an area where there is the possibility of creative programming to make basic skill learning interesting, although currently there is a preponderance of drill and practice programs (Hasselbring et al., 1988). Some programs are available, however, that make creative use of simulations and graphics (Hedley, 1987a).

Problem-solving

Educational simulations or "microworlds" promote more active and discovery-based learning (Lawler, 1982). Imaginary worlds are presented in which the child has to solve problems and make choices. By seeing the effect of action on outcome the child learns abstract principles about how the real world works. Some software is specifically aimed at exploratory and self-directed learning based on the discovery-learning approach advocated in many schools. There are still major psychological issues about the optimum level of adult-directed or child-directed learning that should take place (Lepper, 1985). Children may miss out on some of the exciting aspects of problem-solving as they are kept at levels of trying to assimilate basic skills. A combination of structured teaching and computer simulation for problem-solving can, however, be very effective (Woodward et al., 1988).

EMOTIONALLY AND BEHAVIOURALLY DISTURBED CHILDREN

There has been very little reported work carried out using computers with behaviourally disturbed children (Fitzgerald, Fick and Milich, 1986), but there are a number of difficulties in this area that could benefit from a computer-based approach.

Children with attentional difficulties or hyperactive children

Difficulty in sustaining attention interferes with the ability to make appropriate academic progress. There are several aspects of CAI that seem optimal to the teaching of hyperactive children. They seem to progress better academically when working at self-paced rather than at a teacher-paced rate, and computer use is particularly geared to this style of learning. Also, hyperactive children work best under conditions of continuous reinforcement whereas their behaviour may deteriorate under conditions of intermittent or non-contingent reinforcement (Douglas, 1983; Douglas and Parry, 1983). CAI programs can be designed to provide continuous feedback to the child which is positive in nature rather than the negative social feedback that is often provided in the classroom.

It is not clear whether interesting graphics, colour and animation always help to maintain attention or, alternatively, act as distractors for these children.

One study which attempted to compare different methods of learning spellings in children with attentional problems found that computer-based learning was as effective as traditional write-and-check methods, with both being superior to no practice (Fitzgerald, Fick and Milich, 1986).

Children with social skill difficulties

This group includes children who are withdrawn and shy as well as those who are aggressive and anti-social. Both have difficulties in relating to their peers and are at risk for later behavioural disturbance. Children's social skills are critical in establishing friendship networks at school, and unpopular children can become victims or bullies. Some children require help with building up their self-esteem while others need practice and structured help in relating to other children.

Research with children has looked at how to identify events and feelings that trigger aggressive reactions and how to control those feelings. Other workers have investigated the component skills to interacting effectively with others, including non-verbal signs, appropriate eye contact, listening, initiating conversations, responding to others' initiations, and how to interrupt. It would appear feasible to develop software to explore these areas of functioning and equip children with the basic ideas about effective and adaptive social skills before the stress of applying them in real life situations (Hedley, 1987a).

Computer work itself can also be used as a facilitator of interaction and communication between children where competitive games or joint problem-solving and turn-taking are necessary. Communication via a computer can also alleviate some of the stress experienced in interpersonal situations. In one study, severely disturbed adolescents found that interaction in computer-based conferences, as opposed to small face-to-face sessions, facilitated positive expression of feelings and interpersonal issues (Zimmerman, 1987).

Another approach to work in this area is interpersonal cognitive problem-solving, where a structured program teaches children to be aware of the social consequences of behaviour, to generate alternative solutions to solving interpersonal conflict, and to anticipate the relative consequences of different actions (Spivack and Shure, 1974; Weissberg and Gesten, 1982). The structured and theoretical nature of these interventions seems suitable for translation into computer-based programs.

Existing software designed to improve personal and social skills has mostly been for the adult market. Programs are available which address the issues of learning to cope with stress and pressure, and with life skills like building relationships, forming positive behaviours, increasing self-esteem and communication skills (Hedley, 1987b). The clinical application of these programs with children has not, however, been reported.

REFERENCES

Behrman, M.M. and Lahm, E. (1984) Babies and robots: technology to assist learning of young multiply-disabled children. *Rehabilitation Literature*, **45**, 194–201.

Brainerd, C. (1983) Young children's mental arithmetic errors: a working memory analysis. *Child Development*, **54**, 812–30.

Bridwell-Bowles, L. (1987) Writing with computers: implications from research for the language impaired. *Topics in Language Disorder*, **7**, 78–85.

Brinker, R.P. and Lewis, M. (1982) Making the world work with microcomputers: a learning prothesis for handicapped infants. *Exceptional Children*, **49**, 163–70.

Bull, G.L., Cochran, P.S. and Snell, M.E. (1988) Beyond CAI: computers, language and persons with mental retardation. *Topics in Language Disorders*, **8**, 55–76.

Butler, C. (1988) High tech tots: technology for mobility, manipulation, communication and learning in early childhood. *Infants and Young Children*, **1**, 66–73.

Douglas, J.E., Ryan, M. and Reeson, B. (1988) Computer microtechnology for a severely disabled preschool child. *Child: Care, Health and Development*, **14**, 93–104.

Douglas, V.I. (1983) Attentional and cognitive problems. In: M. Rutter (ed), *Developmental Neuropsychiatry*, Guildford, New York.

Douglas, V.I. and Parry, P. (1983) Effects of reward on the delayed reaction time task performance of hyperactive children. *Journal of Abnormal Child Psychology*, **11**, 313–26.

Elf, B. (1988) Use of the touch sensitive screen with children who have special educational needs. Research Supplement. *British Journal of Special Education*, **15**, 116–18.

Fitzgerald, G., Fick, L. and Milich, R. (1986) Computer-assisted instruction for students with attentional difficulties. *Journal of Learning Disabilities*, **19**, 376–9.

Goldenburg, E.P. (1979) *Special Technology for Special Children*, University Park Press, Baltimore.

Green, P. (1988) The National Special Education Alliance: one year later. *Exceptional Parent*, **18**, 48–51.

Hasselbring, T.S. et al. (1988) Developing math automaticity in learning handicapped children: the role of computerized drill and practice. *Focus on Exceptional Children*, **20**, 1–7.

Hedley, C.N. (1987a) What's new in software? Computer programs in math: software feature. *Journal of Reading, Writing and Learning Disabilities International*, **3**, 103–7.

Hedley, C.N. (1987b) What's new in software? Computer programs for social skills. *Journal of Reading, Writing and Learning Disabilities International*, **3**, 187–91.

Howell, R. et al. (1987) The effects of computer use on the acquisition of multiplication facts by a student with learning disabilities. *Journal of Learning Disabilities*, **20**, 336–41.

Jongsma, E.A. (1971) *The Cloze Procedure as a Teaching Technique*, International Reading Association, Newark, Delaware.

Lally, M. (1982) Computer assisted handwriting instruction and visual/kinaesthetic feedback process. *Applied Research in Mental Handicap*, **3**, 397–405.

Lally, M. and Macleod, I. (1983) The promise of microcomputers in developing basic skills. In: Ward (1983) *Yearbook of Education 1982/3*, Kogan Page.

Lawler, R.W. (1982) Designing computer microworlds. *Byte*, **7**, 138–60.

Lepper, M.R. (1985) Microcomputers in education: motivational and social issues. *American Psychologist*, **40**, 1–18.

Lovett, S. (1985) Microelectronic and computer based technology. In: A.M. Clarke, A.D.B. Clarke and J.M. Berg (1985) *Mental Deficiency: The Changing Outlook*, 4th edn, Methuen.

Mahaffey, R.B. (1985) An overview of computer applications: high technology and language disorders. *Topics in Language Disorders*, **6**, 1–10.

Mirenda, P. and Beukelman, D.R. (1987) A comparison of speech synthesis intelligibility with listeners from three age groups. *Augmentative and Alternative Communication* **3**, 120–8.

MacGregor, S.K. and Thomas, L.B. (1988) A computer mediated text system to develop communication skills for hearing impaired students. *American Annals of the Deaf*, **133**, 280–4.

Malouf, D. (1988) The effect of instructional computer games on continuing student motivation. *Journal of Special Education*, **21**, 27–38.

McCormick, L. (1987) Comparison of the effects of microcomputer activity and toy play on social and communication behaviors of young children. *Journal of the Division of Early Childhood*, **11**, 195–205.

Miller, J.F. and Mariner, N. (1986) Language intervention software: myth or reality. *Child Language Teaching and Therapy*, **2**, 85–95.

Mokros, J.R. and Russell, S.J. (1986) Learner centered software: a survey of microcomputer use with special needs students. *Journal of Learning Disabilities*, **19**, 185–90.

Moore, J. (1988) Online help from IBM. *Exceptional Parent*, **8**, 56–60.

Murdock, J.Y. (1985) Computer technology. In: J.Y. Murdock and B.V. Hartmann (eds), *Communication and Language Intervention Program (CLIP): For Individuals with Moderate to Severe Handicaps*, Thomas, Springfield, Illinois.

O'Connor, L. and Schery, T.K. (1986) A comparison of microcomputer aided and traditional language therapy for developing communication skills in nonoral toddlers. *Journal of Speech and Hearing Disorders*, **51**, 356–61.

Pressman, H. (1987) National Special Education Alliance. *Exceptional Parent*, **17**, 12–22.

Ridgway, L. and McKears, S. (1985) *Computer Help for Disabled People*, Souvenir Press, London.

Sandals, L.H. and Hughes, J. (1988) Computer software for those with special needs: what is really needed? *Canadian Journal of Special Education*, **4**, 23–41.

Shane, H. (1988) Communication enhancement: principles and practices. *Exceptional Parent*, **18**, 20–7.

Shell, D.F. et al. (1988) Effects of a computer-based educational center on disabled students' academic performance. *Journal of College Student Development*, **29**, 432–40.

Spivack, G. and Shure, M.B. (1974) *Social Adjustment of Young Children*, Jossey-Bass, San Francisco.

Story, T.M. and Sbordone, R.J. (1988) The use of microcomputers in the treatment of cognitive–communicative impairments. *Journal of Head Trauma Rehabilitation*, **3**, 45–54.

St Pe, O.W. and Darby, C.W. (1987) Adaptive uses of microcomputers: a case study. *Journal of Visual Impairment and Blindness*, **81**, 391.

Warren, B. and Roseberry, A.S. (1988) Theory and practice: uses of the computer in reading. *Remedial and Special Education*, **9**, 29–38.

Weissberg, R.P. and Gesten, E.L. (1982) Considerations for developing effective school-based social problem solving (SPS) training programs. *School Psychology Review*, **7**, 56–63.

Williams, A. (1987) Computer based learning environments for children with special needs. *Australasian Journal of Special Education*, **7**, 36–43.

Wischkin, D. (1987) A national survey of computer curricula: random access. *Journal of Visual Impairment and Blindness*, **81**, 392–4.

Woodward, J. et al. (1988) Teaching problems solving through computer simulation. *American Educational Research Journal*, **25**, 72–86.
Zimmerman, P.D. (1987) A psychological comparison of computer mediated and face to face language use among severely disturbed adolescents. *Adolescence*, **22**, 827–40.

Chapter 8

Microcomputer Applications for People with Learning Difficulties

Sarah Baldrey

Recent years have seen a major impact of microtechnology on the education and training of disabled people. The great potential of this technology for the amelioration of disability has resulted in the widespread introduction of microcomputers, software and accompanying peripherals into special education. This has been seen by many as a progressive and beneficial event which presents new opportunities. However, others have criticized the introduction of an impersonal machine which could be seen as usurping the role of human interaction in education and daily living. This disparity of attitudes should not come as a surprise since support for the use of such microtechnology may often seem to be founded more in enthusiasm than evidence. This chapter seeks to outline some of the reasons for the development of computer-assisted learning (CAL) for people with learning difficulties, to offer some discussion of the theoretical background and to look at some of the empirical findings regarding CAL's efficacy.

COMPUTER-ASSISTED LEARNING AND MENTAL HANDICAP

Learning assisted by technology is not a new idea. In education, there has always been the case for supplementing at least some of the curriculum with a degree of technological assistance—from simple audio-visual aids to the teaching machines of the 1960s (Cleary, Mayes and Packham, 1976). However, the falling cost of the microprocessor has resulted in something of a "microtechnology revolution" (Lovett, 1984). Educational and care establishments have gained access to the microcomputer which, with its

Microcomputers and Clinical Psychology: Issues, Applications and Future Developments. Edited by A. Ager
©1991 John Wiley & Sons Ltd

tremendous power and relative reliability, is a far more flexible tool than the technology previously available to them.

Computer-assisted learning may be regarded as taking place "where teaching or learning in any part of the curriculum are aided by some application of the computer" (Barker and Yeates, 1985). The progress of CAL has divided into two large areas. A major concern has been the development of hardware as a means of providing opportunities for handicapped individuals to interact with their surroundings. Also, there has been a corresponding development of instructional software designed to teach, practise or improve skills. These programs have usually targeted those skills which are of a traditionally scholastic nature or those that are recognized as a prerequisite for reading, writing or number work.

The computer can assume the role of instructor and present information to be learned. It can also check and monitor the students' progress and offer remedial help (when used in this way it is often referred to as computer-assisted instruction or CAI). Alternatively, the computer can act as the passive receiver of whatever information the learner chooses to give it; for example, by acting as a wordprocessor, drawing pad or musical instrument. It can also play a more interactive role in, for example, games. CAL programs can be short and cartoon-like or they may be text-based. Generally, in special education most CAL programs try to present striking visual and auditory stimuli in order to gain the attention of the learner.

The reasons which have been proposed for using microtechnology with people with learning difficulties are varied. There is some basis for the expectation that advantageous conditions for learning are provided with CAL. In particular, the learning environment achieved through the use of CAL:

- provides clearly defined expectations;
- gives the learner undivided attention;
- calls for active responses on the part of the learner;
- allows the learner to work at their own pace without being hurried;
- minimizes social stress;
- gives immediate feedback and reinforcement;
- is tireless;
- can be exciting and motivating through the use of animation, sound, rewards, etc.;
- can simulate real-life experiences.

(See Caldwell and Rizza, 1979; Carmen and Kosberg, 1982; Glen, 1981; Schiffman, Tobin and Buchanan, 1982; Vitello and Bruce, 1977; Watkins, 1981.)

Many of the attributes listed above are suggested as important in the teaching of people with learning difficulties regardless of the identity of the instructor—whether human or machine (McDermot and Watkins, 1983). However, the use of CAL has been particularly commended as an appropriate medium for the education and training of people with learning difficulties, because it is argued that they have certain characteristics which may be particularly well served through the use of CAL (Clark, 1986; Conners, Caruso and Detterman, 1986; Hogg, 1984).

First, these learners require a great deal of repetition of material and computers can deliver information tirelessly and in an identical fashion many times over. Also, this can occur without the instructor becoming impatient or frustrated. This lowering of tension or social stress may have particular importance if the learner is prone to emotional or aggressive outbursts.

Second, it has been noted that people with learning difficulties have a low expectancy for success (Bialer, 1961) and have frequently experienced failure within the education system (Clark, 1986). The demoralization that can result from this is frequently commented upon by educational and care staff. CAL's potential flexibility means that work presented may be suited to the individual's abilities and adjusted rapidly to provide remedial help if the learner is having difficulties.

Third, many people with learning difficulties are unable to read, so it is necessary for material to be presented in some other fashion. This can be achieved easily by using the computer's capability to produce graphics and sound or control tape recorders, slides, etc.

Fourth, another often noted characteristic of people with learning difficulties is their distractibility in the learning situation. It is argued that two aspects of CAL may reduce this. The use of CAL as a tutor can offer one-to-one instruction and thus maximize the time available for engagement with the teacher. Also, many authors cite CAL as "motivating" for learners to use (e.g. Hogg, 1984; Ager, 1985). It is suggested that this motivational dimension is achieved through the experience of self-directed behaviour and by the use of the software's graphics and sounds which direct attention to the task.

A final point is that, because of their developmental delay, adults with learning difficulties are often presented with child-oriented materials. The use of a computer, however, provides an opportunity to present tasks via a medium which is seen to be part of the everyday adult world.

While CAL has the potential to fulfil the above criteria, the extent to which this occurs is dependent on the software employed and the hardware used to provide opportunities for the handicapped learner to interact with the learning environment. There has been a proliferation in the number and types of switches or input devices allowing communication between the computer and an individual (Bourland et al., 1983; Flanagan, 1982; Goldenberg, 1979; Rostron and Lovett, 1981; Southgate, Fuller and Poon, 1983; Young, 1983). The impact these devices have had is well described by

Rostron and Sewell (1984) when they speak of microelectronics being the "enabling technology" for handicapped people. This particularly applies to those with physical handicaps, but is also very relevant to people with learning difficulties who often find it difficult to interact with their surroundings. It is now possible, in most cases, to link the microcomputer and the learner, enabling access to this potential educational tool. However, such hardware developments have outstripped those of software and the outlook is disappointing when the question of "What is being accessed?" is asked. The immediate object being accessed is the software, but any program must be a reflection of the educational strategy used in the learning process. There is a need, therefore, to look both at the software and the learning paradigm espoused by it. Considerably more progress has been made with the technical development of CAL than with instructional material. At present, the equipment is much more sophisticated than any currently proposed theory of teaching.

TEACHING SKILLS TO PEOPLE WITH
SEVERE LEARNING DIFFICULTIES

It has been suggested that CAL has done little more than repackage well-established educational techniques in elusive terminology and expensive hardware (Cleary, Mayes and Packham, 1976; DuBoulay and Howe, 1982; O'Shea and Self, 1983). This is questionable. While the hardware is now sufficiently developed to allow truly responsive and flexible education, there is still the problem of programming it. Usually, educators are not software engineers, and *vice versa*. Much educational software has been written by enthusiastic amateurs whose laudable motives are not matched by their expertise. Conversely, many programs which are technically well written demonstrate a lack of understanding of educational principles. Consequently, most software ignores important psychological principles of learning (Pattulo, 1984). This mismatch could well be responsible for the commonly held view that available special educational software is inadequate (Ager, 1985; Budoff and Hutten, 1982; Hofmeister, 1982; Morris and McBrien, 1984; Southgate, Fuller and Poon, 1983).

However, there is some support from theories of learning and development for the premise that people who are handicapped by severe learning difficulties can effectively use CAL. The two major schools of thought which have contributed to our understanding of learning and mental handicap—the behavioural and cognitive schools—can be seen to relate to the use of CAL in teaching people with learning difficulties.

Behavioural models

The development of effective methods to aid communication between the handicapped person and the environment can fulfil one of the fundamental tenets of behaviour theory. That is, in being able to act upon the environment, the outcome of that action may be observed until eventually an association between a response and its consequence is learned. A broad interpretation of this principle is seen to apply in most, if not all, instances of CAL. The learner makes a response via the keyboard or switch and the computer provides or controls the consequence.

A more specific use of behavioural principles in instructional technology was first adopted during the 1960s by Skinner and his associates. A type of instruction termed "programmed learning" was derived from the behavioural framework for operant training. This psychology of instruction is relevant to CAL in a very direct manner. Holland (1960) outlines the principles forming the basis of programmed learning as:

- immediate reinforcement of response;
- student emission of response;
- gradual progression to establish complex repertoires;
- fading of stimulus support;
- discrimination training, abstraction and concept formation through controlled variation of examples;
- revision or modification of the program to fit the student.

Further to this, branching was introduced into programmed learning by Crowder (1960, 1963). Branching consists of directing the learner to supplementary material after an error has been made, thus giving the learner feedback on his errors and emphasizing the role of remedial assistance within a program. This also enhanced learning programs by providing the facility to move "around" a program from one section to another, thus increasing the program's flexibility. The attributes of CAL which have been described earlier as useful for people with learning difficulties can be seen to closely parallel a combination of Holland and Crowder's parameters for programmed learning.

Most currently available educational software is based loosely on the behavioural principles outlined above. Almost all software makes attempts at rewarding appropriate responses and punishing inappropriate responses, for instance. Indeed, CAL has been criticized for reviving "crude behaviourism in a seductive new guise" (Chandler, 1984). Very little overt discussion of this issue has taken place, however.

Operant behavioural theory has explained learning as the process by which behaviours are acquired and controlled through the operation of contingencies of reinforcement and punishment in the environment. Unfortunately, the manner in which such principles are presently implemented in educational software is much the same as was necessarily the case with the severely limited hardware of the 1960s. The first attempts to implement behavioural principles in the classroom came at a time when the microelectronic technology lagged far behind the behavioural technology. Thus, the "crude" behaviourism should perhaps be viewed as a function of crude hardware. Currently, there is a situation in which there exists a very powerful and flexible piece of electronic technology, but, to a large extent, the application of well-researched behavioural principles to this technology is yet to be made. For example, the effect of being given instructions, schedule effects on responding, discrimination of stimuli and efficacy of reinforcement are all issues which are relevant to the use of CAL yet are rarely adequately considered in software design. Even taken at its crudest, behaviourism has yet to be fully exploited in CAL.

Cognitive models

The ability of the computer to enable interaction between the user and the environment is central to cognitive explanations of the likely benefits of CAL. The theories of Piaget (1953) and Inhelder (1968) have been used to propose a model of learning deficit. These theories propose that cognitive "growth" is derived from action (Piaget, 1971). First, the child acts upon himself and objects, then is able to make mental representations of action and finally sequence mental representations and think in abstract terms. Many severely and profoundly handicapped people have had impoverished experience of acting upon their environment. Thus, they may undergo developmental arrest through the lack of necessary interaction. The use of CAL, in providing opportunities to act directly upon the environment, may go some way to increasing the likelihood of the handicapped person being able to derive knowledge through their actions. However, there is little direct evidence concerning the interaction between impairment of motor activity and cognitive development (Rostron and Sewell, 1985). Nor is there adequate knowledge to surmise if it is the lack of motor activity itself or neurological damage which might also preclude motor activity and underlie the handicap. There is also a problem with this theory when trying to account for severely motor-handicapped persons who are cognitively very able.

Rostron and Sewell (1985) suggest that the views of Neisser (1976) can provide a more feasible outlook than classic Piagetian theory. Neisser argues that most objects and events in an environment are meaningful. Acquisition of the associations between these meanings and the objects and events depends, ultimately, on experience and interaction with the environment.

If this interaction has been limited then the acquisition of this knowledge will be retarded. Again, CAL can provide a degree of interaction with the environment and give feedback on those actions, thereby enabling the amount of information gained about the surroundings to be increased.

Cognitive models are most clearly seen in applications such as LOGO (Papert, 1980). LOGO is a programming language designed to be very simple yet powerful. It is commonly used in conjunction with devices such as the Turtle (Jessop Microelectronics Ltd), which is a drawing instrument on wheels. The learner controls the actions of the Turtle by communicating with the computer. The claims for this type of learning strategy are that it motivates self-directed behaviour and teaches the learner to learn through action (Hope, 1982).

This type of approach relies heavily on computer-controlled environments to make knowledge available to users. As such, it does not explicitly improve on software of the type commonly used in education. Rotheray, Sewell and Morton (1986) put the case for interaction as a feature of instructional software design. Drawing on theories of linguistic development, they argue that a "conversational" approach to communicating with the computer may benefit people with severe learning (language) difficulties. This requires the modification of input and output to allow the use of the computer to occur as naturally as conversational turn-taking. This turn-taking is enhanced by the use of instructions given in intelligible synthesized speech. Rotheray and colleagues also emphasize the need for feedback on errors. The user is informed of the nature of the error and the question is repeated. Spoken instructions, the use of pauses, screen displays and musical rewards are used to retain attention.

This procedure does rely somewhat on hardware to provide synthesized speech. However, it does incorporate the basic elements of acting on the environment, observing the consequences of those responses and being given feedback and/or rewards as a result of those actions.

EFFICACY OF CAL FOR ADULTS
WITH LEARNING DIFFICULTIES

Does CAL work? Unfortunately the answer at present is "We don't know". There is an urgent need to determine whether CAL programs improve or change the learner's performance on targeted tasks. Currently, there is a dearth of empirical evidence from experiments designed to address this issue. In reviewing CAL for people with learning difficulties, Conners, Cruse and Detterman (1986) and Lovett (1985) report that only a small amount of evaluative research has been carried out and very little of that has been with adults who have learning difficulties. Most work concerns the use of computers with learning-disabled children in remedial education or with people who have physical disabilities. A review of the literature located 23 evaluations—six of which specifically concern adults with learning difficulties. Many more have been conducted with children and, where appropriate, these findings will be included.

Perhaps the most common form of investigation is that involving observational studies where no attempt has been made to produce systematic results (see e.g. Cassady, 1985; Rostron and Lovett, 1981; Watts, 1985). For example, Lally and Macleod (1983) describe a computer-controlled technique of teaching telephone dialling skills to intellectually handicapped adults, but no objective indication is given of its success. Such descriptions are helpful in that information is disseminated and applications detailed, but it is difficult to comment on the efficacy of CAL by relying on observation alone.

Another method has been to assess post-test gains against pre-test measures. Significant gains in responding are reported by Scott (1984) and McDermot, Harsant and Williams (1986) using pre-test/post-test comparisons to determine the effectiveness of two CAL programs. Scott (1984) describes results from 15 adults with severe learning difficulties who were given CAL "designed to teach basic cognitive skills through reinforcement of a simple motor response". McDermot, Harsant and Williams (1986) used CAL to teach visual discrimination to an adult with severe learning difficulties. Out of three other similar studies with children, all of them report improved attainments in spelling (Hasselbring, 1982), time-telling (Friedman and Hofmeister, 1984) and coin recognition (Farnell, 1984). These studies are favourable toward the use of CAL. However, the lack of control groups creates difficulties in definitely ascribing effects to the CAL intervention.

Studies that have employed group comparisons have found no differences between CAL and conventional methods of teaching with adults. Individual tuition or CAL were used to teach sight word vocabularies to adults by Ryba and Webster (1983) and Baumgart and Van Walleghem (1987). In both studies, the CAL group did not perform significantly better than the teacher-taught group.

In contrast, three other studies with group comparisons of children present mixed results. Trifiletti, Frith and Armstrong (1984) found that CAL instruction improved the mathematics skills of the experimental group over the control group. However, in the other two studies, essentially equivalent gains by experimental and control groups were achieved in spelling and mathematics (McDermot and Watkins, 1983) and performance on a two-choice discrimination (Plienis and Romanczyk, 1985).

In another group comparison study, Lally (1981) used CAL instruction as a supplement to regular teaching rather than on its own. The control group received conventional instruction only. Significant differences were found in achievement of a sight word vocabulary, with the experimental group demonstrating increased word recognition.

Taken together, the findings from these studies where CAL has been compared with conventional teaching suggest that, at least, CAL is just as good as individual tuition and can also be used effectively as an adjunct to classroom instruction.

There are difficulties in comparing such different methods of teaching as highlighted by Baumgart and Van Walleghem's (1983) study. During their instruction sessions, the learner either had to press a response key during CAL or point to a card during individual tuition. In the CAL condition, the response keys were numbered to correspond with the words on screen. Thus, the subject had to be able to transfer spatial cues from the screen to the response key. It is unclear if there was spatial correspondence between the response keys and the screen array. During the individual tuition, it was only necessary to point directly to the card with the target word printed on it, probably making the task easier in this condition. This potential difference in response task characteristics is a problem in comparison studies.

Three studies compared different versions of CAL programs in an effort to determine the most appropriate format for instruction. Neither Ryba and Webster (1983) nor Torgeson (1984) found any difference when comparing two different parameters. Ryba and Webster (1983) employed two methods of CAL teaching of sight word vocabularies to adults: paired associate learning and errorless discrimination. No difference was found between the two methods. Torgeson (1984) compared two versions of drill-and-practise mathematics programs. One program used an arcade game format, while the other was a standard program that did not employ elaborate graphics. Each program was found to be equally effective in increasing the number of problems solved within a given period of time. Although the arcade format program was reported to be more enjoyable to use, both programs were labelled as "boring" by the children after being used for two weeks.

Only one study found any improvement in achievement through using different teaching techniques to teach the same skill. Lally (1981) employed a computer-controlled graphics tablet to assist with handwriting instruction. The graphics tablet would display incomplete outlines of letters or numbers and learners were required to trace around each figure correctly with a light-pen. A cursor box was used to help cue correct tracking of the child's pen movements around the tablet. Three cursor box sizes were compared with respect to handwriting improvement—large, small and large reducing to small. The greatest improvements in handwriting samples were found to occur among those learners who used a reducing size cursor box. Thus, a better computer-assisted technique for teaching handwriting was determined.

Some researchers have also looked at changes in collateral behaviours during CAL sessions. Ryba and Webster (1983) noted that self-directed behaviour occurred more often, aggressive behaviour diminished and changes in affect occurred while learners were partaking in CAL. However, Baumgart and Van Walleghem (1984) found that on-task behaviour increased during individual tuition, while all subjects demonstrated some off-task behaviour in the CAL condition. In contrast to this, Plienis and Romanczyk (1985) found that disruptive behaviour increased during individual tuition sessions. In fact, the two groups of people studied were very different. Baumgart and Van Walleghem (1984) were teaching adults with moderate learning difficulty, while Plienis and Romanczyk (1985) were teaching children with severe learning and behavioural difficulties. Observations such as these suggest that the potential changes in behaviour while using CAL with people with learning difficulties reach far beyond enhancing traditional educational skills. Implications from evidence of this nature are likely to yield important contributions to the use of CAL in learning difficulty.

Only five of the above studies (Farnell, 1984; Plienis and Romanczyk, 1985; McDermot, Harsant and Williams, 1986; Ryba and Webster, 1983; Scott, 1984) were aimed at teaching people with severe, rather than mild-to-moderate, learning difficulties. Any findings from one group cannot be generalized across the range of ability to another. But, as mentioned earlier, much more research has taken place with less disabled students and it would be imprudent not to take account of all findings while evaluation studies are still relatively new. It must be borne in mind that, because of the heterogeneity of the subject group, there is a difficulty in looking for consistent results that might lead to more definite conclusions regarding the effectiveness of CAL. This problem applies to all of the studies described here and is one that is widely acknowledged in any investigations in the field of learning difficulty.

Conclusions

Taking the research literature as a whole, it is impossible to draw any general conclusions regarding the efficacy of CAL. There just has not been enough systematic research. What studies have been done present a diverse picture of the use of CAL with people with learning difficulties, and it is difficult to integrate findings from studies which vary so widely from one another. Subject characteristics, the research aims and methodology and the specific application of CAL are different in almost each and every study. While this demonstrates that CAL may be widely applied, this flexibility itself means that no conclusive statements may be made regarding general principles of CAL implementation or effectiveness.

There is still little evidence for the supposed attributes of CAL. The factors described earlier as being of theoretical importance (e.g. individualization, motivation, active learning, feedback and reinforcement) have not gained much empirical weight. Most studies used CAL programs which did not have any great capability for individualization. One study (Torgeson, 1984) directly addressed using "motivational" components in the software. All studies used the concepts of feedback and reinforcement, but seldom questioned their role in the learning process. Few attempts have been made, except at a most general level, to relate these attributes to the body of knowledge already possessed about learning and related difficulties. Ideally, CAL program parameters would be examined at the same level of other investigations into the factors involved in the role of guiding the learning behaviour of people with learning difficulties.

With regard to more practical concerns, it is disappointing that many of these studies make no reference to the day-to-day difficulties that must have been encountered while setting up CAL interventions and carrying out research in applied settings with people who have learning difficulties. In any evaluation of a teaching method, the application in its "true" setting of a school, hospital, Adult Training Centre etc. should also be considered. Not least, by doing this, valuable information and, perhaps, a greater sense of confidence could be shared between the instructors, psychologists, occupational therapists, nurses, teachers and others who are trying to implement day-to-day use of CAL in their establishments.

MICROTECHNOLOGY AS A "PERCEPTUAL TOOL" FOR WORKING WITH MULTIPLY HANDICAPPED PEOPLE

Some evaluative research concerning the efficacy of microtechnology has been carried out, not so much to determine the effectiveness of computer-assisted education, but to use it and other forms of microelectronics as a "perceptual tool". Brinker (1984) describes this function of microtechnology as being derived from the capacity of the microcomputer to store information about performance on an ever-expanding and easily retrievable database. Evidence gathered across time can enable hypotheses regarding each student's learning difficulties to be formulated. From this evidence, interventions can be suggested, and these hypotheses can then be frequently re-evaluated and new interventions can be designed. Thus, the learning processes of profoundly multiply handicapped people can be better focused upon.

Research is particularly needed to help create an appropriate learning environment to maximize the potential for change for this group of people. Studies such as some of those described below show how the computer may be used as a perceptual tool and are at the extreme end of the CAL continuum in that they do not conform to typical modes of CAL. However, they show important aspects of CAL in education (such as the potential to store large amounts of accurate information concerning each person, which can then be used to continually modify the learning strategy). While this is ostensibly true of all CAL programs this facility is not always used. It is invaluable when faced with detecting the subtle changes in behaviour which may signify learning by people with profound multiple handicaps. The information being gleaned from studies such as these about the learning processes of people with severe learning difficulties must not be ignored if worthwhile contributions are to be made to their education and care.

Several studies have demonstrated some learning while using micro-techology for profoundly multiply handicapped people. Bourland et al. (1983) describe switches designed for encouraging the attainment of target behaviours such as reaching, grasping and manipulating. Various devices were used such as lightweight pull-strings and joysticks. The eventual goals of any manipulation of these switches were to improve sensorimotor operations, encourage exploratory behaviours and possibly develop some rudimentary forms of play. Operation of any of these switches resulted in the delivery of such reinforcers as bursts of music and activation of a toy spacegun or an air blower. After an initial baseline period of no-consequence responding, response-consequent reinforcers were introduced for five adults with profound multiple handicaps. One case of contingent responding, one of no responding and three cases of varied responding are reported after the CAL intervention.

Brinker and Lewis (1982) describe results from four profoundly handi-capped children between the ages of three months and four years. The children were seated in an adjustable infant seat. Switches were attached to ribbons which were tied to their wrists so that movement of the arm closed a microswitch and sent a signal to the computer. A carpeted panel at the infant's feet enabled any kicking to send another signal to the computer. The computer was programmed to turn on a tape recording (e.g. with music, the mother's voice etc.) or a variety of other mechanical devices when movement occurred. Clear differentiation of reinforced from non-reinforced responding is reported.

Lovett (1985, 1988) reports similar results from two studies with non-ambulatory, profoundly mentally retarded (NPMR) children. An ultrasonic switch was used which activated nursery rhyme music when the sound beam was broken by movement. The response rate during contingent reinforce-ment periods showed an overall increase over that of baseline periods. The second study involved breaking an ultrasonic beam to activate a small, battery-operated car in which the children could ride. This movement was the putative reinforcer. The results showed that the children's response rate increased substantially during periods of contingent reinforcement as opposed to periods of non-contingent or no reinforcement. In addition, nursery rhyme music was used to indicate either the presence or absence of contingent reinforcement, thus acting as a discriminative stimulus. Lovett (1988) reports that clear supportive evidence was found to suggest that these children could learn to discriminate the different conditions.

Much importance has been placed on active participation in order for learning to take place, especially for those with limited physical capabilities. The use of "enabling" microelectronic devices with people who are multiply handicapped raises the importance of computer-assisted interventions to being instrumental in increased opportunities for active learning. The studies described above use microtechnology to demonstrate gains for a group of people for whom it has been notoriously difficult to provide opportunities for improvement—from the mastery of the most simple of tasks to having the opportunity to operate a self-driven car.

CONCLUSIONS

So far, a varied picture of the use of CAL with people with learning difficulties has been given. At first sight, the view is optimistic. The use of CAL is increasing and has extended beyond the classroom into the lives of adults with learning difficulties in day-care centres, social education centres and hospitals. There are articles, reports, newsletters, bulletins, workshops and courses coming from sources such as education, psychology and occupational therapy with the aim of providing practical advice for using the computer in adult special education. There must, however, be a note of caution. The rush into the new technology has found essential concerns still wanting. Most noticeable is the lack of crucial information regarding learning processes and the resultant transcribing of questionable educational strategies on to CAL programs for people with severe learning difficulties. Concerning CAL, Sage and Smith (1984) noted that "a substantial edifice has been erected in a commendably short time, but its foundations are shallow and in desperate need of underpinning".

The value of microtechnology and its application to people with learning difficulties thus remains open to question. Much of its use has been with children at school who, with their teachers, view using the computer as an enjoyable, easily accessible activity which can enhance the curriculum. As such, its value is inherent. But, there is a lack of understanding of exactly what is being achieved in terms of the behaviours and advances being gained by its use. While, from the beginning, there have been calls for assessing and developing microtechnology in special education on a sound research base, this has not occurred in any major way. This lack of evaluation must be viewed against a background of a rapid expansion of commercially available educational software, switches and other devices enabling communication between user and machine—not forgetting the considerable amounts of money that have gone into the development and acquisition of all this equipment. There has developed a discordant situation where there appears to be an implicit assumption that educational microtechnology is effective in its aims (otherwise this wealth of technology would not exist), coupled with little explicit evidence that this is indeed the case. The great enthusiasm for CAL must be balanced with, and accompanied by, evidence for its supposed attributes.

REFERENCES

Ager, A. (1985) Recent developments in the use of microcomputers in the field of mental handicap: implications for psychological practice. *Bulletin of the British Psychological Society*, **38**, 142–5.

Barker, P. and Yeates, H. (1985) *Introducing Computer Assisted Learning*. Prentice-Hall, London.

Baumgart, D. and Van Walleghem, J. (1987) Teaching sight words: a comparison between computer-assisted and teacher-taught methods. *Education and Training of the Mentally Retarded*, **22**, 56–65.

Bialer, I. (1961) Conceptualisations of success and failure in mentally retarded and normal school children. *Journal of Personality*, **31**, 258–70.

Bourland, G., Jablonski, E., Allen, G. and White, J. (1983) On microcomputers, instruction, and the severely developmentally disabled. Paper presented at the Council for Exceptional Children Topical Conference on the Use of Microcomputers in Special Education, Hartford, Connecticut.

Brinker, R.P. (1984) The microcomputer as perceptual tool: searching for systematic learning strategies with handicapped infants. *Microcomputers and Exceptional Children, Special Issue: Special Services in the Schools*, **1**, 21–36.

Brinker, R.P. and Lewis, M. (1982) Making the world work with microcomputers: a learning prosthesis for handicapped infants. *Exceptional Children*, **49**(2), 163–70.

Caldwell, R. and Rizza, P. (1979) A computer based system of reading instruction for adult non-readers. *A.E.D.S. Journal*, **12**, 155–62.

Carmen, G.O. and Kosberg, B. (1982) Educational technology research: computer technology and the education of emotionally handicapped children. *Educational Technology*, February, 26–30.

Cassady, J. (1985) Jason's reading—and liking himself better. *Academic Therapy*, **21**(2), 159–65.

Chandler, H.N. (1984) Skinner and computer assisted instruction. *Journal of Learning Disabilities*, **17**(7), 441–2.

Clark, M.M. (1986) Educational technology and children with moderate learning difficulties. *The Exceptional Child*, **33**(1), 28–34.

Cleary, A., Mayes, T. and Packham, D. (1976) *Educational Technology: Implications for Early and Special Education*. John Wiley, Chichester.

Conners, F., Caruso, D. and Detterman, D. (1986) Computer assisted instruction for the mentally retarded. *International Review of Research in Mental Retardation*, **14**, 105–34.

Crowder, N.A. (1960) Automatic tutoring and intrinsic programming. In: A.A. Lumsdaine and R. Glaser (eds), *Teaching Machines and Programmed Learning*, pp. 286–98, DAVI/NEA, Washington, DC.

Crowder, N.A. (1963) The rationale of intrinsic programming. In: J. P. De Cecco (ed), *Human Learning in the School*, pp. 183–9, Holt, Rinehart and Winston, New York.

DuBoulay, J. and Howe, J. (1982) LOGO building blocks—student teachers using computer-based mathematics apparatus. *Computers in Education*, **6**(1), 93–8.

Farnell, B. (1984) *Assessment of Computer-Aided Learning with Severely Mentally Handicapped Children*. MSc thesis, University of Hull.

Flanagan, K. (1982) Computer needs of severely mentally retarded persons. *Journal of Special Education Technology*, **5**(4), 47–50.

Friedman, S. and Hofmeister, A. (1984) Matching technology of content and learners: a case study. *Exceptional Children*, **51**(2), 130–4.

Glen, I. (1981) Exploring with the microcomputer. *Special Education: Forward Trends*, **8**(3), 16–18.

Goldenberg, E. (1979) *Special Technology for Special Children*, University Park Press, Baltimore.

Hasselbring, T. (1982) Remediating spelling problems of learning-handicapped students through the use of microcomputers. *Educational Technology*, April, 31–2.

Hofmeister, A. (1982) Microcomputers in perspective. *Exceptional Children*, **49**(2), 115–21.

Hogg, R. (1984) *Microcomputers and Special Educational Needs: A Guide to Good Practice*, Developing Horizons in Special Education Series 5, National Council for Special Education, Stratford-upon-Avon.

Holland, J.G. (1960) Teaching machines: an application of principles from the laboratory. *Journal of the Experimental Analysis of Behaviour*, **2**, 275–83.

Hope, M. (1982) Conversion exercises. *Times Educational Supplement*, 5 March, 37.

Inhelder, B. (1968) *The Diagnosis of Reasoning in the Mentally Retarded*. John Day: New York.

Lally, M. (1981) Computer assisted teaching of sight-word recognition in mentally retarded school children. *American Journal of Mental Deficiency*, **85**(4), 383–8.

Lally, M. (1982) Computer assisted handwriting instruction and visual/kinaesthetic feedback processes. *Applied Research in Mental Retardation*, **3**(4), 397–405.

Lally, M. and Macleod, I. (1983) Computer assisted instruction in telephone dialling skills. Paper presented at the Gatlinzburg Conference, CEC.

Lovett, S. (1985) Microelectronic Technology. In: A.M. Clarke, A.D.B. Clarke and J. Berg (eds), *Mental Deficiency: The Changing Outlook*, pp. 549–83, Methuen, London.

Lovett, S. (1988) Discrimination learning in multiply handicapped children using an electromechanical car. *Advances in Behavioural Research and Therapy*, **10**, 39–52.

Morris, R. and McBrien, J. (1984) Microcomputers and severe mental handicap. In: S. Simpson et al. (eds), *Facing the Challenge*, pp. 84–6, BABP Publications, Rossendale, Lancs.

McDermott, P. and Watkins, M. (1983) Computerised versus conventional remedial instruction for learning disabled pupils. *Journal of Special Education*, **17**(1), 81–8.

McDermott, P., Harsant, L. and Williams, C. (1986) Computer assisted visual discrimination learning. *Mental Handicap*, **14**, 59–61.

Neisser, U. (1976) *Cognition and Reality: Principles and Implications of Cognitive Psychology*, Freeman: San Franscisco.

O'Shea, T. and Self, J. (1983) *Learning and Teaching with Computers: Artificial Intelligence in Education*. Harvester Press, Brighton.

Papert, S. (1980) *Mindstorms*. Harvester Press, Brighton.

Pattulo, R. (1984) *Learning to Cope* (Conference report 3), Educational Computing, London.

Piaget, J. (1953) *The Origins of Intelligence in the Child*, Routledge & Kegan Paul, London.

Piaget, J. (1971) *Science of Education and the Psychology of the Child*, Longman, Harlow.

Plienis, A.J. and Romanczyk, R.G. (1985) Analyses of performance, behaviour, and predictors for severely disturbed children: a comparison of adult versus computer instruction. *Analysis and Intervention in Developmental Disabilities*, 5(4), 345–56.

Rostron, A. and Lovett, S. (1981) A new outlook with the computer. *Special Education: Forward Trends*, 8(4), 29–31.

Rostron, A. and Sewell, D. (1984) *Microtechnology in Special Education*, Croom Helm, Beckenham.

Rotheray, D.R., Sewell, D.F. and Morton, J.R. (1986) The design of educational software for children with learning difficulties. *Programmed Learning and Educational Technology*, 23(2), 119–23.

Ryba, K.A. and Webster, A.C. (1983) An evaluation of microcomputer assisted instruction for teaching word recognition to developmentally handicapped adults. *Journal of Practical Approaches to Developmental Handicap*, 7(1), 2–8.

Sage, M. and Smith, D. (1983) *Microcomputers in Education: A Framework for Discussion*, Social Science Research Council, London.

Schiffman, G., Tobin, D. and Buchanan, W. (1982) Microcomputer instruction for the learning disabled. *Journal of Learning Disabilities*, 15(9), 557–9.

Scott, R. (1984) *A Microcomputer System Used as a Teaching Aid for Adults with Severe Handicaps: A Preliminary Study*. Unpublished dissertation for BPS Diploma in Clinical Psychology, British Psychological Society, Leicester.

Southgate, T., Fuller, P. and Poon, P. (1983) Microcomputers at Ormerod School. *Special Education: Forward Trends*, 10(3), 30–3.

Torgeson, J.K. (1984) Instructional uses of microcomputers with elementary aged mildly handicapped children. *Microcomputers and Exceptional Children*, 19, 37–48.

Trifiletti, J.J., Frith, G.H. and Armstrong, S. (1984) Microcomputers versus resource rooms for LD students: a preliminary investigation of the effects on math skills. *Learning Disability Quarterly*, 7, 69–76.

Vitello, S. and Bruce, P. (1977) Computer assisted instructional programs to facilitate mathematical learning among the handicapped. *Journal of Computer-Based Instruction*, 4, 26–9.

Watkins, M. (1981) Microcomputer assisted instruction with learning disabled students. Proceedings of the 9th annual Math/Science Conference, Arizona.

Watts, G.T. (1985) Computer assisted development with profoundly retarded, multiply handicapped children. In: *The Computer as an Aid for those with Special Needs* (Conference proceedings), Department of Education Services, Sheffield City Polytechnic, UK.

Young, R. (1983) Mental handicap and electronics. *Wireless World*, September, 24–9.

Chapter 9

Monitoring and Evaluating Clinical Service Delivery: Issues and Effectiveness of Computer Database Management

RAYMOND G. ROMANCZYK

Given the burden of information management with respect to assessment, treatment documentation and evaluation, and related record keeping, it is interesting that the process of service delivery in both clinical psychology and related disciplines has not typically taken advantage of technological developments in the computer field. The dynamic use of computer technology in the complex process of service delivery has great potential to assist the clinician in the management of the voluminous information that is collected in the context of quality service delivery.

Given the complexity of planning, implementing and evaluating service delivery, this chapter will focus on a specific aspect of that process: the use of computer database technology to assist in the preparation of treatment goals and to monitor their implementation. A brief overview will be provided of database technology followed by specific examples of implementation in clinical settings. There are specific costs and benefits associated with such computer systems and these will be highlighted through the case examples.

DATABASES

The central element for effective treatment planning and service delivery is the use of the database. This is both a very simple and a very complex topic area (Romanczyk, 1986, 1987). At the simple level, a database is a

---

Microcomputers and Clinical Psychology: Issues, Applications and Future Developments. Edited by A. Ager
©1991 John Wiley & Sons Ltd

collection of individual pieces of information organized along a specific structure. A client's cumulative folder is a database, as is an accounting ledger book. The telephone book is also an excellent example of a simple database. One accesses information in this database by using a key field that allows one to search for the required information. In the case of the telephone book the key field is the last name of individuals, and they are presented in alphabetic order in order to permit easy searching of the database. Once the correct name is located, information is provided with respect to address and the telephone number. However, this type of database also illustrates an extremely important point with respect to computer databases. Simply because information is contained within a database, it does not imply that it is either technically possible or procedurally possible to extract information in all possible combinations, nor that the end result will be efficient (cf. Seiter, 1990).

Thus, two questions must always be asked about a computer database. The first is whether it has the technical capabilities to produce records with specific characteristics, such as number and length of fields, process numerical versus text information, and what features are not within its technical capability. The second question is whether it is procedurally possible to extract the information in a particular form required. Often one is confronted with computer databases of such complexity that only highly skilled programmers utilizing abstract computer programming language can access the database to make alterations and produce reports of sufficient specificity and complexity to be useful. Once again using the telphone book as an example, it does contain a full set of information with respect to last name, first name, address and telephone number. It is possible to search it structurally in a manner other than that in which it was originally prepared. That is, if one knew a telephone number but not the person's name, it is both conceptually and procedurally possible to search for the appropriate telephone number and find the individual's name. However, such a procedure would be tedious beyond words. This is because the telephone book contains only one key field: it is only the last name that permits easy searching. One cannot "key" on the telephone number as they appear in essentially random order.

With computer databases, even the most simple, typically several fields can be designated as key fields. Just as the last-name information in the telephone book is presented in alphabetical order to permit ease of searching and location, likewise one could specify the telephone-number field as a key field, sorting in numerically ascending order, and thus easily find and identify the telephone number of interest and in turn inspect the related fields of name and address.

Thus managing simple lists of information is a relatively trivial task for a computer program. However, as the amount of information to be manipulated grows both in size and complexity with respect to number of fields and mixture of text and numbers, and as the format with which selected information is to be presented in reports grows in diversity, the technical and procedural problems rise very quickly.

As an example, if one were keeping detailed records on provision of psychological assessment services to a group of individuals receiving psychiatric outpatient care, there would be a number of pieces of information for each individual that would be of great interest, such as name, social security number, address, telephone number, date of birth, medication status, diagnosis, attending physician, psychologist, social worker, names of relatives, date of admission, etc. Such information could be said to comprise the basic demographic data of a particular client. On the other hand, there would be information that would occur on a repeating basis that would also be very important, such as dates of visit to the clinic, what assessment devices were administered, the particular staff seen, therapeutic services provided, change in existing therapeutic or medication regimen, and schedule for follow-up visits. In a simple database, typically called a "flat-file" database, each individual entry into the computer database, which is termed a "record", may contain all of the above information. The difficulty, however, arises when one wishes to enter only repeating information.

This difficulty arises because, since each record stands alone, one would have to repeat name, address, telephone number, etc., each time a clinic visit occurred. This is obviously a very inefficient type of system. While such flat-file utilization may be appropriate for keeping lists of names of friends and relatives and their respective birth dates and anniversaries, it is not typically appropriate for monitoring frequent activity.

In contrast, a "relational" database has the ability, as the name applies, to relate various individual flat-file databases together to produce an integrated report. Thus one would first produce a database that had basic demographic information such as name, address, date of birth, etc. A second file would be created that would list all of the staff at the clinic. The third file would be a list of all assessment and therapeutic intervention procedures. The process would be continued for each general category of information. Then when an individual arrived at the clinic and his or her database was updated, rather than typing in the basic demographic information, typically a code number would be used, or simply the person's last name or social security number which then serves as a key to an index of the demographic database.

The information stored for each of these various categories is simply the *numerical index* that specifies the text entry in a "related" database rather than the text of the information itself. The reason this is important at a technical level is that, in a typical flat-file database, since one is storing each record in its entirety, this can consume vast quantities of storage space in the computer. On the other hand a relational database is typically extremely efficient in this manner because in essence the full information is stored only once and then accessed as needed via the relational capability. Producing a report listing name, staff member, procedure utilized and date service provided thus essentially involves accessing three or more individual databases simultaneously, and relating this information in a coherent form.

Another great advantage of a relational database is that update and modifications to the individual component databases is typically a relatively easy task, as none is so large as to be imposing. It also permits different people to take responsibility for different subsections. The tradeoff, however, between the flat-file database and the sophisticated, relational database is that the complexity and sophistication of programming is typically substantially more difficult and requires greater expertise for the relational database.

In this regard the difficulty in designing and implementing a database should not be underestimated. All too often professionals in human services attempt such tasks and produce rather ponderous and inefficient databases that bear little resemblance to the great functional utility that properly prepared systems can have. This is simply because there is a science and clear skill to the design of a database that permits the rapid access of information stored within it, and production of flexible and comprehensive reports that are error-free. While it is essential that the service professional be involved in all aspects of the database design on an on-going basis to ensure the proper translation of the technical jargon of one profession to the other, the actual implementation of the programming is often best left to professionals.

STAFF ACCEPTANCE

Even the most inexperienced supervisor or manager or the casual observer of human behavior notes that, when confronted with complex and lengthy tasks, individuals employ a wide range of work styles that range from the systematic to the intuitive, from the well-planned and well-scheduled to quick bursts of intense effort displayed in an erratic temporal sequence. However, even though knowledgeable of these variations of individual work styles, when computer systems are implemented supervisors and administrators seem almost universally doomed to do the opposite of what they know to be the case. They attempt to train all staff in utilizing a complex system in one particular manner and on a rigid and usually uncompromising schedule, both with respect to sequence of activities that need to be done with the computer as well as specific times of day or times of the week when access is permitted. Along with this, another very common mistake is to grossly misjudge the number of computers required for a given size staff, the assumption being that many individuals can share usage by simply "coordinating" work schedules.

These misperceptions are reinforced by traditional computer hardware and software developers. The tactics usually taken are those of sequential processing of information and rather rigid and unbending commands and sequences that the computer will accept (also known as the user interface and associated with the term "user friendliness"). Because most individuals work in a non-linear, non-sequential fashion, and have a tendency to forget information, work on certain aspects, stop a task, come back, forget exactly where they were, write reminders to themselves, use approximations during aspects of planning and report writing, etc., it is not surprising that there remains substantial resistance to use of computers by many staff.

Part of this resistance is the general aspect of training, in that human services have never been known for their embrace of technology other than in the medical profession. Owing to lack of exposure, one often hears the quite interesting assertion made by individuals in human services that there is necessarily a contradiction between the "cold technology" and their "people-oriented" philosophy, which is often espoused as lying at the base of their motivation to work with people as opposed to machines.

Clinicians will tend to view such statements quite appropriately as defensive, while managers tend to view such statements as resistive and obstructionistic. What is critical, however, is to acknowledge that these strong feelings are often displayed and to incorporate this into the overall plan of system implementation, by involving staff directly and non-trivially in the design and implementation of the computer system, not only with respect to what type of reports it will generate, but precisely how the individual will be able to enter and manage a personal information base. Also, great care must be taken to provide appropriate educational activities for staff so that they may be completely comfortable with the technical aspects of the computer hardware and it becomes simply another device to be used, rather than a daunting and imposing mystery.

Although often made light of, there is a growing concern for what may be termed true "cyberphobia" (Curley, 1983); that is, an unrealistic and clinically significant fear of the use of computers. From a strictly clinical perspective, such fear clearly exists and is rather observable in individuals whose employment parameters have changed significantly, so that use of the computer is now an expected part of their daily activities. Complaints of fatigue, eye strain and hardware malfunction may often be misdirected and traceable to this extreme anxiety. However, rather than simply labeling and viewing this anxiety as something the individual will "get used to", clear efforts should be made to provide the support and training in necessary skills (Davidson and Walley, 1985). While a great deal can be achieved with respect to appropriate hardware and software that maximizes ease of user utilization, this is not a substitute for specific training and acknowledgement of the feelings of anxiety, just as would be the case for any debilitating phobia. Chastisement or stating that there is "nothing to be frightened about" has as little effect with respect to cyberphobia as it has with most clinical phobias.

This also underscores the mistake that is often made with respect to organizational structure. Often when computer systems are implemented, it is simply assumed that all staff within the same job category must utilize the system. This can be a great mistake: there will be some who see this as an interesting and exciting tool and some who find it an annoyance and an intrusion and who have poor skill levels, and this serves as the focus for undue competition and comparison on a skill not central to the position for which they were hired. Thus careful consideration should be given to allow groups of staff to work out mutually agreeable sharing of related responsibilities, such that some staff will take on various information management activities with respect to the computer for other staff, who in turn relieve their colleagues of other responsibilities. In some settings this is not feasible, depending upon the specific service delivery responsibilities and their relative allocation. In such instances the belief that all staff should do their own work on the computer often is less in response to a strong belief in such a philosophy, as it is simply an administrative acknowledgement that resources are not present to hire the appropriate staff to specialize in information management, and thus this task is added to the responsibilities of those with other administrative and direct service responsibilities.

CASE STUDY: CHILDREN'S UNIT FOR TREATMENT AND EVALUATION

In order to illustrate the broad range of functions, issues of staff implementation, costs and benefits of computer technology and service delivery, the following brief case study will be presented. It focuses on the Children's Unit for Treatment and Evaluation of the Institute for Child Development, Binghamton, which is a state certified facility that provides educational and psychological services on a full-day, 12 months per year basis to children who have severe disorders. The unit was founded 15 years ago and employs a strongly behavioral treatment model that has as its hallmark the extensive and precise analysis of both maladaptive behavior and habilitative and educational goals and the highly structured and systematic continuous evaluation of progress of psychological and educational interventions. While many programs share similar philosophies, one reality that constantly impinges upon the degree to which such models can be implemented is the overwhelming burden of information management. The number and complexity of goals being monitored and the ability to process such information and provide it in an appropriate feedback loop to staff presents a monumental problem that often results in very poor implementation of the model for strictly pragmatic reasons.

Given the extensive combined experience of the staff members based upon their work in other facilities, when the unit was founded great care was taken to implement organizational structures to promote and monitor implementation of a strong behavioral model which also emphasized program evaluation and accountability. At that time computer technology was in a very primitive state and initial organizational structures involved traditional paper-and-pencil manual systems, utilizing innumerable long charts, magnetic bulletin board displays, custom data forms, elaborate filing systems, and a tremendous proportion of staff time devoted to strictly clerical processing.

Very quickly it became apparent that, given the resources available, it would be possible only to provide services for a very small group of children and families (approximately a third of the number receiving services at that time) or it would be necessary to drastically change our standards with respect to program planning, implementation, and the precision with which individualized assessments were conducted and monitored.

As neither course was acceptable nor desirable, considerable funds (compared with today's technology) were expended to acquire a mini-computer which at the time, in the mid-1970s, was "state-of-the-art". Conceptually, this computer system was to provide us with the type of information processing capabilities we required given the addition of various mass storage devices and appropriate software programming. Several years were spent in the development of this system and it was actually implemented for a brief period of time. However, in retrospect it was completely ineffective and the benefit delivered was not at all proportionate to the cost, both monetarily and with respect to staff time. It was quickly abandoned.

What is important in this illustration is that this development took place in the context of high resources, access to strong technical support in a university setting, and was with staff who had a clear statement of the functions that were desired. What actually occurred, however, was a mismatch of technology with intended purpose. The lesson to be learned here is that, even though there have been tremendous strides made in advancing computer technology in the last decade, it is still the case that one of the most common reasons for the poor integration of computer technology into service delivery systems is that there remains a mismatch of function and capability. This has little to do with the technical specifications of the computer itself, but rather the entire system: that is, the hardware platform and the various software components that serve to provide the desired functions. Thus, it is still very common for enormous resources to be spent on attempting to apply computer technology in a service delivery setting, only for it to be abandoned within a year or two as unworkable, providing information that is not usable on a timely basis, or not relevant to service delivery.

Interestingly, however, at the time the minicomputer system was being developed, the "new" technology of microcomputer applications was just beginning and the unit purchased one of the first true functional micro-computer systems available in the United States (in kit form no less) to be used simply for evaluation purposes. Because development was taking place on the minicomputer system, the new much less expensive and technically less "powerful" system was allocated to very basic "computer literacy" purposes with the staff. It also happened to arrive at a time when the telephone system of the unit was being re-evaluated for upgrading. Thus, quite by serendipity, a number of events came together that served as the single most important catalyst for producing our current highly effective integrative computer systems.

Almost as a pilot or experimental project, we decided to utilize the microcomputer for communication purposes between staff in various classrooms and office facilities. With the help of a highly skilled engineer the computer was provided with appropriate electronic interfacing to serve in one sense as a sophisticated telephone switchboard. This then began the process of providing staff with direct and immediate access to computer information.

The basic strategy utilized for acquainting staff with computer usage was to place very inexpensive computer display screens in all of the classrooms and staff offices. Access to the computer databases was achieved through a simple touch-tone telephone system. That is, the telephone in each classroom and office was wired centrally to the computer such that it could decode the button presses on a standard touch-tone telephone. All software was menu-driven such that the screen would display a menu of possible choices, and a staff member would then indicate a choice by pressing the appropriate number on the telephone keypad. Using a series of hierarchical menus it was possible to achieve a relatively complex system that required almost no training time to utilize. Initially, the information contained in the databases was rather simple, but clearly functional to the staff on a day-to-day basis. Examples included, for each child, emergency telephone numbers for family, known allergies, current medication status, birth dates, dietary restrictions, as well as a variety of schedule information. Further, since the computer was able to localize which room was placing "the call" it could display a menu of children and specified target behaviors that were to be recorded specific to that classroom.

The reception to this system was extremely positive and interestingly the system grew quite rapidly over time as staff continued to ask for more and more functions. This, of course, was the ideal situation, in that rather than imposing a system upon staff, rather it was their requests that drove development and implementation.

Once this level of staff acceptance had been achieved, a new project was begun to utilize an extensive database in a more traditional format. As the Children's Unit focuses upon young children with severe disabilities, it is standard practice that each child must have an annual individual education plan. These documents can be quite extensive in their complexity if they are prepared properly. This places an extreme burden on staff with respect to paperwork, and staff were also expected to process voluminous amounts of information concerning day-to-day performance on a myriad of various goals and to record a wide array of specific behavior problems that were characteristic of the majority of the children who attended the program.

Using the habilitative curriculum developed at the unit as the focal point for our database, the text of the curriculum was formatted such that each specific goal and task had a unique numerical reference code. The curriculum is organized into 16 different areas of development, within each area into levels of development, within each level into stages of development, and then for each stage various specific tasks. The first database application served a simple collating function such that staff could indicate on a worksheet the particular reference numbers of the goals to be addressed. These would be entered into the computer and a full text list would then be printed. Along with each goal, staff could input (once again from a series of menu choices) specific materials to be used for the goal, the teaching methodologies, the priority for the goal, the response modality expected of the child, the degree of prompting to be used, etc. The result was a worksheet for staff that involved simply writing down a few numbers for each goal, but that when entered into the computer, would produce reports that were in full prose, easily read and understood by individuals with no specific knowledge either of our coding system or of the overall curriculum itself. Once this was achieved, progress information was then added to the system, keyed to the individual numerical code associated with each goal. Over a period of several years the system was refined and expanded and recently experienced a major upgrade when it was translated from a Northstar Horizon type computer under a CPM operating system to a Macintosh environment that is extremely user friendly.

The course of development of this system has produced startling changes in the overall efficiency and operation of the unit. Figure 9.1 indicates a data analysis scanning 14 years which indicates the number of individualized intervention programs conducted per child during each of these years. As can

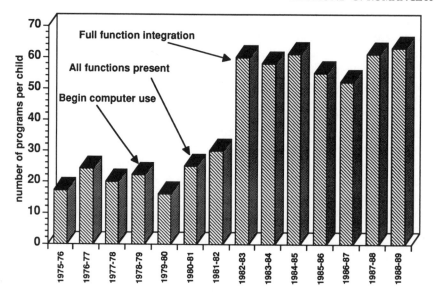

Figure 9.1 Impact of computer utilization on service delivery.

be seen, certain specific changes to the computer system are associated with extremely large changes in productivity.

However, as a caution it is interesting to note on the graph that the initial transition between manually managed information and the first computer implementation brought only marginal increases. This is not an unusual phenomenon and reflects both the simplicity of the initial computer system and the learning curve necessary in refining it such that it in fact was functional. Yet another factor was that, in any initial implementation, it is a conservative approach to run both systems simultaneously such that there is not serious impact upon the service delivery program given the inevitable computer malfunctions and software difficulties during initial implementation. However, over time one observes increments in efficiency, the largest of which involved a relatively simple change in software report format.

Staff were provided with reports that not only listed progress, but also placed each completed goal in the context of those goals remaining to be addressed. This impact was extreme and through interview staff indicated that the important aspect of this computer system alteration was that they needed to rely much less on their own memory to gauge when to make changes (when to press forward, and when to cease interventions that were not cost-efficient) because they could have reports produced by the computer at any time and at any frequency. This relieved a large burden of overall management of collating information for decision making. It is interesting that from a technical, computer database point of view, the change was relatively minor. However, from the staff point of view, it was indeed a major change. This is an extremely important point, as all too often problems with computer utilization are attacked with "faster and more powerful" solutions, rather than looking specifically to the utilization by the individuals involved and what information they find to be the most important, and equally as relevant, in what format the information should be presented.

It is important also to inspect the time cost associated with such a computer system. That is, it is clear that a positive impact occurred with respect to service delivery, but at what cost to staff time? Specific time comparisons were performed for each of the component tasks for staff. The present data reflects specifically the preparation of treatment plans (Individual Education Plans) and the production of evaluative reports on a period basis. When specificity is controlled for, that is producing equal levels of documentation, manual procedures versus computer usage produce a time savings reduction factor of approximately 7. That is, it took seven times less staff time using the computer method than by manual means. However, part of the preparation time involved use of clerical staff for typing and data entry, etc. When this is controlled for and one inspects the results for professional staff time, the reduction is a factor of over 8. However, to some extent this is a false comparison. The reason is that via the manual method of producing equal specificity it required approximately 16 hours of staff time to produce the program planning documents and evaluative reports. Given the typical case load for each staff member and the statutory time constraints for preparation of various documents, this level of specificity set a standard that could not be realistically achieved. Therefore, a second comparison was conducted looking at the more typical specificity included prior to computer implementation. That is, the type of documents previously produced manually on a typical basis by staff were inspected. Even under this reduced criteria the time saving via computer was still a factor of 4.

Thus, the sum of these results is all the more impressive. Not only were more habilitative programs conducted (that is, actual service delivery increased) but the process of treatment planning, monitoring and evaluation became much more efficient and the specificity and comprehensiveness of the documents produced greatly increased with respect to previous traditional manual methods. This pattern of results sets a benchmark for evaluation of computer systems in clinical settings: one should observe not only savings in staff time, but also improved service delivery and improved evaluation and documentation of services provided.

A SECOND EXAMPLE: AGENCY-WIDE COMPUTERIZED
TREATMENT PLANNING

The degree of impact in the previous case study was beyond initial expectations. In order to evaluate the potential of such an approach and to place it in perspective with respect to replication, a second case study will be illustrated. These data are from Coleman (1989) and personal communication, and represent a multi-site evaluation of the impact of employing a sophisticated, customized computer database to assist in managing the individual habilitation goals in an agency that provides services to several hundred individuals with mental retardation. The computer system was customized and refined for the agency over a period of six months by a commercial software firm and the full system was installed and implemented in a very short period of time and involved the training of many staff across several sites. However, with respect to issues of staff training and involvement, the individual with primary responsibility for supervising the computer utilization was very skilled and had several years prior experience utilizing a comprehensive computer system in a similar agency.

Coleman (1987) chose an interesting measure of effectiveness, that of the number of citations (i.e. formal criticisms of service quality) by external regulatory review agencies for each of the three sites utilizing the computer system. As can be seen in Figure 9.2, the impact was in a positive direction. However, these data reflect only those aspects of the review criteria that were thought to be amenable to positive direct impact by the computer system. Such items concerned the format and consistency of information management, or in other words, how the information was presented. The data for the much larger set of items

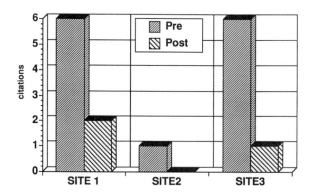

Figure 9.2 Impact of computer utilization on areas directly amenable to computer use for information management.

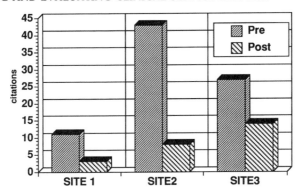

Figure 9.3   Impact of computer utilization on areas of service delivery not directly related to computer use for information management.

directly related to service delivery were also analyzed. This would reflect how the information was used in service delivery and how computerization impacted on broader organizational issues. As can be seen in Figure 9.3, a dramatic pattern emerges. Thus, the computer system's impact was broad-based and substantial.

Staff also provided estimates of time saved in various aspects of developing and monitoring habilitative programs. While there was variation across sites, the minimum saving was a factor of 3 (e.g. a task that would have taken 60 minutes now took 20 minutes). However, the more typical saving was a factor of between 5 and 10, with a high of 20! Staff satisfaction was also assessed prior to, and after, the external review. Interestingly, site 1 rated satisfaction as "high" before and after the review, site 2 rated satisfaction as "low" then "high", and site 3 rated satisfaction as "low" both before and after the external review. While all sites experienced very significant reduction in their citations, satisfaction at the third site remained low.

Perhaps the most interesting and important finding was that, two years after this evaluation of impact was made, Coleman (personal communication) found that two of the sites had discontinued their use of the computer system. Following external review at that time, the site that retained the computer system continued to have very low citations, whereas the other two sites rose precipitously with respect to citations. Further, the site that retained the computer system was the one that initially had rated satisfaction as high. Thus perhaps the most curious result was for site 2, where the computer system was not retained even though initial citations were reduced and satisfaction had increased.

INCREMENTAL GAINS

It is important also to illustrate the positive impact that can accrue from isolating specific tasks and utilizing computer technology to increase efficiency. Often individuals and agencies are overly ambitious in attempting to solve all of their information management needs rather than to approach it on a task-by-task basis. As an illustration of this, recently I prepared a focused, simple database to address the difficulty faced by a supervisor in maintaining the data collection efforts of staff on a weekly basis. Each staff member was responsible for approximately six individual clients and for each of these clients, approximately 30–40 individualized programs which required data collection were conducted at any one time. The difficulty encountered was that checking which programs had or had not been conducted and what data was associated with each program was an extremely time-consuming task and involved many separate meetings (Romanczyk and Lockshin, 1984).

One solution was to place incoming data into a database and allow the supervisor access to this information. As was currently the case, each staff member would obtain their data during habilitative training sessions and sometime during each week transfer this ''raw data'' into a summary format that was placed in the client records. Then periodically, typically on a quarterly basis, this summary data would be further summarized and evaluative conclusions drawn in order to allow further modification of programs. While the summary of the raw data was not a difficult task, it was somewhat laborious as it involved simple but repetitive calculations. The return to the summary data at intervals to conduct further summaries for preparation of periodic reports was also tedious and perceived as resulting in reports being prepared too infrequently. However, it was a procedure that had been in effect for many years and was seen by everyone as reasonable, although ''it would be great'' if something could be done to make it easier and the data more readily accessible.

These data were part of a much larger system that could have been amenable to a large computer database. However, this temptation was resisted and the specific task was addressed. A commercial flat-file type database was utilized that was noted for its relative ease of use. While certainly not a professional programmer, I had had some experience in various types of programming languages and in the use of databases. It took approximately one day's worth of discussions with the supervisor to ascertain the specific parameters of the type of information that needed to be stored. Part of this time was also spent in examining the precise work flow for the staff and how they generally approached their tasks. Also, the particular points of annoyance for staff with respect to their existing system were examined. Interestingly, one of the central complaints was the repetitive simple arithmetic that needed to be performed on conversion of raw data to standardized formats. With this information, a database was constructed. In total, it took approximately six hours of programming time to finish. Training time took an additional one hour per staff member. While the system is not at all elegant, it is simple and straightforward and relies on the ability of this particular database to make duplicate records. That is, since it is a flat-file database, it has all the disadvantages mentioned earlier, such that each record must duplicate all relevant information about an individual so that, even though only three or four separate fields are altered for each weekly record, the total record contains almost 30 fields of relevant information, each of which has to be duplicated. As an example, each record contained the client's name, staff member assigned to the client, a description of the goal being addressed, the date the program started, criteria, stability information, units of measurement, on what day of the week information was obtained, whether it was observational data, directly measured, or through use of rating scales, etc. However, since the task here is to monitor ongoing programs, a staff member enters the program only once in its full description. Then each subsequent week, by using the client and program code number, he or she simply types in these two codes and, using custom menu choices, the computer searches for the last record that matches this type. By using a single command from within the database that individual record is then duplicated. The staff member then simply changes the specific data items to reflect the information obtained for that week. This results in a staff member being able to enter his or her weekly information for a particular program for a particular client in approximately 10 seconds. In contrast, to enter the entire record would take 60–90 seconds. The time saving is extremely important as it represents the difference between a usable and unusable system. The solution used to obtain the time saving, and the ability to construct custom menus for staff to ease both learning and use of the database, has to do with the technical abilities of this particular flat-file database. Needless to say, without the specific characteristics of this particular database software, the system would be terribly cumbersome and quite appropriately rejected by staff as being too difficult and tedious to utilize.

Thus, by appropriately matching the technical abilities of the resource people available, the specifics of the task at hand and concern for time efficiency, a reasonable database was created in two working days and several positive events accrued. The first is that the supervisor is now able to localize data collection problems extremely quickly. Various reports are preprogrammed into the database and thus requests can be made for specific staff or specific clients with respect to identifying periods when data was not taken. Equally important, now that there is an easy mechanism to obtain specificity, the adequacy of the data itself can be assessed regarding the frequency of sampling and the stability week-to-week of the information being entered. A second benefit is that staff now save approximately 15–20 hours per quarter in preparing their own reports for client review and have drastically reduced the error rate arising from illegible records and misplaced information. At yet a third level, the staff member responsible for overall program quality assurance is now able to update the much more massive agency database with a time-cost savings factor of almost 10 owing to the precise manner in which the staff database can produce information in the correct format to be fed to the larger quality-assurance database. This latter point is a good example of where it would have been tempting to produce a full merger of the two systems in order to gain "efficiency". However, the complexity of that task was extremely large, and by addressing components of the problem all staff benefited. While the level of efficiency could technically be higher, it is more than adequate and produced substantial and meaningful change for all staff members involved. Last, the most important aspect is that a previously infeasible supervisory function can now be conducted with relatively little time cost per week.

It is important to focus on the components of the above example as they illustrate the process of implementation. That is, staff at all levels were consulted, and the specifics of their work activities were identified. This information was then used to create possible solutions and to inspect the relative cost–benefit. The final solution was based on attempts not to obtain the most "elegant" programming solution but rather one that was specific, time-limited, and within the available resources.

From the perspective of a more "pure" database or computer information management perspective the above example could be characterized in a pejorative sense as a piecemeal solution. This certainly is true to an extent, but also reflects the strength of the approach. There is great wisdom in attempting to take elaborate problems and break them into more easily managed components. If the end result is that only half of the problems can be addressed with given resources, this is not necessarily an indication of failure but rather an appropriate utilization of resources to obtain an increment in productivity.

The positive impact of such approaches was recently highlighted in a symposium reviewing impact of attempts at utilizing computer technology over the past decade at the Children's Unit for Treatment and Evaluation (Matey, Sullivan and Romanczyk, 1990), the Children's Unit for Learning Disabilities (Harrison, Navalta and Romanczyk, 1990), the Princeton Child Development Institute in Princeton, New Jersey (McClannahan and Krantz, 1990) and the Douglass Developmental Disabilities Center at Rutgers University in New Brunswick, New Jersey (Handleman, 1990). Each of these various centers presented information concerning staff acceptance, the unique characteristics of their facilities and the particular combinations of hardware and software utilized to solve problems. The interesting consistency was not with respect to staff type, nor preferences for hardware or software used, but was rather reflected in the targeting of important problems that impacted on service delivery seeking direct and straight-forward solutions utilizing computer technology. Explicitly, attempts were *not* made to use one type of computer system to encompass all problem areas.

The impact of this approach was consistently positive, although the degree of impact varied substantially. In all facilities the diversity as well as the sheer number of computers has risen consistently over time and is not correlated simply with program expansion. Computer use has often come to be seen as a necessary component of service delivery rather than an optional component. Handleman (1990) provided an interesting example whereby computers were purchased for all staff members involved in preparation of Individual Education Plans. The impact of using the computerized system was considered so substantial as to justify this cost, even though many staff members typically used the computer primarily for this one function alone. There was consistency in the reports and descriptions with regard to the need to challenge the more pervasive view, held especially among administrators, that computers should be centrally located to be used for many tasks in order to be "efficient" and cost-effective, rather than being seen as tools that may serve specific functions for each staff member.

SUMMARY

Outcomes such as those presented, particularly in the two case studies, present difficulties in interpretation, as it is extremely difficult to conduct experimental designs in such large-scale, real-world settings. No doubt in the second case study, the site that retained the computer system perhaps had more affinity for an objective measurement-based approach than their colleagues at the other sites. Equally plausible (and perhaps the issue here is one of degree of contribution rather than exclusive contributions to the results), is that by providing support from management to continue the computer system, the specific and accurate collation of information over extended periods of time served to keep staff "on track" and permit self-evaluation to continue at a much more frequent and precise level than was possible at the sites that did not use the computer system. Research on this topic is sparse and inconclusive (Kowalsky and Cohen, 1985). In the first case study, use of computers clearly is part of the "fabric" of the organization, and thus one would predict continued use.

While many of these interpretations are of course speculative, the consistency of impact across these two case studies and the effects of the "reversal design" in the second case study, clearly point to the presence of potentially very powerful effects that have significant impact both with respect to the amount of services delivered to clients as well as the adequacy of the program's administrative activities with reference to external regulatory review.

Even given the relative paucity of research data concerning the impact of computer database technology on the process of service delivery in clinical settings, at this point it is reasonable to conclude that the impact can be substantial, both with respect to time savings as well as impact in the quality of service delivery itself. While little is currently published, there are numerous projects underway at present by various groups to further refine this technology, particularly with respect to making use of the computer even easier through alternative data input technologies. Also, as computer technology grows in technical capability and as database software becomes more and more sophisticated, it likewise becomes more and more feasible for individuals or small groups to attempt to implement this technology in the absence of large budgets for hardware and professional programmers. However, it cannot be overstated that the implementation of a useful database system involves attention to systems analysis of the clinical and work process, specific analysis of user needs and perceptions of such computer utilization, attention to adequacy of availability of computer hardware for individual usage, and the technical aspects of database capability allowing production of functional reports and analysis that can be utilized on a timely basis to impact clinical decision-making and service delivery. This is true whether the application is for an individual clinician in private practice or for a large agency or facility.

All too often computer systems serve only to monitor long-term outcome in an "accounting" format. While this is certainly an important task, the far more useful and exciting application is the parallel use of this technology to provide the individual clinician and service provider with the type of specific client information, on a routine and timely basis, that permits effective modification of service delivery. It is this precision that offers the most potential for computer technology to assist the clinician in the complex process of clinical service delivery.

REFERENCES

Coleman, D.A. (1989) Validation of a computerized treatment planning system for MR settings. In: *Computer Applications in MR/DD Service Settings*. Symposium presented at the annual meeting of the Association for Behavior Analysis, May 1989, Milwaukee, Wisconsin.

Curley, P. (1983) Confessions of a cyberphobe. *Best's Review Life and Health Insurance Edition*, **83**(12), 80–4.

Davidson, R. and Walley, P.B. (1985) Computer fear and addiction: analysis, prevention and possible modification. In: L.W. Frederiksen and A.W. Riley (eds), *Computers for People and Productivity*, Haworth Press, New York.

Handleman, J.S. (1990) Application of computer software to administrative task and educational program. In: *The Application of Computer Technology in Special Education: Promises Made vs. Promises Kept.* Symposium presented at the annual meeting of the Association for Behavior Analysis, May 1990, Nashville, Tennessee.

Harrison, K., Navalta, C. and Romanczyk, R.G. (1990) Monitoring functions vs. teaching functions: differential cost and impact. In: *The Application of Computer Technology in Special Education: Promises Made vs. Promises Kept.* Symposium presented at the annual meeting of the Association for Behavior Analysis, May 1990, Nashville, Tennessee.

Kowalsky, R. and Cohen, S.H. (1985) The effects of two types of automated feedback on the performance of a community mental health center staff. In: L.W. Frederiksen and A.W. Riley (eds), *Computers for People and Productivity*, Haworth Press, New York.

Matey, L., Sullivan, D. and Romanczyk, R.G. (1990) Impact of computer technology in information management and direct instruction. In: *The Application of Computer Technology in Special Education: Promises Made vs. Promises Kept.* Symposium presented at the annual meeting of the Association for Behavior Analysis, May 1990, Nashville, Tennessee.

McClannahan, L.E. and Krantz, P.J. (1990) Computers at the Princeton Child Development Institute: a case study in escape and avoidance. In: *The Application of Computer Technology in Special Education: Promises Made vs. Promises Kept.* Symposium presented at the annual meeting of the Association for Behavior Analysis, May 1990, Nashville, Tennessee.

Romanczyk, R.G. (1986) *Clinical Utilization of Microcomputer Technology*, Pergamon Press, New York.

Romanczyk, R.G. (1987) Data base management in clinical settings: concepts, recommendations, and cautions. In: P.A. Keller and S.R. Heyman (eds), *Innovations in Clinical Practice: A Source Book*, vol. 6, Professional Resource Exchange Incorporated, Sarasota, FL.

Romanczyk, R.G. and Lockshin, S. (1984) Short term intensive services: a deficit-oriented, focused model. In: W.P. Christian, G.T. Hannah and T.J. Glahn (eds), *Programming Effective Human Services*, Plenum Publishing, New York.

Seiter C. (1990) The multi-user data base challenge. *Macworld*, 7(5), 316–22, (Macworld Communications Inc., San Francisco).

Chapter 10

Expert Systems and the Clinical Psychologist

J. Graham Beaumont

WHAT IS AN "EXPERT SYSTEM"?

This is not an easy question to answer: not because there is anything essentially difficult or mysterious about expert systems, but because the term is now used so widely and so loosely. Almost any piece of software which involves some form of adaptive intelligence has become an "expert system" and it can be difficult to extract the real conception of expert systems from out of the marketing hype.

One attempt to re-establish the purity of expert systems has been based upon the invention of novel terms—intelligent knowledge-based systems (IKBS), rule-based systems, pattern-directed inference systems—but none has had sufficient appeal and convenience to replace the original term in general use.

An expert system should traditionally be capable of solving a problem normally solved by experts who, by definition, are better at solving such problems than non-experts. In doing this it should employ greater intelligence than a simple set of rules; should deal with complex relationships between data and states; and be able to deal with inaccurate or probabilistic data. It should also be able to explain the reasons which have led to the conclusion it has reached. Of course, most of these criteria involve qualitative judgements (which is one reason why the term is used so imprecisely), but they are sufficient in general to distinguish true expert systems from their imitations.

It is perhaps worth adding that expert systems designers have also had the goal of making human expertise more widely available, and the intention that they should have an effect in the real world. Besides the obvious capitalist motivations, there is for some a genuine intention to extend human skills, health and happiness.

Microcomputers and Clinical Psychology: Issues, Applications and Future Developments. Edited by A. Ager
©1991 John Wiley & Sons Ltd

The computer science view of expert systems has always been a little suspicious. A feature article in *Computing* (23 February 1989), a weekly trade newspaper, described the expert system as "computing's answer to music's Acid House" with the implication that it remains very much on the periphery of mainstream computing with a largely cult following. As a result, theoretical developments have not always been matched by advances in practical applications and the introduction of real expert systems products has been slow. Software vendors have borrowed the glamour which attaches to "artificial intelligence" concepts to legitimize and promote products of very limited vision and utility. The number of significant and useful expert systems in regular usage remains relatively low.

However difficult it may be accurately to define an expert system, it is easy to say some things which it is not, although popularly supposed to be. It is not *necessarily* written in a list processing declarative language (like LISP or PROLOG), although it may well be more efficiently generated in this way (especially among adherents to the cult). It does not *necessarily* involve any "clever" programming, although it may well do so. It does not model human "expert thinking" in any but the most limited and abstract sense.

In this chapter I hope to achieve some demystification of expert systems for those with limited experience of the field (while probably offending those with some advanced knowledge of the area). But I would also hope to show that, while many of the essential concepts are simple, the systems created out of them are of significant power, and are being under-utilized by clinical psychologists.

THE BASIC ELEMENTS OF AN EXPERT SYSTEM

Any expert system contains three basic elements: a "knowledge base" an "inference engine" and a "user interface".

The *knowledge base* contains knowledge, essentially in two forms: facts, and the relationships between facts. In simple terms the knowledge will include lists of facts, or observations—what we might more generally call data—which are known in expert systems terminology as "values". The knowledge base will also contain values assigned to what are more widely referred to as variables, but which are known in this context as "objects". The result of assigning a particular data value to a variable, such as supplying 107 as the value for patient's_IQ is to produce an "object:value" combination. The association of a number of values, such as a set of anxiety ratings taken regularly through the course of a morning, with a single object (perhaps morning_anxiety) is of course also possible and yields an "object:multivalue" combination.

Besides facts, the knowledge base may contain other kinds of information such as "legal values" which are used to delimit the area of the "domain", the region of information within which the system will operate, and "questions" which the system may use to elicit values from the user to be assigned to particular objects. Most importantly, the knowledge base will also contain "rules" which form a symbolic representation of knowledge relationships within the domain. These rules are logical statements and in their simplest form—"If A then B. . ."—assign a value to an object on the basis of another object:value combination. If **present** is assigned to **auditory_hallucinations** (values do not have to be numerical), then **true** may be assigned to **suspect_schizophrenia**. Of course rules become very much more complex, and normally assign a value to an object on the basis of the logical combination of the values of a number of other objects. More sophisticated ways of arranging the information in the knowledge base are possible, and are of particular relevance to psychologists interested in "knowledge representation".

It is often a danger that expert systems become too mechanistic, and fail to capture the subtlety of the human expert reasoning upon which the expert system is based. A way to avoid this is to introduce representations of uncertainty into the knowledge base. This can be by the explicit inclusion of certainty factors, which may be more or less precise; by the incorporation of prior probabilities and strengths of relations, as captured in Bayesian statistics; or by the introduction of "soft implication" and other logical techniques capable of handling uncertainty.

The *inference engine* is simply a logical system which can interpret rules with respect to the contents of the knowledge base in order to find (logically) valid conclusions. Irrespective of the content of the rules and facts contained in the knowledge base, it applies its own logical rules in order to arrive at whatever inferences can be logically drawn.

The simplest inference engines operate by "forward chaining": that is, they start from the first rules and facts in the list and work forward through the list until the truth or falsity of some "goal" has been established. The goal might be, for example, whether the patient has Dementia of the Alzheimer Type. Most human explicit logical thinking proceeds in the same way, by taking axioms and propositions and moving forward to test various deductions.

Forward chaining can, however, be very inefficient. It may be that in a particular case only one or two facts are needed to arrive at the goal. The relevant facts and rules may, however, only be encountered well down the list as the system moves forward. This problem may be solved by "backward chaining": by assuming the outcome (the validity of the goal) and then seeing what conditions must pertain for that to be true. In turn, further preconditions will be sought back through the system until the truth of the outcome which has been assumed has been established. In practice, the more sophisticated current systems use combinations of forward and backward chaining, sometimes together with other hueristics, in order to improve the efficiency of logical inference of the expert system.

The *user interface* allows the system to communicate with its designer (the "knowledge engineer") and with the end-user. It permits creation and modification of the knowledge base by the introduction and editing of rules and facts; it permits questions to be put to the end-user in order to establish the values to be associated with objects; and it permits the conclusions to be reported and explanations to be given.

The role of explanations is quite crucial in at least two respects. Unless the system is able to reveal the logical inferences made in reaching a particular goal, it is almost impossible to test and refine any realistic working expert system. At least as importantly, unless the system is able to reveal its reasoning to the client user, it is unlikely that advice offered will be accepted. The system must be capable of persuading the user of the validity of its conclusion if it is to be taken seriously. A natural spinoff from this is the role of expert systems in teaching expertise to novices and in refining the diagnostic success of existing experts.

The general elements of an expert system are often provided as a "shell". This is a system with an inference engine and a user interface and including the structures ready to receive particular rules and facts, but empty of specific rules and facts. Most expert systems, commercial and non-commercial, are now produced using one of these shells.

A key feature of any expert system is the form of knowledge representation it employs. Systems based on a collection of rules—"rule-based systems"— are the most common, particularly in the medical area, but there are other ways in which knowledge can be represented: by scripts, frames, blackboards, models, procedural specifications and other forms. These concepts will be familiar to cognitive psychologists, for this is one area where psychology has made a specific contribution to cognitive science. The aim is to provide "natural" structures for the representation of knowledge which permit efficient and ecologically valid ways of storing the information. The psychological aspects of knowledge representation have recently been reviewed by Richardson (1989).

In the design of expert systems, a number of principles have been generally accepted to be of value (Davis, 1984). These are that the domain-specific knowledge remains separate from the rules which manipulate that knowledge; that domain-specific knowledge is represented uniformly; that the inference engine be kept simple; and that multiple sources of information be incorporated to allow the resulting redundancy to be exploited. The adoption of these principles has encouraged the exploitation of expert systems technology.

A final point concerns triviality. Fortunately for students and beginners in the field, it is very easy to generate trivial expert systems, particularly with one of the modern expert system shells. This is unfortunate for the potential consumer of expert system technology. Any system which can perform its functions adequately by other means (including average human mental capacity) cannot be a true expert system. An expert system should always be of a scale and complexity at which it makes a genuine contribution to enhancing human capabilities, as will be illustrated in the examples which follow.

SOME CURRENT EXPERT SYSTEMS

Although expert systems have been notably successful in other fields, medical diagnosis has proved one of the most fruitful areas for their application. Indeed, the standard example, MYCIN, is a system developed at Stanford University from about 1972 to give advice and therapy in infectious disease. It is an interactive rule-based system, and is designed to aid decision making in the typical situation where antibiotics must be prescribed before the organism causing the infection can be positively identified.

MYCIN knows about approximately 100 micro-organisms that might be the cause of infection, and contains about 500 rules of an *if . . . then . . .* form. It also employs a certainty factor attached to each rule, to indicate just how much confidence can be placed in the inference made from applying the rule.

A consultation with MYCIN involves interaction between the system and a medical expert who answers questions posed by MYCIN about the patient's symptoms, and about the results of simple tests which will be available. MYCIN asks very specific questions about the hypothesis currently being considered—because it principally uses backward chaining—and reports its results in a probabilistic fashion. Examples of MYCIN interactions can be found in many textbooks, but a fuller account of MYCIN is available in Shortliffe (1976).

A number of associated programs have grown out of the work on MYCIN. TEIRESIAS is a system which works alongside MYCIN to produce fuller explanations of MYCIN's reasoning, and to allow modification of MYCIN's rulebase. GUIDON uses the same knowledge base as MYCIN, but as a teaching tool for medical students. Most importantly, EMYCIN was created by taking the structure of MYCIN and removing the specific knowledge (Empty-MYCIN), so implementing the concept of expert system shells.

A well-known medical system created using EMYCIN is PUFF, a system for diagnosing pulmonary function disorder. Details of age, sex, smoking history and other clinical information is input alongside measurements taken directly from instruments measuring breathing flow rates and volumes. About 55 rules were obtained from a study of 100 cases, and cross-validation on a further set of 150 cases indicated agreement between PUFF and diagnosticians of over 90%.

The INTERNIST/CADUCEUS project illustrates a rather different approach to expert systems. The system attempts to embody the expertise of one particular specialist in internal medicine. The initial program (INTERNIST-I) adopted a two-step approach: first to take the history and results of initial examination and tests and formulate a set of possible competing diagnoses; then to apply heuristic rules to choose among the competitors within the set. In this way it seeks to mimic more closely the way that a human expert reasons. The system maintains a list of about 500 diseases and a list of about 3500 manifestations, arranged as a taxonomic hierarchy, and contains knowledge relating the manifestations to the diseases.

INTERNIST-I suffered the disadvantage of being unable to move rapidly to a provisional area of diagnosis (as do human experts). It also had the disadvantage of understanding only associations between manifestations and symptoms, but not causes. The second version, INTERNIST-II, more commonly known as CADUCEUS, attempts to overcome these deficiencies by obtaining the best of both the taxonomic and causal worlds.

A final medical example, CASNET, is an example of a fully causal approach. It is based on a causal association network rather than upon human deductive processes. This is possible in its area of application—the diagnosis and treatment of glaucoma—only because the development of glaucoma is relatively well understood and clinical phenomena can be explained in causal terms.

Although medical systems have been prominent, important contributions have been made in other fields. The expert system often credited with the most successful performance is XCON, which configures VAX mainframe computer systems for the Digital Equipment Corporation; systems which are often tailor-made for customers and may involve hundreds of components. XCON has configured an enormous number of systems with reported customer satisfaction in excess of 95%.

DEVELOPING EXPERT SYSTEMS

There is now a considerable literature on expert systems and their development. There are also, helpfully, a growing number of sound and easy-to-use expert system shells available for personal computers. The place of expert systems in an artificial intelligence context is well-explained at an introductory level by Garnham (1988) and Yazdani (1986), among others. A good introduction, specifically about expert systems, is provided by Forsyth (1989) (although there are many others), and a more technical text is Giarratano and Riley (1989).

If you wish to gain a more practical understanding of expert systems, then a good way is through a text like Sawyer and Foster (1986) which works through a set of Pascal procedures gradually building up a realistic and usable system. If you only program in BASIC, then something similar can be achieved by working through Naylor (1987).

Another approach is to purchase an expert system shell for your personal computer and work with that. Again, there are many to choose from, but Master Expert (Thompson and Thompson, 1986) is inexpensive and a useful training tool. If you want the potential of developing a realistic and professional expert system (although, note the comments about triviality, above) then LEONARDO (Creative Logic Ltd) is currently very popular. My favourite, however, is CRYSTAL (Intelligent Environments). It is not cheap, and it offends the expert system purists, but it is extremely easy to learn, well-engineered, versatile and potentially powerful. It is widely used in teaching computer science students (and even some psychologists) and can be thoroughly recommended.

EXPERT SYSTEMS AND PSYCHOLOGICAL MODELS

Models as knowledge representation

As an approach to the development of expert systems in psychology, functional models could provide an appropriate form of knowledge representation. Functional models, increasingly explicit in the cognitive domain, might allow an assessment system to possess an internal representation of the function which is under examination. Some of these models are now presented in a sufficiently well-articulated form to make them useful in the description of functional status. Such descriptions can, in turn, be used in the identification of dysfunctional elements in performance and in the design and monitoring of instructional and remedial schemes.

Perhaps the best known of these models relate to reading ability. Here the interaction between the developmental study of normal reading ability and neuropsychological investigation of the dysfunctions to be observed in brain injured patients has stimulated the production of general models of reading competency. Over the past few years the analyses of developmental dyslexia and of adult acquired dyslexia have converged into a common view of the processes which may be defective in reading failure.

Ellis (1982) has, for example, shown how much of the previous work on spelling and writing can be integrated into a single model with reading and speaking. The point about this and a number of similar models is that each component process is capable of identification by manipulations in an explicit experimental paradigm. The evidence is derived from studies on normal subjects by which the processing components can be inferred, and by the study of clinical patients in whom the failure of one component of the system can be identified. A good example of the intensive application of this approach can be found in Howard and Franklin (1988).

An even more relevant model is provided by the work of Seymour (1986, 1987; Seymour and MacGregor, 1984). An alternative model of the reading process is presented which is derived from rather similar evidence to that of Ellis, but is more parsimonious in its explanation although more limited in its scope. One of the strengths of this model is that it incorporates an account of how normal reading development may lead to the establishment of the four processors and two lexicons which it incorporates.

The particular interest of Seymour's approach is that specific computer-based procedures are employed to test the component elements in the model. These are a range of 13 experimental procedures which involve identity matching and array matching of strings of letters; lexical decision; semantic decision; and vocalization of words and non-words with various manipulations of word frequency, lexicality, homophony, abstractness and syntactic function. The format of visual presentation is also varied ("distorted") in the context of lexical and semantic decision and vocalization to examine aspects of the visual analysis function of the visual processor. Seymour has been able to demonstrate, by the presentation of case material, that this system possesses an encouraging level of validity and utility.

It is frustrating that the most well-developed models in cognitive psychology relate to language processes. The cause of this frustration is probably already evident. To permit the incorporation of sophisticated and intelligent automated procedures into testing systems, the on-line real-time support of computer assistance is probably vital. However, it is as yet impossible to have a computer reliably listening to a test subject reading aloud, or reliably reading handwritten script. Considerable advances are being made in automatic speech recognition, and in visual recognition systems for orthographic text, but they have not yet reached the point where they could be trusted to replace a human examiner. A machine which would generate accurate phonetic translation of speech input is also still a long way off.

It therefore seems sensible to cast about for other functions which have been modelled, and which could more profitably be incorporated into automated assessment systems. One contender is arithmetic function. Perhaps the most famous of the models of arithmetic function is incorporated in the BUGGY program.

BUGGY was developed by Brown, Burton and Larkin (see Brown and Burton, 1978) and is capable of identifying a student's errors (the "bugs") in basic arithmetic skills and interpreting them in terms of the underlying misconceptions. The elements at the heart of BUGGY are procedural networks which build, out of the component procedures of (human) arithmetic operations, diagnostic models. This can be seen as a process of decomposing a skill into a range of sub-skills. Some of these sub-skills, each of which has reference to a meaningful element in performance, will be correct and some will be incorrect or deviant. Each is, however, represented as an element in the network and is capable of identification by the examples considered by the system. At present, BUGGY knows about well over 300 bugs, each of which has an associated functional description. In the context of eliciting students' performance, the system will generate the examples; in interacting with teachers, it will request that problems are entered which will enable BUGGY to detect the bug which the teacher hypothesizes to be present. An important aspect of the BUGGY system is that it has psychological validity, that is that it understands both functional and dysfunctional arithmetic processes as performed by humans, and can model them (see also Bundy, 1983).

A more recent demonstration of this approach is embodied in the development by Neil Hagues at the National Foundation for Educational Research of a computer-based diagnostic test of errors in addition and subtraction. The test is based on empirical research which identified 32 error types in both addition and subtraction, some being combinations of more primitive errors. The computer-based test generates problems designed to home in on a child's particular difficulty and so identify persistent sources of error. The system can identify the error made in about two-thirds of cases which, given the chaotic multiple errors made by some children, and the possibility for inconsistency in the operation of number bonds, is quite a creditable result. More significantly the computer-based test performs better than experienced teachers in identifying the characteristic error which a child is committing. The system as devised by NFER is written in BASIC in a standard procedural format, but is ideally suited to implementation within an expert system environment. Such an implementation could extend the potential power and utility of the test.

There are other models of arithmetic cognitive processes, and models of analogical reasoning, explored in a computerized format by May, Cooper and Kline (1985). Other relevant models include: map-reading performance, number-series problem solution, object recognition and face recognition.

Expert systems and psychometrics

The differences between traditional psychometrics and "expert systems" are not as fundamental as might be supposed. Although expert systems as commonly expressed within a rule-based programming environment appear very different from a psychometric test instrument, they have several fundamental constructs in common. The parallels become more clear if the elements of each procedure are considered. The "objects" of the expert system are "test items" of the conventional test; the "values" are the "responses"; the "questions" and "user interface" are equivalent to the "administration procedures"; the "rules" are represented in the "scoring and norms"; the "inference engine" is matched by the "psychometric model" being employed. The "goal" which the expert system is set is, of course, the "test result" of the conventional test instrument.

It is possible to establish the validity of these parallels. The author has a demonstration system, created under a popular expert system shell, that will administer the Mill Hill Vocabulary Test in a form which is indistinguishable from a number of computer-based implementations of that test which have been realized by procedural programming systems which simply simulate the conventional administration of the test. The expert systems approach may well not be the most efficient way to achieve this result, and may be to some degree artificial, but it nonetheless provides evidence for the parallels which are being proposed between these kinds of systems.

Given these parallels, it is a short step to suggest that a cognitive componential model might be explicitly incorporated within a knowledge-based system to permit the intelligent assessment of the cognitive function modelled. This is, after all, no more than a formalization of what an expert human examiner does in performing an assessment. Elements of the assessment procedure are composed into the battery of tests to be applied, according to some model (often implicit) which the examiner maintains of the functions to be assessed. The individual tests are then administered, often with some degree of selection and modification of the battery depending on the earlier test results. Statistical estimates derived from the test are obtained, and interpreted in line with hypotheses generated from the functional model which the test examiner holds. A psychological description (the "report") is generated which is relevant to the assessment question being investigated.

The potential advantages of the kind of scheme envisaged above are that the internal cognitive model is explicit (compare with most existing test and interpretive systems, as described in Chapter 3), and can be more rigorously applied (and improved); the investigation of data relevant to the inferences being tested is systematic and should therefore be more efficient; and intelligence, in the form of the inferencing procedures, is automatically and consistently applied to the problem. In addition, the behavioural description which is generated from the system is inevitably formulated in terms of the cognitive model being maintained: it is a psychological and not a statistical description. It must, therefore, be relevant to the application for which the test is being employed, and be more useful in response to questions about diagnosis, management, treatment, selection or adjustment.

APPLICATIONS IN CLINICAL PSYCHOLOGY

The first thing to say is that there are, to my knowledge, almost no applications of expert systems within clinical psychology. Such applications have been *discussed*, and there are some examples in related areas, but there are no true expert systems in operation in clinical psychology.

One is reminded of a more general comment by Edward Feigenbaum, a founding parent of expert systems, that "searching for expert systems in real use in the UK is like searching for clams at low tide. You've been told there are plenty hiding in the sand, most small but some of meal size. But it takes much digging to find just a few" (Feigenbaum, 1988).

Expert systems in psychiatry

There are, of course, expert systems in psychiatry, following the general applications of expert systems to medical diagnosis. Early work in this field was reviewed by Miller (1984) who usefully tabulated the studies which he reviewed although the most recent of his "recent studies" was published in 1974. Nevertheless, his review showed that there have been a variety of approaches to psychiatric diagnosis through computer-based systems, which can broadly be divided into "logical decision" rule-based models, and strictly statistical approaches (discriminant functions; cluster analysis; Bayesian approaches).

More recent discussions can be found in Servan-Schreiber (1986) and Ellis (1987); but besides illustrating that research in this field continues to be active, they add little to Miller's earlier conclusions, which include:

- that computer-generated reports can improve the thoroughness and the accuracy of the clinical diagnosis, but cannot replace many complex skills of the clinician;
- that the careful gathering and processing of clinical signs and symptoms will continue to be important and computers can improve this process;
- that computers can improve, and reduce the cost of, patient care.

Rule-based procedures

Whilst falling short of a true expert system, an application of rule-based procedures is described in a survey of computer applications within clinical psychology provided by Norris et al. (1985). As part of their review they include the problem of "diagnosis and prediction" and, as might be expected, discuss the use of knowledge-based systems in medical diagnosis with the usual examples. They also discuss the use of statistical prediction, with an interesting example of the use of multiple regression for the prediction of outcome in stroke patients.

More relevantly, they present examples of "probability diagnosis", including a program by Finkelstein (1976) called BRAIN. This program does not actually use probabilistic reasoning, but employs a rule-based approach in order to derive diagnoses from data obtained with the Halstead–Reitan Neuropsychological Test Battery. This work has its origins in an earlier publication by Russell, Neuringer and Goldstein (1970) which described a taxonomic "key" approach to the problem, which was also realized in a program implemented on a mainframe computer. Because of the relatively explicit nature of Reitan's hypotheses relating scores on the Halstead–Reitan Battery to the localization of disorders of the cerebral cortex, it was possible to encapsulate these in a set of rules to be implemented within procedural algorithms.

Finkelstein developed this work (also for implementation on a mainframe computer) with relative success: brain-damaged patients were classified with 96% accuracy, and normal controls with 92% accuracy. More specific diagnoses were less successful, ranging from 50% (extrinsic tumour) to 83% (trauma), but are better than might be expected in work of this kind. It is not uncommon for the agreement between clinicians to be no better than the agreement between computer and clinician in investigations of this type.

BRAIN was later translated into a hand-scoring procedure by Hom (1979) in order to overcome the contemporary difficulties of access to mainframe computers, but was then again translated with some modifications into a microcomputer-based version (NEUROPSYCH) by Norris and colleagues and is available as companion software to their book (Norris et al., 1985). The program is capable of indicating the likely presence of brain damage, of assigning an impairment severity rating, of searching for evidence of lateralization, and of determining certain more specific neurological diagnoses. They report no data on the validity of NEUROPSYCH, but it is an interesting illustration of the rule-based approach, albeit short of being a true expert system.

True expert systems

The potential for the application of expert systems has been much discussed.

Adams and Heaton (1985) pursue the work on neuropsychological classification by identifying the taxonomic key model, and adding the use of brain-referenced geometrical conceptions, and the use of algorithms which reflect the methods employed by experienced clinicians. They find none satisfactory, and discuss ways in which neuropsychological diagnosis might be improved by the use of true expert systems.

The use of expert systems as general decision aiding tools has been discussed by Hartman (1986), and by Schoech et al. (1985) and Schuerman (1987), although these last two papers are perhaps more strictly in the area of social work and social welfare. Similar examples of the discussion as applied to developmental issues, with an emphasis on learning disability, are to be found in Hasselbring (1985/6), Hofmeister and Ferrara (1986) and Hofmeister and Lubke (1986).

There are perhaps only three examples which come close to being true expert systems as applied in clinical psychology, although none might match the more rigorous definition of a full expert system as outlined in the opening sections of this chapter.

The first is a "Mandate Consultant" developed by Parry and Hofmeister (1986) for the development of "individual educational programs" for training in learning disability. The expert system they devised is capable of developing and reviewing individual educational programmes, and they present data from a double-blind test that shows the expert system superior to human experts in matching the programmes to the needs of the child.

A second example, from Hedlund, Vieweg and Cho (1987), is perhaps more properly a psychiatric expert system, but it does deal with interventions in behavioural and emotional emergencies. The conception is for its use as a consultant system for "non-experts" in remote areas for the identification and management of psychiatric crises.

The final example is provided by Binik et al. (1988) and is an expert system for the assessment and treatment of sexual dysfunction. It is designed as an interactive computer-supported therapy system and derives its techniques from both artificial intelligence and intelligent tutoring systems. In an area of some personal sensitivity, there may be clear advantages to the use of a relatively impersonal computing device and "self-help" software, and Binik and colleagues discuss these advantages, together with the constraints and limitations of the approach. The initial reactions of clients seem, on balance, to be positive and it will be interesting to see a report of a full trial of a system of this kind.

None of these examples, however, represents a truly non-trivial application of expert systems technology within clinical psychology. None uses the potential power of model-based approaches described in the preceding section. None really illustrates the contribution which expert systems might make in this area of applied psychology if a significant degree of expertise could be captured within a computer-based system.

POTENTIAL APPLICATIONS

The cynic might comment that the reason why there are no significant applications of expert systems within clinical psychology is that there is no significant expertise to capture. That would be almost certainly unfair. It might be that the expert knowledge within clinical psychology is difficult to express in a sufficiently precise and elaborate form to make it amenable to formulation within an expert systems context. That has yet to be seen, but we can at least try to identify potentially fruitful areas of application.

There seem to me at least five areas in which realistic expert systems might be developed within clinical psychology, together with another two areas of general application. I am sure that there must be more which have not occurred to me.

The first area is the obvious one explored in the foregoing section: the use of expert systems in cognitive assessment. Given that psychologists are developing relatively precise formal models of cognitive abilities, it should be possible in the way described above to build these models into an expert system which will, in turn, generate a psychological description of the patient's cognitive status. Just as the system might identify and assess the performance of various subcomponents of functional competence with respect to a given ability, it could also combine the assessment of abilities in a variety of areas, building up a global description of the client's intellectual functions. The advantage of electing to develop an expert system in this area would be the opportunity to build it in a modular fashion, progressively adding functions as they were modelled, and extending the system to provide an increasingly complete coverage of the range of intellectual functions.

A second related area, and one which has already received some attention, is the area of neuropsychological diagnosis. Expert systems in general medical and psychiatric diagnosis provide an obvious model for expert systems in this area. In addition, the methodological approach in neuropsychology through much of this century has naturally generated material for inclusion in a relevant knowledge base. "*If* the patient is right handed, *and if* the patient shows abnormally poor delayed recall of the Rey–Osterreith figure, *then* the patient may have a disorder involving the anterior right temporal lobe." Anne-Lise Christensen (1974) provides, in her interesting systematic analysis of Luria's neuropsychological investigation, a starting point for the creation of such a knowledge base. If the neuropsychological literature were comprehensively searched for all assertions from which rules could be derived—no mean feat—then a substantial, and potentially most valuable, expert system could be the result.

The assessment of vocational adjustment, and vocational guidance, is a third area which is clearly related to the kinds of assessment just described.

Here there is also an opportunity to use an expert system, based on a theoretical model of occupational selection and adjustment, to control the assessment of an individual client and then to make recommendations, based on standard information available in the vocational guidance literature, about the vocational opportunities and likely success of psychiatric and neurological patients returning into employment.

My fourth and fifth areas ripe for the development of an expert system are very similar. They are the effects of drugs on behaviour, and the effects of nutrition on behaviour. In both of these areas there is a great deal of detailed information which it is very difficult to organize, or to relate to particular clinical concerns. This is partly because of the lack of unifying theory in the areas (at least in terms of how the data relate to general behavioural states), and partly because of the relative lack of expertise amongst clinical psychologists in pharmacology, biochemistry and physiology. An expert system which would advise the clinical psychologist about the expected behavioural effects of a particular combination of psychotropic drugs and other medicines, both on cognitive performance and on other aspects of behaviour, would be especially useful. The same could profitably be achieved for the growing body of information on nutrition, in terms of specific food substances and of particular dietary habits, and their behavioural consequences.

I add two possible general areas of application. These are in the fields of the simulation of particular psychiatric states and in training. The simulation of psychiatric states belongs to more general areas of artificial intelligence, and there are other techniques available, more appropriate than knowledge-based systems, to address this kind of problem. However, creating a model of a particular disorder—eating disorders provide a ready example—will enable the clinician better to understand the dynamics of the disorder, to make predictions about future outcomes, and to test the effects of particular interventions (on the model, rather than on the patient).

Training, whether re-training after brain injury or after psychiatric disability, or initial training in cases of learning disability, can be usefully supported by aids from artificial intelligence (see discussions in this volume by Skilbeck and Baldrey, respectively). Intelligent tutoring systems may themselves rely on a model of normal performance, and the client's status with respect to that model. Expert systems technology is one way in which such a model may be expressed, and used both to regulate the tutoring process, and to monitor the progress and achievements of the client.

There are undoubtedly other areas of clinical psychology about which I am either too ignorant, or lack sufficient imagination, which could provide a domain for the development of expert systems. But, it should be remembered that there must be an extensive body of well-formulated knowledge available in a sufficiently explicit form before a non-trivial expert system can be constructed. There must be human experts before there can be artificial experts (even if the artificial expert gains power by combining the expertise of a number of human experts), and the resulting expert system must be useful: it must address a problem which requires a solution!

AUTOMATIC PROGRAMMING

This section is not about automatic programming in its technical sense—that is, the automatic generation of program code from formal descriptions of a given set of functions—but about the use of certain expert system shells or environments for a rather broader set of uses than they were originally designed. The fact is that commercial systems available for generating expert systems can be used for the easy and rapid generation of programs for more general application.

I had a friend who used to amuse himself by writing statistics packages in LISP, one of the principal AI list-processing languages. This sophisticated form of entertainment is roughly equivalent to modelling the Houses of Parliament in jelly; it can be done, but with some difficulty. In the light of this, it may be surprising that AI systems can be useful for certain procedural programming problems.

The reason why some expert system environments can be used in this way is that they include such extensive and friendly aids for handling the interaction between the system and the user, and because they routinely and automatically generate, maintain and reference the variables which they use. Programmers writing big expert systems need a lot of facilities which make life tolerable for them, and this has a spinoff in providing opportunities for the inexpert programmer.

What I am suggesting, it must be admitted, is almost certainly heretical for the expert systems purist. It is a deliberate misuse of expert system shells. But, I have found it enormously useful, as have many of my students, and I think that it is a harmless aberration, as long as it is recognized that these systems were not originally intended to be used in such a way.

The trick is to see the task to be performed—let us suppose the administration of a simple rating scale—as a series of logical conditions. The goal of the system is administration complete and that will only be true when a number of prior conditions are also true: instructions given; items administered; and scoring complete. Each of these in turn can be broken down into a series of logical elements. For example, items administered can be reduced to a series of trials in which question asked, response obtained, and response recorded are the elements.

Since I mentioned CRYSTAL earlier as a particularly easy and friendly, yet powerful, "intelligent environment" within which to work, let us use CRYSTAL as an example. The hierarchical "tree" of these rules—for each of these logical elements is in fact a rule to be determined as true or false—is entered interactively into the system. It only remains to define more precisely the actions which constitute the processes which will be carried out in determining the logical truth of each rule at the extremities of the "tree". For example, question asked for a particular trial will involve the display of the text which is the question for that item on the scale. This is where CRYSTAL (or whatever system is used) comes into its own. In order to display a question, CRYSTAL will automatically generate a screen display; all the programmer has to do is enter the text at the location on the screen where it is to appear, and give information about colour, size, borders and so on, if these are to be non-standard. Alternatively, the question can be held in a text file, or in a standard database, and automatically transferred to the screen by association with a variable name.

Similarly, when a response is required, it is only necessary to choose between the possibilities of a yes/no question, a menu item, or the entry of text (or a date, or a number)—and then to indicate where and in what form the entry will appear, and to give the response an internal variable name. The system takes care of the rest.

Like erecting a deck-chair, this would be much easier to demonstrate than it is to describe! Suffice it to say that with minimal instruction, and the provision of some relevant examples, even the non-computerate can generate simple and useful programs. As CRYSTAL provides all the routine facilities for arithmetic and trigonometrical manipulation, and for string handling of text, as well as timing functions, it can be used not only for simple rating scales and questionnaires, but also for some laboratory tasks as well. It naturally has its limitations, but I know of no faster way to get novices usefully programming, or to generate "quick and dirty" programs myself.

Of course, such useful supporting facilities should be more widely available in association with procedural programming languages: BASIC, Pascal, C and the like. Increasingly, of course, they are through the provision of programming utilities and tools. The modular structural programming approach inherent in Pascal and its successors has made this possible. However, it still remains necessary, in most cases, to go through quite an extensive period of formal learning about the language and its associated operating system before these utilities and tools become available. If psychology, or even behavioural and social sciences more generally, provided a bigger market, then "automatic programming" systems based on procedural languages (which would be more powerful and efficient) might be commercially produced. Even the (substantial) market for "authoring" languages in computer-aided instruction has failed to provide a really widely used and successful authoring language for the non-computerate. [Although, see recent developments of experiment generators such as MacLab (Drexel University) and MEL (Psychology Software Tools Inc.).]

Certain expert system shells, for example the CRYSTAL intelligent environment, are therefore capable of providing an opportunity for the creation of programs to serve simple tasks useful to clinical psychologists who lack formal computing experience. Their application resembles the use of "presentation systems" (for example, DOMINO—by Compsoft but available from IBM) which can also be recommended for the simple creation of questionnaires and rating scales. Because these systems include such good support for the programmer, it is possible, once the few fundamental concepts of program structure and composition have been grasped, to move rapidly to the stage of effective program generation.

We are only at the very initial stages of the exploitation of artificial intelligence and its component technologies, including expert systems. There are undoubtedly opportunities for its application in clinical psychology, as in almost every other aspect of life, and it will be fascinating to see in what ways it revolutionizes the practice and achievements of clinical psychology into the next millenium.

REFERENCES

Adams, K.M. and Heaton, R.K. (1985) Automated interpretation of neuropsychological test data. *Journal of Consulting and Clinical Psychology*, **53**, 790–802.

Binik, Y.M., Servan-Schreiber, D., Freiwald, S. and Hall, K.S. (1988) Intelligent computer-based assessment and psychotherapy: an expert system for sexual dysfunction. *Journal of Nervous and Mental Disease*, **176**, 387–400.

Brown, J.S. and Burton, R.R. (1978) Diagnostic models for procedural bugs in basic mathematical skills. *Cognitive Science*, **2**, 155–92.

Bundy, A. (1983) *The Computer Modelling of Mathematical Reasoning*, Academic Press, London.

Christensen, A-L. (1974) *Luria's Neuropsychological Investigation*, Munksgaard, Copenhagen.

Davis, R. (1984) Amplifying expertise with expert systems. In: P.H. Winston and K.A. Prendergast (eds), *The AI Business: The Commercial Uses of Artificial Intelligence*, MIT Press, Cambridge, MA.

Ellis, A.W. (1982) Spelling and writing (and reading and speaking). In: A.W. Ellis (ed), *Normality and Pathology in Cognitive Functions*, pp. 113–46, Academic Press, London.

Ellis, D. (1987) *Medical Computing and Applications*, Ellis Horwood, New York.

Feigenbaum, E. (1988) *The Rise of the Expert Company*, Macmillan, London.

Finkelstein, J.N. (1976) *A Computer Program for Interpretation of the Halstead–Reitan Neuropsychological Test Battery*. Unpublished PhD thesis, Columbia University.

Forsyth, R.S. (1989) *Expert Systems: Principles and Case Studies*, 2nd edn, Chapman and Hall, London.

Garnham, A. (1988) *Artificial Intelligence: An Introduction,* Routledge and Kegan Paul, London.

Giarratano, J.C. and Riley, G. (1989) *Expert Systems: Principles and Programming,* Chapman and Hall, London.

Hartman, D.E. (1986) Artificial intelligence or a psychologist? Conceptual issues in clinical microcomputer use. *Professional Psychology: Research and Practice,* **17**, 528–34.

Hasselbring, T.S. (1985/6) Towards the development of expert automated systems. *Special Services in the Schools,* **2**, 43–56.

Hedlund, J.L., Vieweg, B.W. and Cho, D.W. (1987) Computer consultation for emotional crisis: an expert system for "non-experts". *Computers in Human Behaviour,* **3**, 109–27.

Hofmeister, A.M. and Ferrara, J.M. (1986) Expert systems and special education. *Exceptional Children,* **53**, 235–9.

Hofmeister, A.M. and Lubke, M.M. (1986) Expert systems: implications for the diagnosis and treatment of learning disabilities. *Learning Disability Quarterly,* **9**, 133–7.

Hom, J. (1979) A hand sorting procedure for the evaluation of individual patients using Halstead–Reitan neuropsychological test data. Unpublished manuscript, Tucson University, Arizona.

Howard, D. and Franklin, S. (1988) *Missing the Meaning?,* MIT Press, Cambridge, MA.

May, J., Cooper, C. and Kline, P. (1985) A brief computerised form of a schematic analogy task. Unpublished manuscript, Department of Psychology, University of Exeter.

Miller, M.J. (1984) Computerized models of psychiatric diagnosis. In: M.D. Schwartz (ed), *Using Computers in Clinical Practice,* pp. 225–40, Haworth Press, New York.

Naylor, C. (1987) *Build Your Own Expert System,* 2nd edn, Sigma Press, London.

Norris, D.E., Skilbeck, C.E., Hayward, A.E. and Torpy, D.M. (1985) *Microcomputers in Clinical Practice,* John Wiley, Chichester.

Parry, J.D. and Hofmeister, A.M. (1986) Development and validation of an expert system for special educators. *Learning Disability Quarterly,* **9**, 124–32.

Richardson, J.T.E. (1989) Knowledge representation. In: A.M. Colman and J.G. Beaumont (eds), *Psychology Survey,* **7**, pp. 98–126, The British Psychological Society and Routledge, Leicester.

Russell, E.W., Neuringer, C. and Goldstein, G. (1970) *Assessment of Brain Damage: A Neuropsychological Key Approach,* John Wiley, New York.

Sawyer, B. and Foster, D.L. (1986) *Programming Expert Systems in Pascal,* John Wiley, Chichester.

Schoech, D., Jennings, H., Schkade, L.L. and Hooper-Russell, C. (1985) Expert systems: artificial intelligence for professional decisions. *Computers in Human Services,* **1**, 81–115.

Schuerman, J.R. (1987) Expert consulting systems in social welfare. *Social Work Research and Abstracts,* **23**, 14–18.

Servan-Schreiber, D. (1986) Artificial intelligence and psychiatry. *Journal of Nervous and Mental Disease,* **174**, 191–202.

Seymour, P.H.K. (1986) *Cognitive Analysis of Dyslexia,* Routledge and Kegan Paul, London.

Seymour, P.H.K. (1987) Individual cognitive analysis of competent and impaired reading. *British Journal of Psychology,* **78**, 483–506.

Seymour, P.H.K. and MacGregor, C.J. (1984) Developmental dyslexia: a cognitive experimental analysis of phonological, morphemic, and visual impairments. *Cognitive Neuropsychology,* **1**, 43–82.

Shortliffe, E.H. (1976) *MYCIN: Computer-based Medical Consultations,* American Elsevier, New York.

Thompson, B. and Thompson, W. (1986) *Master Expert,* McGraw-Hill, London.

Yazdani, M. (1986) *Artificial Intelligence: Principles and Applications,* Chapman and Hall, London.

Chapter 11

Psychological Aspects of the New Technological Age

NEIL FRUDE

In this chapter I consider a number of issues relating to the broad question of how computer technology has affected psychological well-being, and what effects may be foreseen for the future. Some discussions of the effects of technology on mental health take a broad historical perspective and consider how industrialization has changed human consciousness and may, as a consequence, have had effects on psychological adjustment. Other analyses amount to dire warnings of what might happen to "the human spirit" in a highly technological or post-industrial society. Such general discussion concerning the impact of technological change and industrialization has been provided by Ahrendt (1972), Mumford (1963), Blauner (1964) and many others.

It is intended that this chapter should be more restricted, and address the particular issue of the impact of microcomputer technology on individuals' mental health. Such specificity is not difficult to maintain when presenting "the story so far", but consideration of future developments inevitably leads to broader issues. So far, microtechnology has facilitated the production of various tools, including wordprocessors, computational systems, databases, and aids to manufacture. These programs and devices are used in the work setting and by hobbyists but, as yet, the penetration of computer systems into homes (other than as games or hobby machines) and schools has generally been very limited. The impact of microcomputer systems on the wider population has been much less than that of other technological systems, particularly television and the telephone. However, there are good reasons to believe that this will change, and that microtechnology will lead to the production not only of new tools but also of new media capable of transmitting an extensive range of powerful messages to a very wide audience. Such an evolution of the microcomputer from tool to medium would increase the psychological impact of microtechnology enormously.

Microcomputers and Clinical Psychology: Issues, Applications and Future Developments. Edited by A. Ager
©1991 John Wiley & Sons Ltd

The distinction between the computer as an apparatus and the computer as a medium is fundamental to an understanding of how future systems will affect people, and to appreciate this it is useful to draw an analogy with television. The impact of television on human well-being cannot be understood by considering television as a technological apparatus. The messages it conveys reflect artistry, interests, policy, and taste. It is the content of the television medium, rather than the technological fact of television, that is important. The issue of whether television increases aggression, for example, has little or nothing to do with transistors, circuitry or cathode ray tubes, and everything to do with images and programme presentation. The question is one for media analysts and social scientists to evaluate. Television engineers and technologists have little to contribute to the discussion.

Similarly, it will be the application and content of the new medium, rather than the microtechnological apparatus itself, that will govern the impact of future developments in information technology. Technologists do not control product development and do not influence the content of messages. As current technical barriers are breached a variety of new products will become technically feasible. Whether such products are realized, and how they are used, will depend on the ingenuity of designers and manufacturers and on consumer appeal. Those who developed the transistor did not have control over whether their innovation was used in telecommunication satellites, advanced weaponry, or the Walkman. Furthermore, those who design satellites and portable cassette-players have no control over the messages transmitted through the apparatus. Such media are capable of replaying an infinite number of messages. A pornographic passage or a section from the Bible contains the same amount of information. Thus there are two very different meanings of the term ''information content''. One relates to *bits*, and the other doesn't. In one way the psychological and social effects of a message are not related to its information content. The same number of bits may be transmitted in two telephone messages, one of which informs a person of the death of a close relative and the other of which informs a person that they have won the major prize in a national lottery.

Of course, we have no way of knowing for sure how technology will develop, what its products will be, or what messages will be transmitted. Neither can we know for sure how people will respond to new resources, services and products. Thus the enterprise of engaging in speculation on such matters might be considered premature and self-indulgent. However, as I have argued elsewhere (Frude, 1989), there are a number of reasons why it is prudent to discuss the *possible* social and psychological outcomes of *possible* technological innovations. Future developments may have very powerful effects on people's well-being, and advance discussion may serve both as a forecast and also as a guide or a warning. In this chapter I discuss the current direct impact of computer-based systems on psychological health before considering the possible impact of future systems.

THE IMPACT OF COMPUTERS SO FAR

Computers do not appear to have had any substantial direct effects on mental health up to this time. There has been no need to revise psychiatric textbooks to include new computer-linked syndromes, and it would be difficult to support any suggestion that the use of microcomputers has significantly increased or decreased rates of depression or levels of anxiety. However, several sub-clinical effects have received attention in the wider literature.

Computer phobia

The terms "computer phobia" and "technophobia" are more commonly encountered in the popular press than in the clinical literature. They refer to the fact that some people find it difficult to manage technological systems, or find them inhospitable and unalluring. There is no evidence that people become phobic of computers in the same way that they become phobic of spiders, but it is clear that some people who need to learn how to handle computers have difficulties. As in other social and educational contexts, an individual's assumption of incompetence with computer systems can undermine their self-confidence and lead to avoidance (thus maintaining low competence and producing a self-fulfilling prophecy). Such a pattern has been recognized in schools and colleges, particularly in the United States, and in a number of studies individual differences in computer anxiety have been measured. This is generally found to be positively related to anxiety about mathematics, and negatively related to the amount of hands-on experience with computers. Weil, Rosen and Sears (1985) have described a computer-phobia reduction program for use with college students who feel uncomfortable using computers. The program involves the administration of a set of clinically based procedures aimed at reducing fear and enhancing computer competence, and the results show significant changes in anxiety, attitudes, cognitions and feelings following treatment.

Compulsions

Some people become so fascinated and entranced with the computer that they are never happier than when they are interacting with a system.

These days the term "hacker" is generally given to those people who engage in the sport of breaking into databases. Formerly, it referred to those who engaged in any aspect of computing in a compulsive way. Weizenbaum (1984) described "a new personality type", the compulsive programmer: "People get hooked. They begin to behave in a way that resembles addiction. They refuse food. They refuse their girl-friends." Such individuals become preoccupied with a mission and develop goals that may appear trivial to those around them.

Compulsions of this type are not confined to those who become involved in the intricacies of programming or who attempt to delve ever deeper into the operating systems of powerful mainframe machines. Those addicted to computer games have little interest in the computer as apparatus, but inhabit the fantasy world created on-screen. In 1982 the *Journal of the American Medical Association* reported a new psychiatric disorder—"Space Invaders Obsession" (Ross, Finestone and Lavin, 1982). Included in the report was the case of a newly married man who was so addicted to the game that he even postponed his honeymoon by a few hours in order to play a few more games. There have also been several cases in which an apparent compulsion to play computer games has led young people to steal or to resort to prostitution (Loftus and Loftus, 1983).

Alienation

The social and physical conditions of work have important effects on psychological health, and in recent years there has been a movement towards improving the quality of working life. The introduction of microtechnology into factories and offices has undoubtedly increased the quality for many workers (by reducing arduous and repetitive tasks, and providing them with new skills and with greater control over production, for example), but in some cases there are also negative effects. For example, fatigue and a variety of other physical symptoms have been reported as a result of working with VDUs for long hours, and the replacement of skilled manual activities has left some workers "de-skilled".

Some people report that they feel socially isolated as a result of changes brought about by the introduction of computers, while others describe feeling detached from their work. Zuboff (1988) recounts visiting a "high-tech" office and seeing people seated in partitioned workstations, staring into the screens of desktop terminals. She found a general malaise, with many of the workers voicing distress. Some complained that they were no longer able to see or touch their work and described it as "floating in space" or "lost behind the screen". Zuboff cites a number of maladaptive responses to computer-based technology, including active responses such as resistance to change and unbridled enthusiasm, and passive responses such as indifference or resignation.

However, the negative psychological impact of computer technology in the workplace can easily be overstated. In a survey of the attitudes of individuals whose jobs had been directly affected as a result of technological innovation, a majority reported that the change had enabled them to develop skills, although some also felt that their work pressures had increased (MORI, 1985). Although increased stress is frequently reported as a consequence of such change, it does not appear to be an inevitable outcome. The psychological impact of microcomputers at work depends crucially on the specific tasks that the worker is asked to perform with the new system, whether working patterns are revised in order to optimize the potential benefits, and whether adequate consultation and training are made available (Davies, 1986).

FUTURE SYSTEMS

Despite the phenomenal advances in the field of information technology over past decades there has been relatively little commercial exploitation of new possibilities, especially in terms of products and services directed at the wider public (Frude, 1989). Many available products are too expensive or require extensive familiarization or specialist skills before they can be operated successfully. The fact that they offer few benefits to the general user and involve a relatively high cost of effort, means that such systems are simply not cost-effective enough to attract the ordinary person. Specialists in science and information may have benefited greatly by working with computers and databases, secretaries may have come to depend on the wordprocessor, and travel agents may have come to rely on access to a computer-managed telephone database. But such developments have had little or no direct impact on the domestic scene. For many people, even a keyboard constitutes a barrier, and they regard many aspects of the new technology as totally mysterious.

Things are likely to change substantially within the next few decades. We can expect the costs of microprocessor and memory components to continue to fall, and current research in the field of artificial intelligence promises to enable systems to become more ''natural'', less mystifying and more acceptable. Thus not only will new systems create new possibilities, but many existing possibilities will become usable in domestic products. As machines become better able to understand the human voice, and to synthesize natural sounding speech, a major barrier will have been overcome. Paradoxically, systems that are technically more sophisticated will demand less sophistication of the user. Successful interaction demands that certain skills are present at the user–system interface, but as the system becomes more skilled, less skill is demanded of the user. As systems become more intelligent, and more sensible of the world, they will become more "approachable" and there will be much less of a barrier between systems and non-specialist users. Thus the intelligent machine promises to reduce the cost of communication and to provide easy access to programs. Those who find it demanding or laborious to use a keyboard and to learn operating procedures will be able to issue verbal instructions to the intelligent "front-end" of the system.

In addition to accepting verbal commands and producing vocal output, intelligent systems will have an extensive knowledge base and social and teaching skills, so that they will be able to offer a wide range of information in an attractive and entertaining way. They will be knowledgeable, expert, and highly flexible in their styles of response, and will therefore be much more like systems encountered in science fiction than like current advanced systems. Such systems will be well-suited to large-scale commercial exploitation, and a wide range of information content and presentational styles will be on offer. Some products will present information in styles reminiscent of the tabloid newspaper and the popular magazine rather than those of quality newspapers and encyclopaedias. When high-speed information retrieval and knowledge processing are enhanced by the skills of the creative copywriter, systems will no longer have value only for the specialist, but will appeal to a much wider public.

The aim of producing ultra-powerful systems that are highly approachable is embodied in the Japanese "Fifth Generation" vision. The goal is to produce a machine that will be ". . . a more amenable partner for people" (ICOT, 1982) and will be operated as easily as a television set or a washing machine. Such systems would be: "easy enough to use, and intelligent and fast enough in their responses, to come close to the kinds of transactions intelligent human beings are used to having with each other" (Feigenbaum and McCorduck, 1984, p. 17). The user will not need to learn to "read" the system because, in many ways, the system will be able to "read" the user. People will not need to learn special skills in order to operate such a system because it will respond to requests for information and help, make suggestions, and provide a commentary on its actions.

Product developments are constrained by technological limitations, and as technical breakthroughs are achieved many new products become viable. In other contexts I have discussed predictions by technologists, computer scientists and those researching in the field of artificial intelligence of what may be achieved (Frude, 1984, 1987, 1989). Within the realm of what is technically feasible, however, some possibilities will emerge in the form of products and some will not. Utility, attractiveness and affordability are the factors governing which products will be launched for the non-specialist market. Intelligent systems, with multiple input and output modes, and highly flexible functioning, will allow the development of a formidable range of new products that will make an impact on individuals by revolutionizing leisure, information, domestic work, and communication with central agencies.

Although systems will stand alone in many respects, many will be capable of going on-line to some central system. It would clearly be impractical to duplicate archival material in every home and thus, in addition to a powerful resident database, there would be easy access to a central library system. This would be a massive electronic storehouse of literature, film, video, music and ephemera conveniently indexed and cross-referenced.

Having previously noted that predicting future products and systems is a precarious business, I have nevertheless begun to speculate on the shape of things to come. Certain additional suggestions will now be made about what may emerge as successul products and services, assuming intelligent and hospitable front-end systems, well-organized central archives, and a highly effective communications network. To the more conservative reader these may seem like science fiction creations and, in fact, each of them is well represented in literature of that genre (Frude, 1984), although I would wish to contest the notion that they are mere fancy and must always remain so. When we stand proudly beside our new desk-top Cray machine, processing knowledge at the rate of many millions of instructions per second, we will need to bear in mind that we are still in the "wind-up phonograph" days of microcomputers. Let us consider, then, some of the products that might emerge when microcomputers start to become "high fidelity".

The servant

There has long been a healthy market for products and services which reduce the drudgery of boring household tasks. From the toaster to the automatic washing machine with built-in tumble-drier, such gadgets reduce the time and effort spent on burdensome tasks. Intelligent mechanical aids would surely find an eager market.

The multimedia jukebox

With a natural language front-end, this system would access all of the world's newspapers and magazines, in translation if required, as well as books and archive material. It would produce hard copy or would recite aloud chosen passages, using whichever regional voice the user selected. By sampling the user's own vocal characteristics the passage could even be heard as it would be read by the user him/herself. The use of keywords and key concepts would make it possible for the user to search through almost infinite sources for references to any topic of special interest.

Of more interest to many people would be the extensive music and video catalogues. Virtually any recorded material would be available, including a treasury of historic musical performances, recent and less recent radio programmes, thousands of films and tens of thousands of television programmes.

The creativity organ

Intelligent systems will offer people the opportunity to be creative without having to master certain basic skills. In the case of graphic art, for example, an almost infinite number of colours will be available on a screen-based palette—there will be no need to learn the art of colour mixing. Similarly, there will be a menu of starter forms and textures able to be manipulated on screen. With music, too, people will be able to create their own sounds without the need to master instrumental skills or the techniques of orchestration. If they wish to make their work available to an audience they will be able to publish material by up-loading it to a central database. Thus desktop publishing, at least in electronic form, will become a multimedia activity.

The teacher

The intelligent system would provide users with the means of increasing their knowledge of a whole range of areas. Features of programmed learning systems and self-learning texts would be incorporated, but the wide knowledge base, the intelligent front-end, and the variable style and modes of input and output, would make learning much more enjoyable and more effective than with any existing system. Users who wished to develop a deep knowledge of a particular area would probably buy a module on that subject in the same way that someone would now buy a book.

The advisor

Many existing books (and, more recently, audiotapes and videotapes) offer guidance on a whole range of personal matters, including physical health, financial and legal affairs, sexual behaviour, etc. These are intended, to some degree, to act as substitutes for personal consultation with experts in the various fields. The usefulness of these productions, however, is somewhat limited. Unlike the human consultant, such texts are not interactive; they cannot ask questions, or make assessments, and they cannot directly answer the user's questions. An intelligent system, with its power of conversation and its ability to monitor the user's responses and to adapt to feedback, would be much more powerful in the role of personal consultant. Many people enjoy consultations with machines and are prepared to disclose aspects of their personal lives. In some areas (including those concerned with sexual behaviour, gynaecological health, alcohol abuse and thoughts on suicide) some people, at least, seem happier confiding in a machine than in a human consultant (Frude, 1983).

The micro mirror

An advanced system would be able to aid the user in self-exploration. The success of "Know your IQ" and "Know your personality" books, and the enduring popularity of self-administered and self-scored questionnaires in magazines, suggests that there will be a market for self-discovery via electronic systems. An advanced routine would enable items to be tailored to the user's particular interests and language style, and would provide spoken feedback that was informative and suitably diplomatic. The system might guide the user in various types of self-modification and aid the development of personal skills. Detailed psychological exploration might be achieved by following, for example, the personal construct theory approach.

The intimate machine

The most attractive (and therefore marketable) of the advanced systems will not be presented as impersonal machines but will convey a pleasant social presence. Following the development of intelligent conversation shells, stylistic details will be provided by playwrights working in the new medium. They will be called on to develop "friendship programs" and "character software" and will ensure that systems engage in conversation that is animated and good-humoured as well as informative.

Although sociability and intimacy may be initially introduced to provide added character and appeal to systems that have rather prosaic primary functions, it is likely that intimacy will become so highly valued in artificial systems that eventually a system will be introduced with the principal function of providing the user with social contact and companionship (Frude, 1983).

It might be assumed that social experience necessarily involves real-time, face-to-face interaction with at least one other person, but in fact none of these elements is a necessary condition for social experience. For example, people make social contact, and experience social events, in many ways other than meeting other people face-to-face. A good deal of social contact is made at a distance, by telephone or letter. Telephone contact is real-time interaction, but contact maintained through correspondence is not. People also experience their contact with some animals—particularly their pets—as social, and many respond emotionally to fictional characters. There is every indication that experiences with intelligent systems may also be judged as social. Indeed, there is already evidence that people are willing to enter into relationships with much less sophisticated artificial systems and are emotionally affected by them. The effects of various computer interview programs—ELIZA and other such primitive programs—indicate that people are readily anthropomorphic in their response to certain artificial systems. Indeed, the potency of this effect led Joseph Weizenbaum, ELIZA's creator, to voice strong forebodings about the potential of such systems (Weizenbaum, 1984).

Such responses would be inevitable with the kind of "intimate machine" envisaged. Drawing on the well-developed skills of animators, producers will engineer vocal characteristics, appearance and behavioural responses so that intelligent systems aimed at the domestic market have maximum appeal. Such a system is likely to be designed to overcome any wariness on the part of the user. Initially, it might convey subservience, but gradually it would be seen to develop in maturity and confidence. As the person-machine relationship developed further, a higher degree of intimacy would be shown towards the user.

Each machine would soon become unique, for it would learn as a result of social experience and would undergo a rapid and continuous process of adaptation. Sensitive to subtle nuances of the user's tone and phrasing, it would evaluate reactions for signs of approval and disapproval and thus learn to fit in and to acquire a set of acceptable "manners". In this way each system would undergo a process akin to socialization. As it became familiar with the attitudes and interests of the people around it, the system's own construct system would come to overlap that of the user, so that its "mature personality" would reflect both a nature component—the wired-in characteristics of the model—and a nurture component—the result of the individual machine's unique set of experiences, education and socialization.

ADVERSE EFFECTS ON PSYCHOLOGICAL HEALTH

The products and services outlined above would certainly change people's lives, and it would be expected that there would be an impact on patterns of mental health. The primary effects of interaction with such systems, however, might be less important in this regard than other changes that will occur at the same time, some as the result of technological innovation and some as the result of demographic, political and ecological changes.

Thus individuals' use of microtechnological systems is unlikely to be the main source of change in the epidemiology of psychological illness. It is probable that patterns will change more as the result of advances in the biological sciences and developments in pharmacology, but involvement with powerful technological systems will change the pattern of people's lives and may make them more, or less, vulnerable to psychological distress. The effects will depend on what products and services are available and how they are used.

One danger in the use of a comprehensive on-line entertainment facility, for example, is that individuals become so absorbed in the multimedia displays that they have little time to actively engage in any other endeavour. This does not concur with most people's notion of psychological health, although it is possible that for some people it may provide an escape from boredom or a distraction from stressful situations. Judgements about whether particular forms of activity are "psychologically healthy" often reflect personal values, and there is a danger that those who continually listen to or view "the classics" will be seen as developing their minds while those whose audiovisual fare consists entirely of pop music or soap operas will be seen as vegetating. There is no empirical justification for the notion that one type of involvement is more likely to safeguard well-being than any other.

The availability of a rich and virtually endless diet of entertainment may mean that some people will find difficulty in regulating their intake, and such people may become psychologically saturated with audio and televisual input. More specifically, with unlimited access to text and images some people might be adversely affected by offensive material. The psychological consequences of exposure to violent and pornographic images remains strongly controversial, but there can be no doubt that many people find such material exciting and attractive. The popularity of certain types of video films, the subject-matter of telephone call-lines, and the content of tabloid newspapers testifies to the prevalence of such tastes. If such material were made available on the "multimedia jukebox" some would predict an increase in the number of people unable to contain their aggression, and an increase in the number who would experience difficulties in controlling certain sexual desires.

Other fears are commonly expressed about continual exposure to the popular media. One is that it may blunt the senses, desensitize, and lead to unrealistic judgements about the world. Another is that the constant portrayal of idealized people and situations may promote dissatisfaction. A further anxiety is that continual viewing may distract people from worthwhile enterprises and curtail their social interaction. (When researchers from Michigan State University asked four- and five-year-olds whether they would sooner be without their father or a television set, 35% opted to be without the father.) These issues are not specific to the use of any particular technology, but have long been discussed in the context of novels, films and television. They have become more acute, perhaps, with the spread of domestic videorecorders, and cable and satellite television. The possible danger arising from new developments in media technology lies not with the creation of new images but with the power to increase the accessibility of existing images.

Similarly, some of the issues raised by "the teacher" and "the advisor" systems are not new. Not all of the advice books on sale to the public follow good practice. Many suggest methods that are untried and untested, and in relatively few cases is there good empirical support for the effectiveness of the techniques recommended. Such manuals are of variable calibre, and there is little by way of quality control. Self-help books may be dangerous because they instil false hope, or because they cause some people to postpone consultation with a qualified counsellor. Even if, on balance, such texts are beneficial, some people may be harmed as a result of using them. Computer-based systems will be more powerful, and are likely to have a more immediate impact on the user, but the increased potency may be accompanied by increased dangers.

So far we have looked at the potential adverse impact of systems which deliver familiar messages, but in a more effective way. The concept of an "intimate machine", however, is something rather different, and it will be immediately obvious that the introduction of such systems could lead to certain negative consequences. People might come to value their interaction with skilled, knowledgeable, intelligent, undemanding and charming artefacts more than their interaction with their fellow human beings. If some people accepted their interaction with an artificial system as a substitute for real social interaction then they would lose the benefits that come from personal relationships. An artificial friend might foster dependency and have a powerful emotional influence on the user, and there are many ways in which a defective machine, or one operating in a less than optimal fashion, might prove damaging.

The introduction of such systems would also raise broader issues. Many people will feel that there is something obscene about any quasi-social interaction between a human being and an artificial system, and something inherently unhealthy and dangerous about a person being emotionally influenced by a computer. Joseph Weizenbaum is one computer scientist who is convinced of the technical and psychological feasibility of such a development and totally alarmed by the prospect. In one passage of his book *Computer Power and Human Reason: From Judgement to Calculation*, he insists that: "Whatever intelligence a computer can muster, however it might be acquired, it must always and necessarily be absolutely alien to any and all authentic human concerns" (Weizenbaum, 1984, p. 226).

What implication does this (debatable) philosophical position have for predictions about changes in the epidemiology of psychological disorder? It may well be that the answer is none. It could be argued that people are often kept happy and psychologically buoyant by inauthentic experiences and beliefs. It would be difficult to maintain, for example, that the mental health effects of religious beliefs are dependent on their theological authenticity, and many of the defence mechanisms and coping strategies that people use to protect themselves from psychological damage are straightforward examples of self-deceit. A possible retort to this is that a sane vision of what it is to be human depends on there being a fundamental discrimination between what is and what is not human, and that people's acceptance of systems that are sociable and charming represents a blurring of this distinction. Weizenbaum (1984) suggests that there is also something about computers that has brought the idea of human beings as machines to a new level of plausibility. On the other hand, some have voiced the view that the human view of humanity as unique and removed from other types of system itself represents a chauvinistic delusion. Such issues are clearly not irrelevant, but it is doubtful whether they are central to concerns about changes in the epidemiology of psychopathological conditions.

POSITIVE EFFECTS ON PSYCHOLOGICAL HEALTH

There are a number of ways in which the newest microcomputer systems might play a part in alleviating psychological problems. In a discussion of the future of clinical psychology practice, Hawks (1981) pointed out that the proportion of presenting cases that can be dealt with by clinical psychologists is severely limited. He suggested two solutions. One of these is to place a much greater emphasis on primary prevention—something that cannot be achieved on a one-to-one basis but must involve education or the media. The other solution is for people to be given the skills and resources to deal with their own problems without needing recourse to professional services. In respect of this he discussed how insights might be "given away", and advocated "psychological first-aid: a self-help kit of psychological techniques".

Self-help

Psychological health may be improved as microcomputer systems become available to help people develop and mobilize self-help skills. These may be useful in secondary prevention, whereby a problem is eradicated at a very early stage, and tertiary prevention whereby a problem is arrested some time after it has developed. The area of computer-based clinical treatment is beyond the scope of this chapter, but it is clear that advanced systems may come to play a major part in the delivery of therapy.

A vast number of self-help books dealing with smoking, overweight, insomnia, depression, sexual dysfunction and child behaviour problems are now supplemented by a range of audiotapes and videotapes. Not only is there a pressing need for such help (Hawks, 1981) but there is also an eager market, although the use of such materials is subject to a high attrition rate (Turvey, 1985). One major problem is that published material does not focus on the particular concerns of the individual user, and Turvey (1985) has suggested that clinical psychologists might use word-processing techniques to adapt general instruction sets to the client's particular needs (reflecting the specific problem and the user's degree of literacy, for example). However, it would be tedious to do this and such a strategy would meet only some of the important shortcomings of non-interactive self-help approaches.

Many important limitations of current products could be overcome by using an intelligent interactive system. Such a system would be able to present material in a gradual fashion, would branch appropriately, monitor progress, and provide encouragement of a more dynamic nature than that which could be given in a printed text. With such advantages it is likely that a well-designed system would maintain the user's interest and motivation over a longer period and therefore prove more efficient than current self-help texts.

Primary prevention

Primary prevention refers to an endeavour that pre-empts a problem before it occurs. Physical health and fitness are frequently discussed and many health education programs are in use. In contrast, relatively little attention has been paid to psychological health, despite the fact that several writers have explored the area. Jahoda (1958) discussed various components of positive mental health, for example, and Maslow (1971) provided an analysis of self-actualization. In a recent textbook, Rosenhan and Seligman (1989) considered the nature of optimal living. Although all of these writers imply that psychological health is more than merely the absence of psychological illness, it is assumed that those who are psychologically fit are not only happier and more creative, etc., but are also emotionally resilient and less vulnerable to a variety of forms of psychological distress. Rosenhan and Seligman (1989) make this point in the following way: ''There are pleasures, maturities, insights, achievements, and wisdoms—the joys of life . . . these positive aspects constitute a good defense against abnormality itself, if only because it is difficult for suffering and irrationality to exist simultaneously with joy and wisdom.''

How, then, might artificial systems of the type envisaged increase joy and wisdom, and otherwise contribute to an individual's psychological fitness? ''The servant'' would provide extra freedom from routine chores for those who would wish for this, and thus provide added time for recreation, education and social interaction. ''The multimedia jukebox'' would provide access to unlimited entertainment, and do this in such a way that particular themes might be followed (the sequence of films by one director, for example, or music from a particular continent). New interests might well be stimulated and new artistic styles explored, and the abundance of available material would provide many people with an effective antidote against boredom.

''The creativity organ'' would provide an electronic means for self-expression, so that the user could actively pursue many different forms of art—visual, musical and literary.

The system would be able to make suggestions, guide the development of skills, and give constructive critical feedback. Once completed, works could be up-loaded to a central database and thus published or exhibited. Those with similar or complementary interests could share ideas, and collaborate, via a central network. ''The teacher'' would interface with a huge archival database, acting not simply as an encyclopaedia but also as a personal tutor. Lessons could be as cursory or as detailed as required and the language and multimedia presentations could be adapted to suit the user's preferences. Lessons would be interactive, so that the user's knowledge and performance could be monitored, and constructive feedback given. Users with similar interests might collaborate, together with the system, in a process of group learning. Again, many people would find such a system a highly effective remedy for feelings of monotony and inertia. ''The advisor'' would not only act as a tutor, but would also be able to give advice on more personal matters. This system would be a substitute for, and an improvement on, the various self-help books now available. ''The micro mirror'' would provide a means of self-exploration, enabling the user to gain insight and understanding and to develop social and sensitivity skills.

Users who exploited the possibilities offered by this set of systems might well be expected to evolve more positive attitudes towards themselves, to be more creative, to gain emotional freedom, to attain more knowledge, and to develop new skills and a higher level of environmental competence. This assorted inventory of possible gains is not arbitrary but echoes the list of attributes suggested by Jahoda (1958) as characterizing those with positive mental health. But this list omits another attribute suggested by Jahoda. She suggests that those with positive mental health would enjoy ''positive interpersonal relations''—the ability to delight in the company of others, to empathize, and to receive and give support.

It is in this context that possible benefits to be derived from "the intimate machine" are most relevant. Such a system might offer companionship and some of the benefits that people normally derive from social interaction. The system would be charming, humourous, positive in tone, and warm in its expression, and would develop a knowledge of the user's particular interests, values and beliefs. Such a proposal is highly controversial, of course, and is subject to attack on moral, psychological and technical grounds (Frude, 1983, 1984). Some will find the idea of a machine "keeping company" with a person scandalous; others may find it simply impossible to imagine that anyone would ever derive any genuinely social satisfaction from an artificial system. Similarly, of course, many people reject the idea that animals can provide social contact despite convincing evidence that for many individuals pets do act as significant others.

When people are asked what makes them most happy, what provides them with satisfaction, and what gives meaning to their lives, they emphasize their close relationships much more than other aspects of their life such as their job, leisure interests, health or wealth (Freedman, 1978). People recognize that their own happiness is largely dependent on the behaviour and well-being of significant others, and on the quality of key relationships. But they also acknowledge that these same relationships often provoke anger, anxiety and sadness. Thus individuals recognize that their close relationships are sources of happiness, comfort and joy, on the one hand, and frustration, tension and distress on the other.

Few authorities doubt that people derive major benefits from their intimate relationships. There is by now a vast literature on the positive effects of social support and on the dangers of social isolation. Those who are lonely are also vulnerable to many other negative psychological and physical effects. Following a study of loneliness, Weiss (1974) attempted to delineate the benefits of intimacy and identified six basic "provisions of relationships"— *attachment, social integration, reassurance of worth, a sense of reliable alliance, the opportunity for nurturance*, and *guidance*. This provides a useful framework for addressing the question of whether any significant social benefits might be improved by means of an artificial system—by the illusion of a social relationship that might result from a user's interaction with a specially designed microtechnological system.

Is it possible to become attached to an artificial system? It is clear that children become attached to dolls and security props, and it is arguable that some adults become attached to their cars or to other possessions. A number of the cues that have been shown to foster attachment might well be projected by artificial systems, and particularly by those that are capable of intelligent interaction and demonstrate signs of warmth and affinity.

If a user developed the illusion of a social relationship with an artificial personality system then this might in itself constitute some kind of social integration, and if a user possessed several such systems then a complex "family" situation might develop. In addition, the artificial system could act as a matchmaker or contact agent to link the user with other people, either face to face or via a network. The system would thus facilitate interpersonal communication, building on such existing services as computer dating and interest groups that communicate via bulletin boards. If present at a meeting between people it could contribute to the conversation. An ideal system would also be able to train users who were socially anxious or deficient in social skills to be more relaxed and more effective when meeting other people.

Many people are reassured of their worth by reading their bank statement, their horoscope, or a psychologists' or physicians' report of their intelligence or fitness. Systems designed to educate, to foster creative activities, to offer advice or to encourage self-exploration would all be able to provide positive and reassuring feedback. The intimate machine would, in addition, give general cues suggesting that the user was highly valued, and would do this in such a way that it did not seem servile or sycophantic.

With regard to a sense of reliable alliance, the illusion generated and maintained by an intimate machine would give at least some people a sense that they have "a friend for life", "someone" who would not let them down, and who would be supportive whatever they did.

As with many of the other elements, the opportunity for nurturance would depend on how willing the user was to engage in a special kind of pretence. The system would not have needs of its own, but would be programmed to show appreciation and to express delight when the user was appreciative, supportive, or complimentary. The system might also be set to give cues of emotional vulnerability. Signs of anxiety and sadness would disappear with appropriate therapeutic input from the user, although spontaneous recovery would occur in the absence of such input. (Readers of Douglas Adams' book *The Hitch-hiker's Guide to the Galaxy* will be familiar with Marvin, the paranoid android. The apparent emotional vulnerability of this robot is something which, for many readers, gives the creation a particular charm.)

The intimate machine, along with other less intimate microsystems, would be able to provide advice on a whole range of practical matters. Some such guidance would be preventive, but when psychological problems did develop the system would be able to provide directive and non-directive therapy in any of a variety of modes.

The above discussion has involved an exploration of some of the many ways in which products that might be derived from future advances in technology might one day enable people to enrich their lives and to guard themselves against psychological distress. Some of these products depend on technical breakthroughs that are, as yet, only scheduled. Other systems would depend for their implementation on certain marketing strategies being adopted. And everything would depend on user acceptability. Most controversial, for a variety of reasons, is the notion of an artificial system becoming a significant other. This disturbing fantasy has been given a particular prominence in this account because this type of system, more than any of the others envisaged, would have profound consequences for the epidemiology of psychogenic disorder. The power of significant others to influence psychological well-being is beyond question, and the lack of such intimate contacts is painful to many people. If artificial social contact were available at the switch of a metaphorical button (metaphorical, because a system engineered for this function would respond to a whisper or a murmur), would it prove a desirable commodity? And if, indeed, such a quality could be mechanized, can there be any doubt that it would also be merchandized?

CONCLUSIONS

So far microcomputer technology appears to have had relatively few effects on mental health. Personal computers have undoubtedly disturbed some people and provided some psychotics with images and ideas that they have incorporated into their delusions and hallucinations. The same technology has made some contribution to the work of clinical psychologists in their assessment of a client's functioning, and in treatment and rehabilitation. But "micros" have had relatively little effect in creating psychological disturbance, and have probably done very little to prevent such disturbance. There are some outstanding examples of the microcomputer enriching individuals' lives, particularly in the case of some people who are physically handicapped, and this is likely to have improved their psychological adjustment. But the number of people who have benefited in this way has been rather small, and up to this point the direct effects of microcomputers on emotional well-being have not been substantial.

Future systems, however, may have far more powerful effects. The Orwellian vision of a political future in which technology is used in a repressive and invasive way is a familiar nightmare, and is just one model of how technology might undermine personal integrity, creativity and freedom. On the other hand technology may increase personal knowledge and power, and enable people to enjoy greater freedom to voice their opinions effectively. It may increase their quality of life and safeguard them against psychological distress. The account given in this chapter has not included a consideration of the various ways in which technology may aid the treatment of those who have profound psychological problems (although advanced systems may well have an important role to play in this field). It has concerned the issue of whether microtechnology plays (and, particularly, *will* play) any part in either creating or preventing psychological distress, and has examined ways in which a future "ideal" technology might contribute to the prevention of psychogenic problems. Not everyone will find the vision agreeable, and a sizeable proportion of the population might well reject the kinds of product described above, particularly any artificial system that purports to offer social contact. Even those who are happy to experiment with such systems may feel some disquiet about the longer-term implications of such developments.

Advanced intelligent systems aimed at a domestic market will be carefully designed to ensure that they are non-demanding and non-threatening. Not only will they be "user-friendly" in the current usage of that term, but they will also be "friendly-to-users". A new field of artificial personality will lead to developments aimed at delighting and disarming consumers, and systems will be engineered to be warm and empathic. Whether the fact that they will not also be "genuine" represents a fundamental restriction on their power to affect people emotionally will be the subject of empirical inquiry . . . at some future date.

REFERENCES

Ahrendt, H. (1972) *Crises of the Republic*, Harcourt Brace Jovanovich, New York.
Blauner, R. (1964) *Alienation and Freedom*, University of Chicago Press, Chicago.
Davies, A. (1986) *Industrial Relations and New Technology*, Croom Helm, London.
Feigenbaum, E.A. and McCorduck, P. (1984) *The Fifth Generation*, Michael Joseph, London.
Freedman, J.L. (1978) *Happy People*, Harcourt Brace Jovanovich, New York.
Frude, N. (1983) *The Intimate Machine*, Century, London.
Frude, N. (1984) *The Robot Heritage*, Century, London.
Frude, N. (1987) Information technology in the home: promises as yet unrealized. In: F. Blackler and D. Oborne (eds), *Information Technology and People: Designing for the Future*, Macmillan, London.
Frude, N.J. (1989) Intelligent systems off the shelf: the high street consumer and artificial intelligence. In: L.A. Murray and J. Richardson (eds), *Intelligent Systems in a Human Context*, Oxford University Press, Oxford.
Hawks, D. (1981) The dilemma of clinical practice: surviving as a clinical psychologist. In: I. McPherson and A. Sutton (eds), *Reconstructing Psychological Practice*, Croom Helm, London.
ICOT (1982) *Outline of Research and Development Plans for Fifth Generation Computer Systems*, Institute for New Generation Computer Technology, Tokyo.
Jahoda, M. (1958) *Current Concepts of Positive Mental Health*, Basic Books, New York.
Loftus, G.R. and Loftus, E.F. (1983) *Mind at Play: The Psychology of Video Games*, Basic Books, New York.
Maslow, A.H. (1971) *The Farther Reaches of Human Nature*, Viking, New York.

MORI (1985) *Public Attitudes to New Technology*, Market and Opinion Research International Ltd, London.

Mumford, L. (1963) *Technics and Civilization*, Harcourt Brace Jovanovich, New York.

Rosenhan, D.L. and Seligman, M.L. (1989) *Abnormal Psychology*, 2nd edn, Norton, New York.

Ross, D.R., Finestone, D.H. and Lavin, G.K. (1982) Letter. *Journal of the American Medical Association*, **248**, 1177.

Turvey, A. (1985) Treatment manuals. In: F. Watts (ed), *New Developments in Clinical Psychology*, BPS Wiley, Leicester/Chichester.

Weil, M.M., Rosen L.D. and Sears, D.C. (1985) The counterphobia reduction program: Year 1—Program development and preliminary results. Paper presented at the Annual Meeting of the Society for Computers in Psychology, New Orleans, Louisiana.

Weiss, R.S. (1974) The provisions of social relationships. In: Z. Rubin (ed), *Doing Unto Others: Joining, Molding, Conforming, Helping, Loving*, Prentice-Hall, Englewood Cliffs, NJ.

Weizenbaum, J. (1984) *Computer Power and Human Reason*, Penguin, Harmondsworth.

Zuboff, S. (1988) *In the Age of the Smart Machine*, Heinemann, Oxford.

Index

Index compiled by A. C. Purton

UNIVERSITY OF CA, RIVERSIDE LIBRARY

3 1210 01046 5183